The Semiperiphery of Academic Wri

*Also by Karen Bennett*

ACADEMIC WRITING IN PORTUGAL I: Discourses in Conflict

ENGLISH ACADEMIC DISCOURSE: Hegemonic Status and Implications for Translation

# The Semiperiphery of Academic Writing

## Discourses, Communities and Practices

Edited by

Karen Bennett
*University of Lisbon, Centre for English Studies (ULICES), Portugal*

Selection, introduction, conclusion and editorial content
© Karen Bennett 2014
Individual chapters © Respective authors 2014
Softcover reprint of the hardcover 1st edition 2014 978-1-137-35118-0

First published 2014 by
PALGRAVE MACMILLAN

Palgrave Macmillan in the UK is an imprint of Macmillan Publishers Limited,
registered in England, company number 785998, of Houndmills, Basingstoke,
Hampshire RG21 6XS.

Palgrave Macmillan in the US is a division of St Martin's Press LLC,
175 Fifth Avenue, New York, NY 10010.

Palgrave Macmillan is the global academic imprint of the above companies
and has companies and representatives throughout the world.

Palgrave® and Macmillan® are registered trademarks in the United States,
the United Kingdom, Europe and other countries.

ISBN 978-1-349-46870-6        ISBN 978-1-137-35119-7 (eBook)
DOI 10.1057/9781137351197

A catalogue record for this book is available from the British Library.

Library of Congress Cataloging-in-Publication Data
Bennett, Karen, author.
The semiperiphery of academic writing : discourses, communities and
practices / Karen Bennett, University of Lisbon, Portugal.

pages cm

Includes bibliographical references and index.
1. Academic writing—Cross-cultural studies.   I. Title.
P301.5.A27B46 2014
808'.042—dc23                                    2014022906

Typeset by MPS Limited, Chennai, India.

Transferred to Digital Printing in 2014

# Contents

# List of Figures and Tables

## Figures

## Tables

# Acknowledgements

We would like to thank all the people who participated in the interviews reported in Chapters 7, 8 and 9 for their time and efforts, without which those chapters would not have been possible. Thanks too to the authors of the extracts and blogs reproduced in Chapters 1 and 12, respectively, for giving permission to use their material.

# Notes on Contributors

**Mirela Bardi** is Associate Professor in the Department of Modern Languages and Business Communication at the University of Economics, Bucharest. She teaches Business English to undergraduates as well as Academic Writing for International Publication and Qualitative Research Methodology to MA students. For 12 years she worked for British Council Romania as manager of the PROSPER project and of European Accession projects after the closure of PROSPER. She is very keen to develop her expertise in teaching academic writing to professional researchers, as one of her main current academic duties is training lecturers in the University of Economics, Bucharest, in writing research for international publication.

**Rita Queiroz de Barros** is Lecturer in the Faculty of Letters of the University of Lisbon, where she teaches various courses within English Linguistics to both BA and MA students. She has an MA in Sociolinguistics (1994) and a PhD in English linguistics (2004), from the University of Lisbon. Her main research interests are Historical Sociolinguistics and, more recently, English as an International Language.

**Karen Bennett** lectures in English for Academic Purposes, Scientific Communication and Translation at the University of Coimbra, Portugal, and is a researcher with the Centre for English Studies, University of Lisbon, in the field of Translation Studies. She is particularly interested in the epistemological issues involved in the transfer of knowledge across linguistic and cultural borders. In addition to numerous articles on translation and academic discourse, she is the author of *Academic Writing in Portugal I: Discourses in Conflict* (2011) and *English Academic Discourse: Its Hegemonic Status and Implications for Translation* (2012).

**Sally Burgess** is Lecturer in English at the University of La Laguna. Her main research interests are in cross-cultural rhetoric, the contribution of language professionals to the preparation of research publications and the teaching of writing in the university context. She has published on all of these topics.

**Olga Dontcheva-Navratilova** is Assistant Professor of English Linguistics at Masaryk University in Brno, Czech Republic. She specializes in discourse analysis, stylistics and pragmatics, with a focus on political and academic discourse. She has published many articles on topics related to her research interests and is the author of *Analysing Genre: The Colony Text of UNESCO Resolutions* (2009) and *Coherence in Political Speeches* (2011). She is the co-editor of *Coherence and Cohesion in Spoken and Written Discourse* (2009) and the linguistics journal *Discourse and Interaction*.

**Anna Gonerko-Frej** is Head of the Department of English at Szczecin University, Poland. She graduated from A. Mickiewicz University in Poznań and holds postgraduate diplomas from Ruskin College, Oxford (British Studies) and Warsaw University (Methodology). She obtained a doctorate degree from Greifswald University (Germany) with a dissertation on the subject of culture in ELT. Her professional interests focus mainly on ELF, linguistic imperialism, language policy, World Englishes, ELT methodology, intercultural education and British Studies.

**Ana Marušić** is Professor of Anatomy and Chair of the Department of Research in Biomedicine and Health at the University of Split School of Medicine in Croatia. She is an active member of the Croatian branch of the Cochrane Collaboration, Chair of the Board of the Croatian Institute of Global Health and creator of the first Croatian public registry of clinical trials. She was the editor in chief of the *Croatian Medical Journal* for 20 years, and is now editor in chief of the *Journal of Global Health*. She has been the President of the World Association of Medical Editors (WAME), President of the Council of Science Editors (CSE), Council member of the European Association of Science Editors (EASE) and member of the International Committee of Medical Journal Editors (ICMJE).

**Matko Marušić** is the founder (1991) and editor in chief (until 2009) of the *Croatian Medical Journal*. He is a graduate of Zagreb University School of Medicine (1970), where he also obtained his PhD (1975) and professorship from the Department of Physiology (1980). Since 2000, his research interests have shifted to medical education and research responsibility. He was one of the founders of the foundation of University of Split School of Medicine and also helped the establishment of medical schools in Osijek and Mostar.

**Laura-Mihaela Muresan** is Professor of English at the Bucharest University of Economic Studies, where she co-ordinates an interdisciplinary, English-medium MA on Research and Teacher Education in Economics. She is founder president of the Romanian Association for Quality Language Services QUEST and an associate member of

EAQUALS, and she has coordinated several European projects on quality management in language education. Her research interests include genre- and corpus-based approaches to academic/research writing, as well as the interdependence between professional development and quality assurance in education.

**Raffaella Negretti** is Associate Senior Lecturer (Assistant Professor) in English linguistics in the Department of English at Stockholm University, where she teaches courses in genre analysis and English for academic purposes for the Centre for Academic English. Her research focuses on academic writing, English for Academic Purposes, metacognition and self-regulated learning and genre awareness.

**Bojana Petrić** is Lecturer in the Department of Language and Linguistics at the University of Essex, UK. She has published papers on student citation practices, plagiarism, students' conceptions of voice and student writer identity and on diachronic developments in published writing in Serbian. She has also published a book on education reform (in Serbian).

**Małgorzata Sokół** is Assistant Professor in the Department of English at Szczecin University, Poland. Her major fields of professional interest include computer-mediated communication and computer-mediated discourse analysis, professional and institutional discourse analysis, genre theory, corpus linguistics and, recently, digital humanities. She has researched into aspects of digital genre development and evolution in professional and organizational communication, and investigated patterns of identity construction and evaluative language use in digital genres. She edited *Perspectives on Othering and Stereotyping: Language, Literature, Culture* (2010), co-edited *Us and Them – Them and Us: Constructions of the Other in Cultural Stereotypes* (2011) and authored *Discoursal Construction of Academic Identity in Cyberspace: The Example of An E-Seminar* (2012).

**Hacer Hande Uysal** is Assistant Professor at Gazi University, Ankara, Turkey. She received her Master's in English Education and her PhD in Foreign Language/ESL Education from the University of Iowa, USA. Her research interests are second language writing, intercultural rhetoric, academic discourse, language planning and policy, performance assessment and teacher education. She is the editor of the *Journal of Language Teaching and Learning* and the author of *The Interplay between Culture and Writing: Rhetorical and Process Patterns in L1 and L2 Argumentative Writing within a Cultural Context* (2008).

**Dimitra Vladimirou** teaches linguistics on the undergraduate and postgraduate programmes offered at Hellenic American University, Athens, Greece. She holds a PhD in Linguistics from the Department of Linguistics and English Language, Lancaster University, UK. She has co-authored papers published in the *International Journal of Applied Linguistics* and the *Journal of English for Academic Purposes,* and she is a member of the International Pragmatics Association and the European Association for the Teaching of Academic Writing. Her research interests include computer-mediated communication, politeness and impoliteness theories, cross-cultural pragmatics, critical approaches to academic discourse practices and English as a lingua franca.

# List of Abbreviations

EAD  English Academic Discourse
EAP  English for Academic Purposes
EFL  English as a Foreign Language
ELF  English as a Lingua Franca
ELFA  English as a Lingua Franca in Academic Settings
ERPP  English for Research and Publication Purposes
ESL  English as a Second Language
ESP  English for Specific Purposes
L1  First language (mother tongue)
L2  Second language
NES  Native English speaker/-ing
NNES  Non-native English speaker/-ing

# Introduction: The Political and Economic Infrastructure of Academic Practice: The 'Semiperiphery' as a Category for Social and Linguistic Analysis

*Karen Bennett*

For some time now, the terms 'centre' (or 'core') and 'periphery' have been a common feature of discussions about academic writing in recognition of the many inequalities that exist in the world of scholarly publishing. One of the most significant works in this regard was Canagarajah's 2002 book, *The Geopolitics of Academic Writing*, which highlighted some of the material and institutional constraints affecting researchers in economically disadvantaged parts of the globe. Since then, the issues raised (which include themes like access to material resources and disciplinary networks, institutional infrastructures, academic cultures and so on) have been developed and extended by authors such as Lillis and Curry (2010), Salager-Meyer (2008) and Ferguson (2007), while the traditional concern with the linguistic constraints facing non-native English speaker (NNES) researchers has also been recast in terms of the core/periphery dichotomy (for example, Flowerdew 2001, Giannoni 2008, Uzuner 2008). The resulting picture is of a global academic system that is neatly split between a prosperous centre, endowed with ample resources and characterized by a rigorous meritocratic culture based on sound Enlightenment principles, and a disadvantaged periphery where academic departments are run like 'minifiefdoms' (Canagarajah 2002, p. 195) and researchers are deprived of even the most basic equipment such as good-quality paper and photocopiers.

However, this picture is highly misleading. For between the two extremes described by Canagarajah lie many countries that are by no means as well-endowed as the United States, where that author now works, yet are not as destitute as the war-torn Sri Lanka of his early career. That is to say, there exists an intermediary category in the global academic order where the constraints described by Canagarajah still

1

exist, but in a less severe, less debilitating form. It is this second division that forms the 'semiperiphery' of the academic system, the zone that constitutes the subject of this book.

The connections between a country's economic situation and its academic status are well known. Bibliometric studies (for example, King 2004, Lee et al. 2011, May 1997) have consistently pointed to a firm correlation between a country's wealth and its scientific achievement, as measured by parameters such as published research papers, citations and (in some cases) patents. Topping all the studies are inevitably the United States, the United Kingdom, Canada, the non-Anglophone countries of northern Europe, Japan and so on (the precise order varies in accordance with the discipline being tested and the precise parameters used for measurement), while the countries of Southern and Eastern Europe make an occasional appearance, as do those of the BRIC grouping;[1] the poorer countries of Africa, South America and Asia are notably absent.

It is not difficult to see why this should be the case. Material resources are an important prerequisite for any research, whether in the form of well-equipped laboratories, up-to-date libraries or fast internet connections, and these in turn provide access to the all-important disciplinary networks that set the ground rules for community membership (Canagarajah 2002, Lillis and Curry 2010, Salager-Meyer 2008). Similarly, it is a country's economic situation that largely determines its level of social development, and ultimately, its academic culture. The rigid hierarchies typical of universities in less developed countries offer little incentive to produce research (Canagarajah 2002, p. 196) nor are they very conducive to critical debate (May 1997); hence, it is unsurprising that most of the leaders in the ratings are modern liberal democracies with meritocratic academic cultures.

The concept of the semiperiphery was first introduced by Immanuel Wallerstein (1984) within world systems theory, and was developed by the sociologist Boaventura de Sousa Santos (1985) in the specific context of Portugal. According to these two authors, semiperipheral countries are located between the centre and periphery of the world system, both economically and geographically, and have characteristics of each of those two regions. They thus provide a buffer zone between rich and poor countries and mediate change across the system as a whole. It is no accident that these frontier nations have often served as traders and transporters of economic and cultural assets: in the 18th century, for example, Spain and Portugal played a crucial role in the world economy, physically transporting goods and knowledge between the economically powerful countries of northern Europe and the poorer countries of South America, Asia and Africa that were their colonies.

A similar pattern can be seen with regard to the production and transmission of knowledge in the modern world. Universities and research units located on the semiperiphery tend to act as conduits for knowledge flows emanating from the centre (received via transnational partnerships, visiting lecturers, participation in international conferences or scholarships to centre institutions), which is then conveyed to the outer rim of the system through their own events and publications, thereby serving communities for whom the more prestigious international ones may be inaccessible (Lillis and Curry 2010, Nunes and Gonçalves 2001). Indeed, these semiperipheral institutions are often the hubs of subsidiary networks that disseminate knowledge back and forth across the language barrier: for example, Portugal and Spain produce scholarly journals in their national languages for distribution amongst the countries of their former colonies, and in some cases translate knowledge produced in those languages into English for wider circulation. Similarly, countries from the former Eastern bloc that are culturally and geographically oriented towards the West serve a similar function with relation to others that are farther removed or more oriented towards the East (see Marušić and Marušić, Chapter 11; Petrić, Chapter 10).

As a direct consequence of this mediating role, academic production on the semiperiphery is often more concerned with replicating accepted models and techniques than with generating new knowledge, which has caused it to be criticized as unoriginal and derivative (Nunes and Gonçalves 2001, p. 19, Gizycki 1973[2]). What is more, these countries' dependence upon the centre for funding and partnerships also tends to engender an attitude of uncritical subservience to that centre, often accompanied by a concomitant scorn for anything local or peripheral (an attitude that I have elsewhere termed the 'butler' syndrome [Bennett forthcoming]).

On the other hand, the semiperiphery is also less constrained than the centre by the need for 'rigour', which means that it can afford to be more heterogeneous and open to outside influences. Consequently, a great deal of 'boundary work'[3] takes place there (Nunes and Gonçalves 2001, p. 22), which may have long-term repercussions upon the evolution of the system as a whole (Bennett forthcoming, Gizycki 1973).

All in all, the semiperiphery has an essential role to play in the functioning of the academic system as a whole, simultaneously sanctioning the values emanating from the centre while refreshing it with new perspectives brought from outside.

## I.1   Academic culture on the semiperiphery

As we have seen, the semiperiphery forms a kind of 'middle class' in the global system, neither as privileged as the centre nor as deprived as the outer periphery. This has repercussions on all aspects of academic life, with inevitable consequences for research productivity.

On the level of material resources, semiperipheral universities rarely enjoy the kinds of benefits that centre institutions take for granted. Their equipment is unlikely to be state-of-the-art and may well be in need of replacement or repair; libraries are often understocked and not very up-to-date; and subscriptions to the main international journals may be only fitfully maintained in accordance with oscillating budgets. Yet their situation is rarely as severe as the case of Sri Lanka in the early 1990s (Canagarajah 2002), where even good-quality paper and photo-copiers were difficult to come by. Semiperipheral researchers are thus not entirely off-network, and they have the basic conditions to produce, though this might sometimes require more effort and dedication than in the centre universities where everything is readily at hand.

As regards the incentive to publish, once again the semiperiphery falls between the two extremes described by Canagarajah (2002). The 'publish or perish' ethos that dominates centre countries is reduced or even absent, due to the persistence of an older tradition that values institutional service and systems of patronage above individual merit. However, the centripetal force that acts upon all the countries of the semiperiphery is gradually bringing change in this area as in others, with the result that legislation is being promulgated in many places to ensure the implementation of a modern meritocratic culture. In some cases, this may lead to a conflict between state policy and actual institutional practice (see Uysal, Chapter 9).

As regards publishing practices, journals and volumes produced on the semiperiphery are not always peer-reviewed, and the selection process may be conducted in a much less rigorous way than would be expected in centre countries (an editorial board is unlikely to refuse an article by a prominent figure in the community, for example, even if it does not come up to the desired standards). There is also a weaker sense of intellectual property, and certain practices that would be con-demned in centre institutions are often tacitly condoned (see Gonerko-Frej, Chapter 4). Once again, though, the situation is by no means as extreme as that described by Canagarajah for Sri Lanka (2002), and there seems to be a growing tendency to assimilate to centre values on this issue as well as others.

Finally, the scientific paradigm, which in centre countries is considered to be the only valid form of knowledge,[4] may not have quite the same centrality on the semiperiphery, where it may face competition from traditional or alternative epistemologies. While none of the chapters in this volume report the persistence of a religious research paradigm similar to that described by Canagarajah (2002, p. 189) at the University of Jaffna, many of the countries involved do have strong humanities traditions that are deeply embedded in the national or regional culture. It is these that are most obviously under threat by globalization, as researchers are encouraged to publish in English and make their research relevant to the international community.

All the semiperipheral countries covered in this volume have experienced rapid change in recent years, usually as a result of measures like the Bologna Agreement designed to standardize academic systems across different geographical regions. Consequently, they are in the process of abandoning their traditional practices (which are becoming viewed as markers of backwardness or underdevelopment) in favour of those espoused by the centre. While this has not occurred at the same speed everywhere, it is clear that this centripetal tendency is an important characteristic of the semiperiphery

## I.2 The semiperiphery in the European context

This volume concentrates exclusively on the European context, despite the fact that the undisputed world centre is on the other side of the Atlantic. There are a number of reasons for this. First, Wallerstein's initial formulation of world systems theory was overwhelmingly Eurocentric in its perspective (and indeed has been criticized for this). As a result, this part of the world has been much more thoroughly theorized than any other, and the concept of the semiperiphery has been applied in fields as diverse as law, literature, commerce, medicine and science.[5]

Second, in the context of the sovereign debt crisis and the much-debated prospect of a 'two-tier' Europe, the notion of the semiperiphery seems particularly pertinent in this part of the world. The term overlaps to some extent with the pejorative 'PIGS'[6] designation that groups the countries along the Mediterranean border that were considered to be most at risk of defaulting on their sovereign debt; but it has the advantage of also including the new or aspiring members of the European Union, located along the eastern borders and geographically and economically comparable to them. All of these countries are clearly perceived as occupying a subordinate role in relation to the richer countries in the north.

The third reason for focusing upon the European context is an entirely practical one. The idea for this volume arose during the course of a conference in Poland, in June 2011,[7] where the term 'semiperiphery' came up several times. It appeared in the original title of a paper by Petrić about academic journals in Serbia[8] (apparently in deference to Lillis and Curry's [2010, p. 5] fleeting reference to the work of Boaventura de Sousa Santos), and was then developed in more depth in my own paper about the academic culture in Portugal (Bennett forthcoming). The notion generated such recognition amongst the participants present that it seemed eminently worthwhile to try to refine the concept and apply it to the concrete realities of the various countries represented.

Hence, this volume brings together contributions not only from the so-called 'PIGS' countries of Southern Europe (Portugal, Italy, Greece and Spain), but also new and aspiring members of the EU located in the east of the landmass (Croatia, Serbia, Czech Republic, Romania, Poland and Turkey). Despite being culturally and linguistically very diverse, all these countries are united by the fact that they are geographically and economically peripheral to the European centre, a fact that seems to have conditioned their academic cultures in the ways described above. Indeed, what this collection brings out is the similarity of the experiences recounted on a whole gamut of issues ranging from the kind of discourse used in academia to practices and procedures relating to academic production and the transmission of knowledge.

A number of the studies included in this book specifically point to the humanities as the most problematic area for the semiperiphery, and as a result, these disciplines acquire particular emphasis in this volume. Many of the cultures represented have traditional scholarly discourses that are very different from the hegemonic English discourse, but which are currently coming under pressure to 'modernize' (that is, conform to the epistemological premises underlying English). This is clearly perceived as problematic by many of the practitioners operating in the field, as the various interviews and surveys show. On the one hand, these semiperipheral players are eager to participate in the international community; on the other, they are aware that a significant part of their identity will be lost in the process – an ambivalence that is in keeping with the findings of similar research done elsewhere (see Ferguson 2007, pp. 25–26, for an overview).

Indeed, almost all the contributions to this volume describe some kind of tension between different academic cultures, whether this is presented as a conflict between sciences and humanities, or between East and West, local and global, traditional and modern. Some (for example, Uysal,

Chapter 9; Gonerko-Frej, Chapter 4; Marušić and Marušić, Chapter 11) also describe a significant gap between official discourse and actual practice, possibly resulting from an inability of the culture to adapt to centre norms at the pace that the national authorities would desire.

The resulting lack of 'rigour', though condemned by some of the authors in this book, may actually prove very fruitful for the global academic system as a whole. For, as some world systems theorists[9] have pointed out, established centres tend to stagnate after a while, entering into decline through lack of competition. The periphery, on the other hand (or, more properly, the semiperiphery, which is near enough to the core to actually participate) is stimulated by the need to compete; and despite ostensibly upholding the values and norms of the centre, the inevitable gap between policy and praxis means that it is more tolerant of non-standard models and procedures, often permitting practices that would not be accepted by the centre. Over the long term, these aberrant practices may ultimately serve as a source of renewal and change for the system as a whole.

The semiperiphery, then, should perhaps be seen as a place of tension, a contact zone where different attitudes, discourses and practices meet and merge. As such, it is effervescent with possibilities, allowing dominant attitudes to be challenged and new paradigms to arise in a way that would be unthinkable in centre countries, where the monopoly over what is considered valid knowledge holds more sway.

\*\*\*

This volume is thus organized into three distinct sections, each dealing with a different aspect of semiperipherality. **Part I** focuses on the question of discourse and the tensions that are generated when traditional scholarly writing styles come into contact with a hegemonic model that may be grounded on quite different epistemological principles. **Bennett** examines the way Portuguese history writing appears to be changing through contact with English, postulating its eventual demise given the pressures that are currently bearing upon Portuguese researchers in this area. **Dontcheva-Navratilova** looks at the textual strategies employed by Czech linguistics scholars in their attempts to represent themselves as members not only of the local but also of the global academic discourse community, and suggests that these complex negotiations may be having an effect upon Czech academic discourse, causing it to change. **Vladimirou** also focuses on scale shifts in the context of a Greek linguistics conference, but in this case concludes that, despite the symbolic value of English, a balance is maintained between locally produced knowledge in Greek and internationally accepted knowledge in English. Finally, **Gonerko-Frej** describes some of the problems faced by Polish students of English academic writing, advocating a non-normative approach that encourages the expression of specific meanings and identities through the medium of the foreign tongue.

**Part II** focuses on academic practitioners and their subjective responses to the pressures of globalization. **Burgess's** opening chapter describes its effects upon humanities scholars in Spain, identifying sites of acceptance and resistance to the principles underpinning the evaluation policy implemented by the country's research funding body. Staying within the Iberian Peninsula, **Barros**, writing from Portugal, also focuses on humanities researchers, reporting that they have a much greater reluctance to use English than do their colleagues from the hard sciences, despite the pressures exerted upon them. **Bardi and Muresan**, for their part, explore the perceptions and attitudes of Romanian researchers at the Bucharest School of Economics towards the implementation of international standards in research writing; and **Negretti** interviews Italian humanities scholars to gauge their attitudes towards the discursive and cultural practices they have left behind.

**Part III** turns to the question of knowledge flows and publication practices, opening with a chapter by **Uysal**, which focuses on the gap between official state policy on academic publication and scholars' actual practice in two different Turkish universities. The next three chapters look specifically at certain channels of research dissemination in the current geopolitical context. **Petrić** questions the role of English-medium journals in Serbia, particularly those that have not been accorded 'international' status, but may instead be aiming at a primarily regional public. **Marušić and Marušić** home in on one particular journal operating in that region, offering a fascinating case study of an English-language journal in Croatia that has been instrumental in implementing centre norms in that part of the world, and providing authorship training and publication opportunities for researchers that might otherwise be excluded from the international scientific community.

**Sokół's** chapter, which closes the section and the book, represents a new departure: instead of focusing upon a particular geographic region, she applies the term 'semiperipheral' to the emerging genre of the academic weblog, understood as an informal response to the 'publish or perish' ethos that is so entrenched in centre countries. This modulation serves to remind us of the increasingly virtual nature of the spatial metaphor that underpins this book. For, as commentators have already suggested, it may well be the new technologies, with their remarkable capacity to evade the control mechanisms set up by global capitalism, that ultimately allow the centre–periphery dichotomy to be transcended, bringing about a decentralization of power relations that can only be in the interests of the quest for knowledge.

## Notes

1. The world's fastest-growing economies (Brazil, Russia, India, China and now also South Africa).
2. Gizycki does not use the term 'semiperiphery', but distinguishes between the countries of the outer periphery and those nearer the centre, which tend to be characterized most by 'patterns of emulation'.
3. This term was coined by the sociologist Thomas Gieryn to refer to activities that define, redefine or dissolve the frontiers between different domains of knowledge.
4. According to Halliday and Martin (1993, p. 220), the scientific paradigm and the discourse that it spawned are so overwhelmingly dominant in Anglo-Saxon culture that even the humanities subscribe to it: there is 'an essential continuity between humanities and science as far as interpreting the world is concerned'.
5. See for example the numerous articles and volumes produced on the subject by the Centre for Social Studies at the University of Coimbra, Portugal, under sociologist Boaventura de Sousa Santos.
6. Portugal, Italy, Greece and Spain (in some analyses, Ireland is included instead of or as well as Italy, though as an English-speaking nation, it clearly has less relevance in the context of this book).
7. PRISEAL 2 (Publishing and Presenting Research Internationally: Issues for Speakers of English as an Additional Language) on the theme of 'Occupying niches: interculturality, cross-culturality and aculturality in academic research', Katowice/Sosnowiec, June 2011.
8. Petrić's paper is reproduced in this volume under a slightly different title.
9. See, for example, Gizycki (1973) on the scientific system and Evan-Zohar (1990/1979) on literary systems.

# Part I
# Discourses in Tension

# 1
# The Erosion of Portuguese Historiographic Discourse

*Karen Bennett*

## 1.1 Introduction

Traditional Portuguese historiographic discourse is a very different creature from its mainstream English counterpart. Delighting in syntactical complexity, Baroque flourishes and emotivity, it clearly does not subscribe to the empiricist paradigm that underpins most scholarly endeavour in the Anglo-Saxon world, and which has established transparency, objectivity, economy and precision as the cardinal virtues of academic prose. On the contrary, its overt rhetoricity betrays a philosophical affinity to the hermeneutic episteme favoured in much of continental Europe, which, in this domain, has found its most potent form of expression in the work of the Annales school, first developed in France in the 1930s.

Indeed, until the last decades of the 20th century, it was French culture rather than English that exerted the greatest influence upon Portuguese historians, an orientation manifested in these academics' mobility patterns and publication practices, not to mention the contents of their libraries.[1] However, since the turn of the millennium, there has been a significant shift in the direction and intensity of these knowledge flows. With the inexorable expansion of English as the lingua franca of academia, Portuguese researchers of all disciplines have come under pressure to publish in Anglophone journals rather than in Portuguese, Spanish or French ones, as they used to. In the case of historiography, this has had profound epistemological implications. For one, the traditional discourse now seems to be on the retreat, beaten back by another, that has to all intents and purposes been calqued upon English and therefore transports quite different assumptions and values.

This chapter describes a study designed to chart the changes taking place in Portuguese historiographic discourse over a 15-year period

(1998 to 2013), and discusses some of the ideological and epistemological implications of the colonization process that is clearly under way in this discipline.

## 1.2   Background

A survey of humanities and social science researchers conducted in 2002 and 2008 (Bennett 2010a, 2011a) revealed a clear perception amongst this community of the differences between Portuguese and English scholarly writing in these disciplines. Though attitudes varied as to the relative merits of the two approaches, Portuguese was consistently described as more complex, elaborate and poetic than English, which was seen as clear, precise, objective, concrete and grammatically straightforward.

However, the concept of 'discourse' as a circumscribed community-defined subset of language was notably absent from the comments put forward in this survey. Respondents tended to consider these characteristics as inherent properties of the two languages, something that is belied not only by the indisputably rich tradition of literary writing in English, but also by the existence in Portuguese of another academic style that is, to all intents and purposes, indistinguishable from mainstream English academic discourse (EAD).

In view of this situation, a second study was carried out in 2008 in order to gauge the relative prevalence of the two discourses in Portuguese academic writing (Bennett 2010b, 2011a). A corpus made up of 408 academic texts of different genres and disciplines (1,333,890 words), which had been submitted for translation between 1998 and 2008, was analysed for the presence of particular discourse features not usually considered acceptable in English academic discourse,[2] and on the basis of this, the texts were graded to indicate their degree of deviation from the EAD norm. It was found that the elaborate poetic style, dubbed the 'traditional' discourse, predominated in the humanities and some social sciences (with a 'postmodern' variant evident in 'artier' subjects such as musicology, architecture, art and literary studies), while the 'modern' style, apparently calqued on English, prevailed in the sciences.

Particularly interesting were the number of hybrids found, that is, texts that fell between the traditional and modern camps because they contained features of each. In accordance with previous studies that have charted the influence of English upon other languages (for example, Ammon 2001, Anderman and Rogers 2005, House 2008), this was taken as evidence of discourse change, probably resulting from the cultural reorientation away from French models towards Anglo-Saxon ones in the early years of the 21st century and a concomitant realignment with the empiricist paradigm dominant in the Anglo-Saxon world. Five years after the closure of that initial corpus, it now seems pertinent to see how that assumption bears out, and whether evidence can indeed be found of a shift towards a more Anglicized style of academic writing.

The decision was taken to focus exclusively on the discipline of history because, in the multidisciplinary study, that subcorpus had contained particularly clear-cut and coherent examples of the traditional discourse, as well as a considerable number of hybrid texts. This new study now sought to compare that body of history texts (hereafter referred to as the *2008 Corpus*) with a second group submitted for translation since then (the *2013 Corpus*) in order to find out, first, if the anticipated shift away from the traditional discourse towards a more modern one has in fact taken place, and second, whether this was having any effect upon the kind of history that was being practised.

## 1.3 The traditional and modern styles in Portuguese historiography

The *2008 Corpus* contained 19 history texts of various academic genres, making up a total of 137,456 words. Of these, over half (52.6 per cent if calculated by text; 66.3 per cent if calculated by word) were classified as examples of the traditional style, while the remainder were hybrids. There were no cases of the modern style – unusually, because in the other humanities and social science disciplines studied at the same time (that is, archaeology, geography, education, geography, law, linguistics, and literary studies), the modern style coexisted alongside traditional and hybrid styles. In the *2013 Corpus*, however, there were several examples of the modern style, which may itself be indicative of a discourse shift across the discipline as a whole.

Let us look at each of these discourses in more detail.

### 1.3.1 The traditional style

The traditional style is so called because it seems, in many respects, to be a direct descendant of the grand style of Classical Rhetoric, widespread throughout Europe prior to the Scientific Revolution of the 17th century. It is characterized above all by a degree of linguistic complexity not commonly seen in English texts of the same type. The sentences are frequently long (60 to 150 words on average, and often much longer) and highly subordinated, and the main topic is not usually presented in initial position, but instead is deferred, adorned or embedded, often within an interpersonal structure that emphasizes the author/reader relationship. This interpersonal focus is reinforced by the abundant use of first-person verb forms and pronouns (such as the magisterial 'we' for authorial self-reference, and various forms of the inclusive 'we'), as well as by the use of emotive or poetic diction, and literary or rhetorical devices designed to create a particular effect upon the reader.

Another characteristic that distinguishes this discourse from mainstream English history writing is the use of the so-called 'historical' tenses (that is, the present and future tenses to refer to events located in the historical past). As this is rarely maintained for very long, but is usually interspersed with conventional past tenses, it would appear to be a device mobilized at particular moments to make descriptive episodes more vivid (as indeed occurs in English in non-scholarly narratives, such as television documentaries or informal first-person accounts).

This chronological blurring is complemented by a similar vagueness with respect to logical relationships. It is common, for example, to find the present participle form (known as the *gerúndio* in Portuguese) used where English might favour more precise connecting devices, such as temporal, conditional, consequential, concessional or other structures. This generates an ambiguity as to the precise nature of the relationship, in keeping with a phenomenological orientation towards the past.

All of these features together, then, suggest that Portuguese traditional discourse is more akin to literary than to scientific or technical writing. Clarity, precision and economy are clearly not its main objectives; for rather than presenting a series of neutral or objective 'facts' about the past, the focus seems to be on the historian's subjective perception of that remote reality and his/her rhetorical relationship with the text's readers.[3]

Perhaps the most representative example of the traditional style in the joint corpus is an article by a canonical figure of Portuguese historiography, Victorino Magalhães Godinho, which was first published in 1968 and then translated into English in 2004 for inclusion in a bilingual volume. With its *longue durée* perspective on shipping in the Indian Ocean, it appears to be emulating Fernand Braudel's famous work *La Méditerranée* (1949) in approach and style.

The extract given below[4] (Extract 1) consists of a single sentence 93 words long, organized in a way that is quite alien to English, as can be immediately seen by the punctuation. In terms of literary devices, there are inversions for rhetorical effect (*'sem que a sua vida por ele seja penetrada'/'sem que por ele se aventure'*) and poetic effusion (*'mole de terra firme sem respiração marinha'*), as well as the use of the present and future tenses to refer to events that occurred in the contextualized completed past. All in all, considerable reformulation was required before this could be rendered acceptably in EAD.

---

## Extract 1: Vitorino Magalhães Godinho, 1968

Enquanto a Europa se desenvolve até a era quatrocentista, à beira do oceano
*While Europe develops up to the fourteen hundreds era alongside the ocean*

mas sem que a sua vida por ele seja penetrado, e sem que por ele se aventure,
*but without its life by it being penetrated and without that across it is ventured,*

ao redor do Índico as diferentes populações vão-se interligando pelas vias marítimas
*around the Indian Ocean the different populations go interconnecting by sea routes*

e as suas economias não dispensam tais conexões longínquas de navegação;
*and their economies do not dispense (with) such distant connections of shipping;*

o complexo europeu é predominantemente mediterrâneo e não se abre a poente
*the European complex is predominantly Mediterranean and does not open to the West,*

onde é merely costeiro: a África setentional liga-se ao complexo mediterrâneo,
*where it is merely coastal: northern Africa connects to the Mediterranean complex,*

a ocidental permanence mole de terra firme sem respiração marinha; em contraste
*the western (part) remains a mass of firm land without sea breath; in contrast*

o Oriente afro-asiático é oceânico.
*the Afro-Asian East is oceanic.*

Source: 'O oceano Índico de 3000 a.C até o século XVII: história do descobrimento, navios, rotas, supremacias' in *Ensaios, Vol. 1*. Lisbon.

Extract 2, by another highly respected historian, is from an article that was published in Portuguese in 1998 and submitted for translation in 2006. This is a good example of the kind of syntax that predominates in the traditional style as, in each of these two sentences, the main clause is not only deferred but also constantly interrupted by circumstantial information. In the first, the 'facts' are also characteristically embedded in an interpersonal framework (*'este horizonte de expectativas levou a que, desde cedo, se tornasse patente que...'*), which has a hedging effect, as well as generating a rhythmically pleasing build-up of suspense.

---

**Extract 2: Fernando Catroga, 1998**

Simultaneamente, e no que à chamada Geração de 70 se refere,
*Simultaneously, and as far as the so-called '70s Generation is concerned,*

este horizonte de expectativas levou a que, desde cedo, se tornasse patente que,
*this horizon of expectations meant that, from early on, it became clear that,*

se existiam alguns postulados comuns, as divergências filosóficas e políticas
*if there existed some common postulates, the philosophical and political divergences*

no seio dos intelectuais mais apostados na democratização do país
*in the bosom of the intellectuals most committed to the democratization of the country*

eram igualmente significativas. Isto é, se quase todos faziam uma análoga
*were equally significant. That is, if almost everyone made an analogous*

avaliação decadentista da realidade portuguesa e se a grande maioria defendia
*decadentist evaluation of the Portuguese reality and if the great majority defended*

a prioridade de se pugnar por uma revolução cultural (intelectual e moral)
*the priority of fighting for a cultural (and intellectual and moral) revolution*

que seria a condição prioritária para as transformações sociais e políticas subsequentes,
*which would be the priority condition for subsequent political and social changes,*

as divergências eclodiram no que concerne às legitimações filosófico-históricas,
*divergences erupted as regards the philosophical-historical legitimations,*

bem como à responsabilização de instituições políticas (como a Monarquia)
*as well as the responsibilization of political institutions (like the Monarchy)*

na aceleração da decadência nacional.
*in the acceleration of national decadence.*

Source: 'Decadência e Regeneração no Imaginário do Republicanismo Português dos finais do século XIX', *Los 98 Ibéricos y el Mar.* Madrid, Comisaría General de España, pp. 423–445.

Extract 3, concerning the arrival of the Jesuits in Portugal, was written more recently (2011), but it nevertheless contains many features that mark it out as an example of the traditional style. The main sentence is less complex than the previous ones, but it has been organized around a series of parallelisms (which in Portuguese are phonological as well as grammatical and lexical), indicating that the author's concern is primarily aesthetic and rhetorical rather than informative or discursive. This rhetorical orientation is reinforced by the use of the historical present and future tenses to create immediacy, and by the grammatical incompleteness of the last two periods, which allows the rhythm gently to wane to a close. Particularly significant here is the use of the inclusive 'we', which effectively collapses the distinctions between author, reader and object of study, generating a discourse that is subjective, emotive and ideologically engaged.

## Extract 3: Maria de Lurdes Craveiro, 2011

Para este grupo de apóstolos letrados, como ficarão conhecidos na sua chegada a Coimbra,
*For this group of lettered apostles, as they will be known on their arrival at Coimbra,*

> não se trata de invadir mas de discutir, já não de impor mas de propor,
> *it is not about invading but discussing, no longer about imposing but about proposing,*
>
> não são mãos fechadas que se abatem sobre uma cultura que se hostiliza
> *they are not closed hands that fall upon a culture that becomes hostile*
>
> mas mãos abertas que aguardam uma resposta. A resposta de um outro
> *but open hands that await a response. The response of another*
>
> que queremos como outro. Como um outro de nós.
> *that we want as other. As an other of ourselves.*
>
> Source: *A Sé Nova de Coimbra*, Coimbra University Press, p. 22.

As these examples show, traditional Portuguese scholarly discourse is very difficult to translate into English in a form that would be acceptable to the international discourse community. In order for such a text to be publishable, the translator usually has to make radical alterations that go far beyond the splitting-up of long sentences and removal of framing references to include whole paragraph reorganization, sentence-pruning and tense conversion. The ideological implications of this procedure have been discussed elsewhere (Bennett 2007a, 2007b).

## 1.3.2   The modern style

The modern style, in contrast, can be rendered into English with only minor alterations. It is so-called because it was felt to reflect the 'modern' (rationalist, capitalist, democratic) mindset that developed in England with the Scientific Revolution of the 17th century.[5] Its orientation is empiricist, in the sense that it aims to describe and explain aspects of reality in a transparent objective fashion, and consequently it values clarity, concision and rational argument above aesthetic or interpersonal factors. Hence, the syntax is mostly simple, with a single idea per clause and limited subordination. Impersonal forms tend to predominate (often realized in Portuguese through the reflexive voice), and personal forms, when they appear, are used in much the same way as in English (that is, for authorial self-reference, to evoke the discourse community, or, occasionally, for textual positioning). The SV word order is generally maintained, though there may be verbal fronting in reflexive or passive formulations. Lexis is used referentially, rather than figuratively, and terms are clearly defined. As regards text organization, this corresponds to what would be used in an English text of the same type, with a clear statement of theme followed by a development at all ranks.

The first example of this style in the corpus dates from 2009 (Extract 4 below).[6] Unlike the previous extracts, it was not published in Portuguese, but was written specifically for translation into English, which may be significant. Indeed, it complies with English discourse norms in almost all respects: the sentences are relatively short and simple, with limited subordination; the information is presented directly, rather than embedded in an interpersonal framework; and the main facts (dates, names, events) are given in initial position. Indeed, the only real concession to Portuguese grammar in this extract is the use of the gerund in the second line (*'tendo por missão'*).

---

**Extract 4: João Gouveia Monteiro, 2009**

Em inícios de 1384, Nun'Álvares foi nomeado pelo Mestre de Avis,
*At the beginning of 1384, Nun'Álvares was appointed by the Master of Avis*

como fronteiro do Alentejo tendo por missão controlar os movimentos
*as frontier commander of the Alentejo, having as his mission to control the movements*

das tropas castelhanas na zona sul de Portugal e evitar a sua progressão até Lisboa.
*of the Castilian troops in the southern zone of Portugal and prevent their progress to Lisbon.*

Em 6 de Abril de 1384, averbou um primeiro grande sucesso militar, na Batalha dos Atoleiros
*On 6th April 1384, he had a first great military success in the Battle of Atoleiros*

(região de Estremoz), derrotando com um pequeno exército uma força de cavalaria
*(region of Estremoz), defeating a small army, a cavalry force,*

ao serviço de D. João I de Castela. Segundo o cronista português Fernão Lopes
*at the service of D. John I of Castile. According to the Portuguese chronicler Fernão Lopes*

---

(meados do século XV), Nun'Álvares foi o primeiro que, em Portugal,
*(middle of the 15th century), Nun'Álvares was the first in Portugal*

travou batalha desmontado e a venceu.
*that waged war unmounted and won.*

Source: 'Nun'Álvares Pereira'. Reproduced with the kind permission of the author.

Extract 5 below is also an example of the modern style, although it is not quite a straightforward to translate as the previous one, largely due to the inversion of subject and verb in the second sentence (*'foi construído um edifício de escala gigantesca'*). It should be pointed out, however, that the agentless passive is uncommon in Portuguese humanistic writing; hence, its very presence effectively marks the text's subscription to the empiricist paradigm. As for the verbal fronting, this is a very common feature of Portuguese scientific and technical prose (see Bennett 2011b, Johns 1992) and indeed probably developed precisely to allow the natural emphasis (through end-weighting) to fall upon the non-human subject.

### Extract 5: Maria Helena Souto, 2010

Em 1867, a França do Segundo Império organizou aquela que foi a quarta exposição universal,
*In 1867, France of the Second Empire organized what was the fourth universal exhibition,*

de acordo com um projecto lançado por Napoleão III. No centro da grande planície
*in accordance with a project launched by Napoleon III. At the centre of the great plain*

do *Champ de Mars* em Paris, foi construído um edifício de escala gigantesca, planetária,
*of the Champ de Mars in Paris, was constructed a building of gigantic planetary scale,*

com uma planta elíptica, formada por sete alas concêntricas; estas separavam
*with an elliptical ground plan formed by seven concentric wings; these separated*

os produtos expostos segundo a sua natureza, enquanto uma série de alas radiais
*the exhibits in accordance with their nature, while a series of radial wings*

delimitavam os países em sectores. A arquitectura do *Palais du Champ de Mars*
*delimited the countries into sectors. The architecture of the Palais du Champ de Mars*

representou, antes de mais, um esforço sério de integrar um princípio classificador
*represented, first and foremost, a serious effort to include a classification principle*

neste tipo de mostras, em sintonia com os dois aspectos básicos da sua organização
*in this type of display, in keeping with the two basic aspects of its organization*

– nações e produtos – constituindo-se num sistema coerente.
*– nations and products – forming a coherent system.*

Source: 'A secção da *Histoire du Travail* na Exposição Universal de 1867 e a museologia em Portugal'. Portuguese version reproduced with the kind permission of the author.

### 1.3.3 Hybrid discourses

As mentioned above, many of the texts in the *2008 Corpus* include features of both the traditional and the modern styles, and were thus considered to form a kind of hybrid discourse. Unlike the other two, this is not really a coherent category, but rather seems to reflect a certain indecision on the part of authors as to which discourse to adopt. Some of the texts begin in a simple straightforward style that seems to indicate subscription to the empiricist paradigm, but slide into a more traditional style as the text proceeds; others, in contrast, use the modern style for the presentation of the main arguments and/or data, reserving the traditional style for the introduction and conclusion.

The example given below[7] (Extract 6) is one of several texts that actually mix the two styles throughout. Although the paragraph and sentence structure is largely modern, the interpersonal dimension is more marked than is usual in English history writing, with many references to author and reader (in the form of first-person singular and plural verb forms and pronouns), rhetorical questions (for example, '*De que fontes dispomos para a reconstituição do combate de Aljubarrota?*') and interpersonal framing devices (for example, '*Creio, portanto, que é o momento de voltar a chamar a atenção para ...*'). There are also some verbless sentences, taking the form of detached subordinate clauses ('*Guerra essa que, em 1367, trouxera até à Península Ibérica ... os exércitos inglês do Príncipe Negro...*').

---

### Extract 6: João Gouveia Monteiro, 2007

Ao tomar conhecimento (tardiamente) do desbarato da linha da frente,
*Upon learning (belatedly) of the disarray on the front line,*

a batalha de Juan I decide avançar, provavelmente a cavalo e acompanhada
*Juan I's battalion decides to advance, probably on horseback and accompanied*

pelas duas alas. Lopes (que concentra a sua narrativa nesta segunda fase da
*by the two wings. Lopes (who concentrates his narrative on this second phase of the*

batalha) realça o aparato da arrancada castelhana. Mas as alas depressa
*battle) highlights the Castilian display of starting-off. But the wings quickly*

ficaram de fora, pois os obstáculos naturais dificultavam o acesso ao planalto.
*got left out, as natural obstacles impeded access to the plateau.*

Quanto aos restantes, ao aproximarem-se da posição portuguesa apercebem-se de que
*As for the rest, in drawing near to the Portuguese position, they realise that*

o combate tem de ser travado a pé. Por isso, os castelhanos desmontam e caminham
*the combat has to be done on foot. Therefore the Castilians dismount and walk*

> umas centenas de metros até alcançar os adversários; ao mesmo tempo,
> *a few hundred metres until they reach the enemy; at the same time,*
>
> cortam as suas lanças.
> *they cut their spears.*
>
> Source: 'A Batalha de Aljubarrota (1385): uma Reaprecião'. Portuguese text reproduced with the kind permission of the author.

The existence of a large number of hybrid texts in the *2008 Corpus* was assumed to be evidence of the influence of English upon Portuguese history writing. Hence, the new study, described in this paper, was designed in order to find out if the modern style was indeed taking over from the traditional style.

## 1.4   Data sources

In order to gauge whether or not there was any noticeable change in the discourse used by Portuguese historians, the history subcorpus from the 2008 multidisciplinary study (now dubbed the *2008 Corpus*) was compared with a new corpus of history texts submitted for translation between 2009 and 2013 (the *2013 Corpus*). The former contains a total of 137,456 words (19 texts), while the latter has 544,974 words (28 texts).

In both cases, various academic genres were represented. The most common genre was the article (this category included conference papers and book chapters, as well as conventional articles for publication in journals), but there were also dissertations (Masters and PhD), full-length monographs, research proposals, and abstracts for all the above. Hence, the texts ranged widely in terms of length, from 78 to 214,444 words, across the two corpora.

In terms of subdisciplinary orientation, the corpora include works generated within the domains of social and economic history, cultural history, history of ideas and history of art/architecture, though these allegiances are not always overtly marked in the text. Some had previously been published in Portuguese, though others were written specifically for translation and publication in English (an aspect that possibly conditioned the style of discourse used, as discussed below). Of those, some were destined to be published in international journals or volumes, or presented at international conferences, while others were to be published in Portugal, usually in bilingual or parallel English/

Portuguese editions. With regards to the dissertations and research proposals, these were being translated usually in order to enable access by non-Portuguese examiners, supervisors, reviewers or consultants, a phenomenon which itself reflects the increased openness of Portuguese historiography to the international community.

## 1.5    Method

The method used in this study of history texts was basically the same as that employed in the 2008 multidisciplinary study. The texts were first anonymized, standardized (through removal of bibliographies, diagrams, figures, and other non-textual information) and labelled using a code that reflected the discipline, year, genre and author. Then they were manually analysed by a single researcher to assess the extent to which their discourse differed from the EAD norm. On the basis of this analysis, each one was awarded a grade called a Variance Factor (VF), which indicates the perceived difference between the discourse used in a particular text and mainstream EAD. Then, the results of the two corpora were compared in the hope that this might yield some indications about changes taking place in Portuguese historiographic discourse.

### 1.5.1    Variance Factor

In the 2008 multidisciplinary study, the VR ranged from 0 (the 'modern' style, when the discourse was essentially the same as what might be expected in an English academic text of the same discipline and genre, with allowances made for aspects determined by the language) to –4 (the so-called 'postmodern' style, when the text organization, syntax and lexis were radically different from EAD). However, as the history subcorpus in that study did not contain any postmodern texts, it was not considered necessary to extend the range beyond –2 (the 'traditional' style) in the new study.

On the other hand, it soon became clear that the –1 band, representing the hybrid texts, needed to be fine-tuned in order to account for the various degrees of hybridity presented by the corpus. Hence, this was divided into three subcategories: –0.5 (attributed to texts that were mostly modern with the occasional intrusion of features from the traditional style), –1 (presenting a roughly equal balance of modern and traditional characteristics) and –1.5 (inclining towards the traditional).

The first level of analysis involved a global impression of the text's general 'translatability' (that is, texts that would require extensive reformulation in order to become intelligible in English would tend to be awarded a higher VF than those in which the surface structure resembled English). However, as this was a rather vague concept, a more detailed analysis was also performed in order to identify the presence of certain characteristics considered alien to mainstream EAD. These Distinguishing Discourse Features (or DDFs), as they were called, were identified manually (most did not lend themselves to electronic tagging) and marked in the text using a system of colour coding. They are described in more detail below.

Another factor taken into account in this study was the presence of bibliographic references that explicitly suggested an epistemological orientation towards non-English theoretical models. Hence, references to historians like Braudel, Ariès, Bloch, Le Goff, Duby, and so on were taken to reveal the influence of the Annales school of historiography.

Other factors that were taken into consideration, as they seemed to indicate a traditional or Romance orientation to humanistic text production, were punctuation devices (such as the use of French guillemets rather than English inverted commas; double dashes instead of brackets; ellipsis marks after a list; the capitalization of words like *Mundo* ['world'], *Terra* ['earth'] or *Homem* ['man']); and certain referencing habits (such as the abbreviation *AA.VV* to refer to various authors). In full-length works, the placement of the table of contents at the end of the text rather than at the beginning was also considered significant.

### 1.5.2  Distinguishing Discourse Features (DDFs)

Of the various parameters used in the attribution of VR, the presence of DDFs was considered to be the most important. Hence, texts that contained the most DDFs would usually be attributed a higher VR. However, this process was not an entirely linear. A clustering of certain kinds of DDFs together was generally felt to be more significant than the persistent use of just one kind, which could be idiosyncratic. For example, the appearance of interpersonal framing devices alongside historical tenses, gerunds and personal references in the main body of a text was felt to indicate a phenomenological orientation to the historical data, while the use of poetic diction alongside grammatical inversions, verbless sentences and rhetorical questions, particularly in introductions and conclusions, was seen as a vestige of the grand or sublime style of Classical Rhetoric.[8]

i. *Complex syntax (CS)*:
This is probably the most obvious marker of the traditional style and one of the first things that Portuguese authors try to change

when they are writing for an Anglophone public (as claimed in the survey reported in Bennett 2010a). Traditional Portuguese sentences tend to be long by English standards (sometimes up to 350 words), but it is not length in itself that counts. More important is the syntactical structure. While English academic style manuals invariably advocate coordinated rather than subordinated structure with one main idea per sentence, the traditional style of Portuguese tends to be heavily subordinated and dense with information. For example, it is common to find 'both ... and' (*quer ... quer / tanto ... como*) or 'on the one hand/on the other' (*por um lado/por outro*) structures coming on top of 'if' or 'although' clauses, all of which may be packed inside an interpersonal framing device (see below). As well as this kind of embedding, the main clause may also be deferred by cataphoric cohesive devices or inversions used for rhetorical effect (see below), or may be constantly interrupted by relative clauses, participle phrases or elements in apposition.

Examples of this DDF can be found in Extracts 1 and 2 above.

ii. *Deferred topic (DT)*:

This is where the main idea is not placed in initial position but is deferred, creating an effect of suspense. It can occur at all ranks of the text. On the level of the sentence, it is manifested by a taste for cataphora (for example, *'Espelho da cultura humanista em Coimbra, o Colégio das Artes começou a funcionar em 1548 sob a chefia do Principal André de Gouveia'* ['Mirror of humanist culture in Coimbra, the College of Arts began functioning in 1548 under the direction of Principal André de Gouveia']), while at the clause level it appears as an inversion of the normal word order, usually for rhetorical effect (*'Recentíssimo é o belo contributo do historiador português Rui Loureiro'* ['Very recent is the beautiful contribution from the Portuguese historian Rui Loureiro']). It is also very common for topics to be deferred to the end of the paragraph instead of presented in initial position as we might expect in English.

iii. *Framing devices (FD)*:

It is common in Portuguese academic discourse for assertions and observations to be presented indirectly, embedded in a main clause that emphasizes the interpersonal dimension. Some of these Framing Devices have specific semantic content (expressing attitude, epistemic modality, emphasis, and so on), but others do not seem to have any obvious purpose other than perhaps pad out the sentence (for example, *'constata-se que'* ['it is noted that']; *'diga-se que'* ['let it be said that']). Other examples include *'não será erro sustentar que ...'* ['it will not be an error to argue that ...']; *'não deixa de ser interessante notar que ...'* ['it does not cease to be interesting to note that ...']; *'na mesma linha se insere o facto que ...'* ['in the same way is inserted the fact that ...']; *'não será presumir em demasia afirmar que ...'* ['it will not be presuming too much to claim that ...']; *'só uma ideia excessivamente elitista dos comportamentos colectivos poderá acreditar que...'* ['only an excessively elitist idea of collective behaviours could believe that ...'].

iv. *Verbless sentences (VS):*

Sentences that do not have a main finite verb are very prevalent in Portuguese traditional style. In most cases, they take the form of relative clauses, participle phrases or appositional elements that have been detached from their main clause for rhetorical effect, such as the following examples from the corpus: *'O que facilmente se compreende'* ['Which is easily understood']; *'Debate que alguns autores têm tendência a classificar em tipos ou categorias históricas'* ['Debate that some authors have the tendency to classify into types or historical categories']; *'Uma situação que evolui para autêntico centralismo político'* ['A situation that evolved into authentic political centralism']; *'Documento raro este, por revelar o momento exacto em que as dignidades são ocupadas'* ['Rare document this, for revealing the exact moment when the dignitaries are occupied'].

However, there are other kinds of verbless sentence that cannot be categorized in this way. They usually seem designed to create a specific rhetorical or aesthetic effect, as in the following examples: *'A 10 de Fevereiro seguinte novo requerimento do seu pai'* ['On 10th February new solicitation from his father']; *'Grandes homens, grandes amigos, grandes vencedores com a vida'* ['Great men, great friends, great winners in life']; *'Sem Humanismo, nenhuma Reforma'* ['Without Humanism, no Reformation'].

As Verbless Sentences are firmly prohibited in the English academic style manuals, their presence is considered an important marker of the Traditional Style.

v. *Historical tenses (HT):*

This is an aspect of Portuguese that has no correspondence in English (except perhaps in more colloquial storytelling registers or popularizations). It involves using the present or future tenses to refer to events that took place in a contextualized past. For example: *'Na segunda metade do século II a.C. Eudoxo de Cízico /.../ alcança mesmo a Índia, e os Gregos continuarão traficando/.../ ao longo da costa da Somália...'* ('In the second half of the 2nd century BC, Eudoxo of Cizico even <u>reaches</u> India; and the Greeks <u>will continue</u> trading along the coast of Somalia …'). Other examples may be found in Extracts 1, 3, and 5 above.

vi. *Personal references (Pers):*

Many of the personal references used in traditional Portuguese humanities writing derive directly from the humanistic preference for active rather than passive or impersonal structures. In particular, the first-person plural is very common, used with a number of different functions. Some of these have correspondences in English (such as the inclusive 'we' to refer to author and reader, or to the discourse community), but others do not, and thus operate as markers of the traditional style. These include (a) a magisterial 'we' for authorial self-reference:[9] *'Como já sublinhámos em outro lugar…'* ['As we have stressed elsewhere …']; *'No nosso entender …'* ['In our opinion …']); (b) an inclusive 'we' to refer to the Portuguese nation: *'Éramos um país com apenas cerca de um milhão e quatrocentos mil habitantes …'* ['We were a country with only about one million four hundred inhabitants …']; *'construções monásticas … tiveram um grande desenvolvimento entre nós'* ['monastic constructions … had a great development amongst us', that is, in Portugal]; (c) a temporally inclusive 'we' to refer to people that are alive today: *'o seu testament … não chegou até nós'* ['his will has not survived till us', that is, until now].

vii. *Gerunds (Ger):*

The verb form the Portuguese call the *'gerúndio'* is very widespread in written discourse of all types and can be used to express a wide range of syntactical relationships, including temporality (anteriority, posteriority, simultaneity), causality, consequence, purpose, condition and concession. For this reason, it can sometimes blur the relationship between the elements in question, generating ambiguity. Examples from the corpus include '<u>Sendo</u> Portugal vizinha de Castela e de França, corriam-se sérios riscos…' ['<u>Being</u> Portugal /**As Portugal was** a neighbour of Castile and France, serious risks were run …']; *'<u>Sendo</u> dois grupos de natureza diferente, são minorias …'* ['<u>Being</u> two groups of a different nature/**Although these two groups are different in nature**, they are (both) minorities …']; *'Só era possível aceder <u>superando</u> um declive com 10% de inclinação …'* ['it was only possible to reach it /by/ <u>climbing</u> a slope with a 10% gradient…']; *'<u>Tendo</u> a frota britânica ancorado no Tejo, foi o soberano ingles…'* ['<u>Having</u> the British fleet anchored in the Tagus/**After the British fleet had** anchored in the Tagus, it was the English sovereign...']; *'Apenas 7% declaravam-na negativa, sendo o número de indecisos de 26,7% ...'* ['Only 7% gave a negative response, being the number of undecided 26.7% / while the number of undecided was 26.7% ...']; *'Cruzando estas informações com o que sabemos sobre ...'* ['Comparing/If we compare this information with what we know about...'].

viii. *Rhetorical questions (RQ):*
Rhetorical questions are particularly common in Portuguese traditional style, in keeping with the interpersonal orientation of this discourse. Examples from the corpus include: *'Quem eram então estes dois homens que chegam a Portugal em 1540?'* ['Who then were those two men that arrived in Portugal in 1540?']; *'Quais os novos nomes que alguns revolucionários escolheram para seus filhos?'* ['What were the new names that some revolutionaries chose for their children?'];*'Estava o rei disponível para dar uma quantidade de especiarias suficiente para carregar três navios?'* ['Was the king available to give a large enough quantity of spices to load three ships?']

In some cases the question is presented in an elliptical form that, in English, would be considered more appropriate to an oral rather than written form: *'O caso português deveria ser analisado em 11 de Fevereiro de 1963. Tal não aconteceu. Porquê?'* ['The Portuguese case should have been analysed on 11 February 1963. That did not happen. Why?']

ix. *Poetic, figurative or high-flown diction (PD):*
Some Portuguese history writing uses a high-flown literary style that is entirely alien to EAD. For example, we often find the city of Coimbra referred to as *'Lusa Atenas'* ('Lusitanian Athens' or 'the Athens of Portugal') or *'Morada de Sabedoria'* ('the Residence of Wisdom'), without any hint of quotation or irony. The grand or emotive style is particularly common in concluding paragraphs, as in the following examples which describe, respectively, a botanical garden and a university archive: *'... este Jardim se talhou no contraponto entre a Arte e a Ciência, no equilíbrio entre o sonhado e o alcançado, entre o desejado e o possível.'* ['... this Garden was carved at the counterpoint between Art and Science, in the equilibrium between the dreamed and the achieved, between the desired and the possible']; *'...é, antes de tudo, um tabernáculo, ou seja, um lugar considerado quase sagrado. O silêncio, a luz coada dos depósitos, a imponência dos códices e livros, o respeito obrigatório por pergaminhos e papéis centenários, para isso contribuem'* ['... it is, first and foremost, a tabernacle, or rather, a place considered almost sacred. The silence,

the filtered light of the deposits, the imposing quality of the codices and books, the mandatory respect for age-old parchments and papers, to this contribute'].

The use of high-flown or emotive diction is often accompanied by other overt rhetorical or literary devices, such as inversions of the usual SV word order (as in the final three words of the above quotation), parallelisms, verbless sentences and rhetorical questions.

x. *Terms from continental philosophy*:
The presence of certain words and phrases derived from 'continental' philosophy[10] were also taken to be indicative of an orientation towards a non-empiricist theoretical model. These include: *'o imaginário'* (Portuguese translation of Lacan's term *'l'imaginaire'* referring to the symbolic universe a child enters upon being initiated into language and other culturally construed semiotic systems); *'a realidade'* ('reality') used not in the empiricist sense but rather to refer to the experiential domain of culture (as in *'a realidade portuguesa'* ['the Portuguese reality']); *'inscreve-se em'* ('to be inscribed in', also derived from French, this often collocates with words like *'imaginário'*, *'realidade'* or *'discurso'* ['discourse']);*'conjuntura'* (translation of the French *'conjuncture'*, popular in the writing of the Annales school, to refer to a particular combination of political, economic or social conditions occurring at a given moment);[11] *'fio condutor'* (Portuguese translation of 'fil conducteur' or 'fil rouge' in French, referring to the central idea that organizes or 'runs through' a text; it invokes a rather loose, non-hierarchical attitude to text production). Certain non-standard grammatical usages, such as the verb *'pensar'* ('to think') used with the direct object (that is, *'pensar Europa'* = 'to think Europe'), were also considered to suggest a constructivist orientation to knowledge.

## 1.6   Results

The first fact of interest about these two corpora is the sheer increase in the number of history texts submitted for translation. In the five-year period from 2009 to 2013, 28 texts (544,974 words) were submitted, as opposed to 19 (137,456 words) in the ten years between 1998 and 2008. The average word length also increased from 7234 words in the *2008 Corpus* to 19,463 words in the *2013 Corpus*, reflecting the fact that more long texts (long articles, dissertations and full-length monographs) were being translated. Though there are of course other factors that could have contributed to this development (such as the translator's decision to specialize in the area of history and her growing reputation in this field), the increase may also reflect changes in policy at national level (see below).

In terms of the VR allocated, there are also interesting changes. In the *2008 Corpus*, 52.63 per cent of texts were attributed a VR of –2, while 47.37 per cent were awarded –1 (there were no cases of 0). In the *2013 Corpus*, however, only 7.14 per cent of texts were classified as –2, with 78.57 per cent considered to be –1 and 14.29 per cent to be 0. The change is even more remarkable when the data is analysed by word rather than by text. Now, 66.29 per cent of the *2008 Corpus* is classified as –2 and 33.71 per cent as –1, while of the *2013 Corpus*, only 5.69 per cent is –2, with 93.44 per cent as –1 and 0.87 per cent as 0 (the difference between the two counting systems clearly reflects the fact that the various full-length texts in the *2013 Corpus* were all awarded a VR of –1).

In fact, given the overwhelming predominance of –1 in the *2013 Corpus*, it was felt necessary to subdivide this category to take account of some of the nuances observed between the various texts classified in this way. Hence, three subcategories were introduced: –0.5 (attributed to texts that were mostly modern with the occasional presence of more traditional features), –1 (texts that presented a roughly equal balance of modern and traditional features) and –1.5 (texts that inclined towards the traditional). The *2008 Corpus* was reviewed in order to implement these subdivisions, but no changes were made to the classifications given. In the *2013 Corpus*, on the other hand, of the 22 texts initially categorized as –1, 13.6 per cent (3 texts) were considered to be –1.5; 54.55 per cent (12 texts) to be –1 and 31.82 per cent (7 texts) to be –0.5. (By word, the results are a little different, reflecting the fact that the 2 of the 3 texts categorized as –1.5 were book-length works: 51.95 per cent of the total word count is –1.5; 21.60 per cent is –1; and 26.45 per cent is –0.5.)

This does suggest, therefore, that there has been a 'modernization' of Portuguese historiographic discourse in the period spanned by the two corpora. Whether the analysis is done by text or by word, the proportion of –2s in the *2013 Corpus* is considerably less than in the *2008 Corpus*, while the proportion of –1s has increased. The fact that the *2013 Corpus* contains examples of VR 0 is also significant.

The final analysis undertaken with the *2013 Corpus* involved redistributing the gridlines so that the VRs of –2 and –1.5 were grouped together to create a category that could be considered 'traditional and near-traditional', while 0 and –0.5 were grouped together as the 'modern and near-modern'. Now, the shift away from the traditional style towards the modern is even more marked: there are only 5 texts (17.86 per cent) that could be considered as tendentially traditional, with 11 tending towards the modern (39.28 per cent) and 12 hybrids (42.86 per cent).

## 1.7  Discussion

The results of this study would seem to suggest a shift of orientation, on the part of Portuguese historiography, away from French or Romance discursive models towards English ones, with significant repercussions on the level of epistemology. Indeed, one of the assumptions underpinning this study is that discourse encodes ideology in its very structure. The various DDFs that were used as markers of the traditional style reflect an epistemological attitude that is hermeneutic rather than empiricist (in that the emphasis is on human perception and interpretation rather than upon the presentation and analysis of independently existing 'facts'), and which values the aesthetic and emotive aspects of verbal communication as much as the referential. Hence, the shift to a simpler, more 'transparent' mode of discourse is not merely cosmetic. It implies the substitution of this epistemological paradigm by another that is grounded on a completely different philosophy of knowledge, namely the positivism, empiricism and linguistic realism that is dominant in the Anglo-Saxon world.

There are a number of factors that seem to influence the individual author's decision about which discourse to employ: age (younger researchers are more likely to favour the modern style than their older colleagues); place of publication (articles aiming from the outset at international publication tend to be couched in a more modern style than those destined to be published in Portugal); and subdisciplinary identity (we might, for example, expect a more modern style in social and economic history, which is often of Anglophone inspiration, than in the Francophone-influenced history of ideas). However, public policy may also play a significant role in choices of this type. Since 1997, research in Portugal in all domains has been overseen by a body known as the *Fundação de Ciência e Tecnologia* or *FCT* ('Foundation of Science[12] and Technology'), whose funding policy is laid out in a document entitled *Regulamento do Programa de Financiamento Plurianual de Unidades de I&D* ('Regulations of the Multiannual Funding Programme for R&D Units'). Comparison of the 2002 and 2007 versions of this document[13] shows an increasing emphasis upon 'internationalization', not only in research dissemination, but also with regard to the organization of projects and, crucially, the constitution of the evaluation committees responsible for judging a team's worth. In 2013, the pressure to publish in high-impact English-language journals intensified even more when an automated system of bibliometric analysis was introduced to assess the output of individual researchers and centres. As the system counts only publications listed in Elsevier's Scopus database,[14] research published in Portuguese and any that is not conducted within the dominant empiricist paradigm is effectively sidelined.

These developments are in themselves sufficient to explain both the increase in translation activity in the field of historiography and the changes in discourse style. That is to say, historians that were once content to publish in national journals in Portuguese now find themselves obliged to produce texts in English in order to secure funding and career advancement. It is therefore reasonable to assume that many of the works included in the *2013 Corpus* will have been written with an international readership in mind. Given the degree of cultural awareness that exists amongst Portuguese academics with regards to Anglophone discourse expectations,[15] it is highly likely that many authors would have deliberately eliminated most of the DDFs from their texts before submitting them for translation.

The internationalization of Portuguese historiography has aroused mixed reactions from the local discourse community. Many of the contributions to a debate on the subject hosted by the *E-Journal of Portuguese History*[16] considered the development to be a positive one: for example, António Costa Pinto, writing in Vol. 1, No. 2 (2003), criticized the traditional parochialism of Portuguese historiography and praised the FCT for its efforts to stimulate international participation. In contrast, the historian António Araújo, interviewed in the newspaper *Expresso* (Castanheira 2012), claimed that Portuguese historiography would be 'asphyxiated' by the pressure to publish in top international journals: an international readership, he argued, would not have the background knowledge or the interest to process texts of a highly specialized nature.[17] Indeed, the marginalization, through 'parochialization' or 'exoticization', of culturally embedded non-Anglophone scholarship is one of the most worrying consequences of the globalization of knowledge, as a number of researchers have pointed out (see Lillis and Curry 2010, pp. 141–145, Flowerdew 2001, p. 135, Bardi and Muresan, Chapter 7, this volume).

## 1.8 Conclusion

In the present context, in which English is the indisputable lingua franca of the academic world, it is scarcely surprising that the traditional

Portuguese scholarly discourse should be under threat. Even without the FCT policies that urge Portuguese researchers to publish in high-impact international journals, the general drift away from French models towards English ones would probably end up affecting Portuguese history writing sooner or later at the epistemological level, bringing repercussions on the level of discourse. As it is, the pressures are even more direct. The requirement to produce texts in English obliges authors to develop different mental habits (different lexical categories; different ways of organizing material at the grammatical and textual levels), and it is natural that this should eventually filter through to their mother-tongue writing. When Portuguese texts are written specifically for translation, this process is accelerated (at least for the individual author) as untransferrable features are eliminated at source, either to facilitate the work of the translator or to avoid misunderstandings.

It is too soon to say what the outcome of this process will be. But further studies could shed some light on the issue, particularly if they focus not on texts submitted for translation, as these were, but on works published in Lusophone journals. Ideally, such studies would attempt to eliminate some of the variables that marred this particular work (that is, by using texts of a single genre produced under similar conditions for a similar purpose) and would take a broader time span in order to get a better idea of the long-term changes taking place.

Whether the process results in the irretrievable demise of the traditional style or in a situation of discursive diglossia (in which one discourse is used at home and another for international communication) will probably depend on how the local discourse community reacts to the situation. At present, Portuguese historians are divided, as we have seen, with some applauding the expansion of vision and scientific rigour resulting from internationalization and others lamenting the loss of specificity that it entails. However, we should not overlook the fact that there is also a very large and increasingly powerful academic community in Brazil, which, given its location and growing economic clout, is less likely to be browbeaten than Portugal. Ultimately, the fate of the traditional historiographic discourse probably lies over there, on that huge landmass on the other side of the Atlantic, rather than with a little country on the periphery of Europe that no longer has the autonomy or the will to defend itself against an academic hegemony of global proportions.

In the meantime, there is very little that concerned scholars can do besides trying to alert all the stakeholders to the various risks implicit in the globalization of knowledge. Whether this will be sufficient to counter its various allures remains to be seen.

# Notes

1. A 2011 study of the holdings of the Institute for Social and Economic History at the University of Coimbra revealed that, of the foreign works owned by the library (which account for 35 per cent of the Institute's total acquisitions since 1985), 58 per cent of the untranslated works were in French and 57 per cent of the translated works had originally been written in French. The authors in question were almost exclusively from the Annales school (Braudel, Ariès, Bloch, Le Goff, Duby and so on) (Bennett 2012a).
2. All claims regarding the characteristics of English academic discourse were derived from a survey of the academic style manuals on the market (Bennett 2009), supplemented by a review of the vast body of literature that exists in the field of descriptive linguistics into how expert academic authors actually do write in practice (see periodicals such as Elsevier's *Journal of English for Academic Purposes* and *English for Specific Purposes*, and specialized volumes such as Swales 1990; Hyland 2000, 2009, 2012; Flowerdew 2002, and so on).
3. This non-empiricist underpinning is explained by British historian Peter Burke (1991: 6) in his comments about the importance of cultural relativism for French historical writing: 'Our minds do not reflect reality directly. We perceive the world through a network of conventions, schemata and stereotypes, a network which varies from one culture to another. ...'.
4. This passage was first analysed in Bennett 2012a. The material is reused with the kind permission of the *Centro de Estudos Anglísticos da Universidade de Lisboa*.
5. See Halliday and Martin (1993), Atkinson (1999) and Ding (1998) on the historical development of scientific discourse in English.
6. This passage was first analysed in Bennett 2012a. The material is reused with the kind permission of the *Centro de Estudos Anglísticos da Universidade de Lisboa*.
7. This passage was first analysed in Bennett 2012a. The material is reused with the kind permission of the *Centro de Estudos Anglísticos da Universidade de Lisboa*.
8. The tropes and figures of Classical Rhetoric are still taught in Portuguese schools. For example, a 12th-year Portuguese textbook, commonly used by students on the Science and Technology course (*Abordagens*, by Zaida Braga, Auxília Ramos and Elvira Pardinhas, Porto Editora, 2007) requires knowledge of terms such as 'hyberbaton', 'apostrophe' (in the rhetorical rather than grammatical sense), 'oxymoron', 'pathos', and so on.
9. This is justified in the style manuals on the grounds that it expresses 'modesty'. Estrela et al. (2006, p. 43) claim that 'this discursive option creates the effect of collective thought, softening the imposing effect created by personal affirmations' (my translation), while Eco (1997, p. 168) argues that it 'presumes that one's claims are shared by one's readers' (my translation).
10. This is a rather blunt term used by the Anglo-Saxon analytical school of philosophy to group together the non-empiricist philosophical currents emanating principally from France and Germany (such as German idealism, phenomenology, hermeneutics and poststructuralism). They share a belief that our experience of reality is limited to or filtered by our consciousness and our sign systems.

11. Burke (1990, p. 97) discusses the difficulties of rendering this term into English and decides that it is 'virtually impossible to translate, and extremely difficult for British historians to understand – let alone accept'.
12. In Portuguese, the word *'ciência'* has traditionally had a much broader range of meaning than its English cognate, and includes research carried out in the humanities, social sciences and arts. However, the policy shifts that are currently taking place suggest that the word is gradually being redefined in order to bring it into line with the English notion of 'science'.
13. Both are available on line at: http://www.fct.pt/apoios/unidades/legisla caoregulamentosnormas. Accessed 26 January 2014. An extract from the FCT's Evaluation Guidelines is also quoted and discussed in Lillis and Curry (2010, pp. 56–58).
14. Of over 3850 journals listed on Scopus, only 29 are in Arts and Humanities, and of those, only a handful are in the field of history.
15. Most of the researchers interviewed in the 2002/2008 survey claimed consciously to change their style when they wrote in English, becoming more succinct and precise, and making less use of rhetorical or figurative devices (Bennett 2010a, pp. 202–203).
16. This is an entirely English-language journal published jointly by the University of Porto and Brown University in the United States.
17. 'For example, if someone wants to write a 10- or 12-page article about Duarte Pacheco in a foreign journal, first he will have to explain what the *Estado Novo* was, then he has to compare it with other regimes, and only in the last 4 or 5 pages will he be able to write something about Duarte Pacheco himself' (translated by me). That is to say, Anglophone knowledge of Portuguese history is considerably lagging behind the state of the art in the Lusophone context.

# 2
# The Changing Face of Czech Academic Discourse

*Olga Dontcheva-Navratilova*

## 2.1 Introduction

It is now generally acknowledged that the globalization of academia has created a geolinguistic centre–periphery tension stemming from the privileged status of English as the global medium of academic knowledge production, evaluation and distribution (see Swales 1997, Canagarajah 2002, Tardy 2004, Salager-Meyer 2008). As recent descriptive and pedagogical investigations into the dynamics of international academic communication have demonstrated, the ever-growing dominance of the Anglophone centre threatens the future of peripheral academic literacies and epistemologies, and often relegates multilingual scholars from geographically, economically, socially and/or culturally peripheral discourse communities to marginal participation in the activities of the global academic world (see Flowerdew 2000, Canagarajah 2002, Ferguson 2007, Uzuner 2008, Lillis and Curry 2006, 2010). Yet the centre–periphery divide is better conceptualized as a continuum comprising a fuzzy area – the 'semiperiphery' – that mediates between the two poles and encompasses discourse communities that share some features with the centre but also display characteristic traits of the periphery (Lillis and Curry 2010; Bennett, Introduction to this volume). In the European context, the group of post-communist countries that are now members of the European Union (for example, Czech Republic, Poland, Hungary, Romania, Bulgaria) are typical of discourse communities with semiperipheral status, since, after breaking out of their imposed isolation under a communist regime, they are currently striving to be integrated in the European and global academic discourse community. This study explores the changes the Czech academic discourse community is undergoing as a result of the globalization and marketization of academia.

When aspiring to partake in the academic knowledge exchange, Czech scholars, like other non-Anglophone scholars from various cultural backgrounds, are forced to face the difficult dilemma of staying local or going global (Lillis and Curry 2010). Commitment to locality involves association with the national discourse community, its research interests and epistemological and literacy tradition, while seeking membership of the international academic discourse community forces multilingual scholars to face the demanding task of presenting their views and interacting with their readers using a foreign language, and to accommodate themselves to different epistemological and literacy conventions. Since non-Anglophone scholars who write in English for an international audience use English as an academic lingua franca (Mauranen 2012), their academic discourse is likely to show features of both Anglophone literacy and of their native language. Views on the acceptability of non-native speakers' academic English vary. It is only recently that the role of the educated native speaker as a language model, and the position of the Anglo-American tradition of academic writing as the norm for intercultural communication have been problematized by scholars (for example, Jenkins 2009, Mauranen and Ranta 2009, Mauranen et al. 2010, Seidlhofer 2011), who point out that we are witnessing an expansion of the discourse communities that can claim ownership of English (Mauranen 2012). Yet it is rather obvious that in the realm of written academic interaction 'linguistic, rhetorical and genre norms are not only expected but are also actively enforced' (Chovanec 2012, p. 7), which may lead to the stigmatization of multilingual scholars by institutional gatekeepers, such as journal editors and peer-reviewers (Flowerdew 2008).

This chapter studies the academic discourse of Czech authors writing in English in order to find out whether and to what extent it bears signs of interference between the Czech and Anglophone academic literacies. The investigation is carried out on a specialized corpus of linguistics research articles and chapters in books published in national and international contexts. The choice of linguistics as the disciplinary discourse under scrutiny reflects my belief that the English academic discourse of Czech linguists – who themselves study language, publish both in Czech and in English and typically teach (academic) English at Czech universities – is particularly revealing for an analysis of the influences to which the Czech academic literacy is exposed. The chapter opens with a description of the distinctive features of Czech academic discourse, followed by a discussion of the differences between Czech and Anglo-American academic literacies. Then the study examines ways in which

Czech scholars resolve the tension resulting from these differences based on an analysis of citations and the use of personal and impersonal structures for establishing authorial presence in their English-medium texts. Finally, the investigation considers how the differences between Czech and English academic writing traditions are reflected in the teaching of academic writing in English in Czech universities.

## 2.2 The Czech academic discourse tradition vs Anglophone academic discourse

Czech academic culture – with its crossroads geographical location 'at the heart of Europe' – seems to follow a historically motivated tendency to adapt to and confront dominant cultures (Čmejrková 1996; Čmejrková and Daneš 1997, p. 41). As is the case with the majority of Central and Eastern European academic cultures, Czech academic discourse conventions were formed under the influence of a Teutonic epistemology and literacy oriented towards the establishment of authority through the presentation of disciplinary knowledge, theorizing, and the avoidance of making the author's position clearly recognizable (Clyne 1987, Duszak 1997a, Čmejrková and Daneš 1997, Kreutz and Harres 1997, Dontcheva-Navratilova 2012a). In addition, due to numerous contacts and common Slavonic origins, Czech academic culture was affected by the Russian scientific tradition with which it shares a tendency to approach the issues under consideration from a general perspective and a preference for a reader-oriented, depersonalized style associated with the use of impersonal constructions and the exclusive 'editorial *we*' (Čmejrková and Daneš 1997, Vassileva 1998, Yakhontova 2006). It is therefore obvious that the Czech academic discourse community operated under a mixture of various influences even before being exposed to the pressure of the Anglophone centre, which, as Čmejrková and Daneš (1997, p. 42) claim, has profoundly affected Czech academic writing.

Before considering the tensions experienced by the Czech semiperipheral academic discourse as a result of contact with the powerful Anglophone centre, it is essential to contrast the literacy traditions of the respective discourse communities. Previous research (for example, Chamonikolasová 2005, Čmejrková 1994, Duszak 1997a, Stašková 2005) has evidenced several divergences between the Anglophone and Czech academic discourses concerning primarily the way they approach discourse organization and writer–reader interaction. These are summarized in Table 2.1.

*Table 2.1*   Academic discourse traditions: Czech versus English

| Anglophone academic discourse | Czech academic discourse |
| --- | --- |
| – competitive large discourse community | – small discourse community avoiding tension |
| – explicit discourse organization | – low on explicit discourse organization |
| – strict discourse norms | – absence of strict discourse norms |
| – negotiation of meaning | – conceptual and terminological clarity |
| – interactive, dialogic | – low-interactive, monologic |
| – reader-oriented | – writer-oriented |
| – marked authorial presence | – backgrounded authorial presence |

Some of the divergences may be attributed to the impact of the difference in the size of the respective discourse communities on solidarity and power relations among their members (Čmejrková and Daneš 1997). Since the members of small academic communities (such as the Czech one) typically know each other personally and share most of their research interests and methodological principles, they tend to adopt patterns of interaction marked by symbiosis and avoidance of tension. This allows Czech authors to convey their views using more narrative, implicit and less structured discourse when communicating with their local discourse community. When discussing the composition and arrangement of Czech academic texts, Čmejrková and Daneš (1997) attribute their problematic surveyability to the following distinctive features: the use of non-specific headings often expressed by noun phrases with modifying prepositions (for example, *O koherenci v mluveném diskurzu* 'On coherence in spoken discourse'); frequent lack of clear topic formulation in the introduction; absence or rare occurrence of subheadings reflecting the instability of generic conventions and the sparse and inconsistent use of metadiscourse.

The situation is quite different in the potentially global and highly competitive English-speaking academic discourse community, whose members strive to find a gap in a research territory densely packed with occupied 'niches' (Duszak 1997a). When interacting with a culturally heterogeneous depersonalized readership, researchers working within the Anglophone academic tradition tend to rely on established disciplinary and generic conventions, which are not only acquired but also explicitly taught during the socialization of novice writers into the academic discourse community (Swales 1990, 2004). Anglophone academic texts typically have focused and eye-catching headings and systematically use subheadings to indicate discourse structure. They open with a clear statement of the topic and the hypotheses the author undertakes to verify and are densely packed with metadiscourse facilitating the reader's path through the text by previewing the content of upcoming discourse, staging and signposting. Yet while academic writing in English is generally seen as 'explicit' in terms of presentation of ideas and indication of text organization (for example, Hyland 2002a), Biber and Gray's corpus-based diachronic research (2011) has recently shown that over the last century Anglophone academic writing has developed a more compressed, structurally complex and thus less explicit style of presentation of meaning.

In their efforts to persuade the implied audience to accept their views, Anglophone scholars typically adopt a more reader-friendly attitude associated with a higher level of interactivity, as it is the writer who takes responsibility for making the text understandable (Thompson 2001, Hyland 2002a, 2005). This interpersonal dimension of discourse is conveyed by attitudinal markers (for example, hedges, boosters, personal intrusions) modifying the force of the argument and appealing to the reader in seeking agreement with the viewpoint advanced by the author. The dialogic character of the Anglo-American academic discourse favours a higher degree of authoritativeness and collaborative discussion of differences, helping writers to negotiate claims and debate views with the implied audience (Hyland 2012). Despite the persistence of the so-called scientific paradigm in academic English related to 'clarity, economy, rational argument supported by evidence, caution and restraint' (Bennett 2009, p. 52) and the avoidance of explicit reference to human agency (Hyland 2001), current practice in published academic articles has evidenced that Anglophone authors increasingly use self-promotional pronouns (Harwood 2005) for 'maintaining the writer-reader relationship and allowing the writer an authorial voice' (L. Flowerdew 2012).

Unlike that of the Anglo-American tradition, the focus of Czech academic discourse is on conceptual and terminological clarity, rather than on persuasion and negotiation of meaning. As in all writer-oriented discourses, it is assumed that the reader follows carefully the writer's argumentation (Mauranen 1993), which is presented with a lesser degree of assertiveness, expressed by the use of face-saving devices and qualified language (Čmejrková 1996, Čmejrková and Daneš 1997). Characterized by a preference for a low level of interactiveness, Czech academic texts tend to background authorial presence, which concurs with the use of impersonal structures, and, in the case of personal structures, with the use of exclusive first-person plural forms (Čmejrková and Daneš 1997, Chamonikolasová 2005).

The significant differences between the Czech and the Anglophone academic discourse traditions in terms of how they handle discourse organization and writer–reader relationship suggest that these are the features of the academic discourse of Czech authors writing in English that may be most significantly affected by a transfer of writing habits rooted in the Czech academic literacy.

## 2.3   Data and methodology

This investigation into the academic discourse of Czech linguists writing in English employs both quantitative and qualitative approaches, comprising frequency counts and discourse analysis of selected features in published research articles and chapters in books. The study is carried out on a specialized corpus which consists of English-medium texts published in the last ten years (2002–2012) by 15 Czech linguists, all of whom hold PhDs, are affiliated with well-established Czech universities (for example, Charles University, Masaryk University), conduct research and write for publication. The English academic discourse of each author is represented by one single-authored text taken from local English-medium academic journals published by a Czech academic institution (a university or the Czech Academy of Sciences) or edited collections published by an international academic publisher. The corpus comprises six chapters in edited collections published by an international academic publisher (John Benjamins, Peter Lang and Cambridge Scholars Publishing) and nine articles published in national English-medium journals (*Linguistica Pragensia, Brno Studies in English* and *Discourse and Interaction*); the absence of articles in international journals is due to the lack of such single-authored texts. The total size of the material is 80,200 words; the length of the individual texts ranges from 3,500 to 10,300 words, although the majority of the publications oscillate around an average word count of 5,300 words. The publications were selected to represent the most typical audience which each of the authors addresses.

The Czech linguists can be grouped in four categories according to their experience as academics, academic position and publication history, as shown in Table 2.2. In order to allow for a comparison between the academic writing habits of the different groups, the corpus was further subdivided into four sub-corpora each comprising the texts of one of the categories of scholars described below.

As all the Czech authors specialize in the field of English linguistics, they are expected to have proficient command of English. It should be

*Table 2.2*  Categorization of Czech linguists included in corpus according to academic experience, position and publications

| Categories | Scholars | Years in academe | Academic position | Publications per person |
|---|---|---|---|---|
| Group A | 3 | 40+ | Full professor | 150 |
| Group B | 4 | 25+ | Full professor/ Associate professor | 55 |
| Group C | 4 | 15+ | Associate professor/ Assistant professor | 35 |
| Group D | 4 | 5+ | Assistant professor | 15 |

mentioned, however, that the majority of them have developed their knowledge of English as well as their academic writing skills in local settings. Obviously, the four groups of Czech linguists have been socialized into the academic discourse community at different stages of the development of the national academic literacy and the globalization of academia; this suggests that they may differ in terms of the schooling in academic writing they have received and consequently in their writing habits. In addition, since the availability of international journals and other scholarly publications, opportunities for study stays, contacts and cooperation with scholars from the Anglophone centre have changed over the years, it is possible to hypothesize that the academic discourse of the scholars in the four groups would show variation both in the degree of interference from the Czech academic literacy and in the choice of strategies adopted to resolve the tension between the Czech and the Anglophone traditions of academic writing.

As to the publication records of the Czech linguists, the majority of their texts are research articles published in local English-medium journals and chapters in books/edited collections or proceedings published in the Czech Republic or neighbouring countries, which reflects an orientation towards the local discourse community, a focus on topics typical of the local research tradition, and, arguably, a reluctance to risk rejection by prestigious, Anglophone-centre international journals. Apart from three of the youngest authors, all the Czech linguists have published in both Czech and English, although the number of English-medium publications considerably exceeds the number of Czech ones. It is symptomatic of the peripheral status of the Czech academic discourse community that of the 870 publications produced by the 15 linguists included in the investigation, only 12 are research articles that appeared in a prestigious international academic journal (seven of these are (co-)authored by one of the Group A scholars, who has established close contacts with colleagues from the Anglophone centre). The number of co-authored books and chapters in edited collections published by international academic publishers, however, is considerably higher (approximately ten per cent of all the publications). The low visibility of Czech linguists in an Anglophone context is also mentioned by Newmeyer (2001, p. 102), who notes that international acknowledgement of the work of Czech scholars within the functionalist approach to syntax was hindered in the second half of the last century by its appearance in local or peripheral English-medium publications not easily obtainable in North America.

Since the approach to writer–reader interaction has been identified as one of the aspects of academic writing marked by most prominent cross-cultural variation, especially in the humanities and social sciences (Duszak 1997a, Flowerdew 1999b, Vassileva 1998, Mur-Dueñas 2007, Shaw and Vassileva 2009), this investigation focuses on citation choices and the construction of authorial presence in the English-medium discourse of Czech linguists. The importance of citations in academic discourse has been shown by several corpus-based and interview-based studies, which have explored their rhetorical functions, the motivation of writers for the making of particular choices, and the potential of citation to contribute to the construction of the author's identity as a member of the academic discourse community (see Hyland 1999, Hyland 2000, Charles 2006, Harwood 2009). The analysis of citation practices in this study draws on the approach suggested by Hewings et al. (2010) for the study of the geolinguistic dimension of citations as an interpersonal resource for claiming affiliation to a particular disciplinary discourse community. The reference lists of the 15 articles in the corpus were analysed along four dimensions: language, publication type, recency and the occurrence of self-citation. The bibliographical references were categorized according to the language of publication into four categories: a) English, b) Czech-English, referring to English-medium publications of Czech authors, c) Czech and d) other, including any language other than English and Czech. The publication types and the recency of bibliographical references were considered in order to explore how Czech linguists access disciplinary knowledge. The estimation of the ratio of more prominent publication types, such as research articles, books and chapters in books, as against other publications, comprising encyclopaedias, reference grammars and internet sources, was complemented by the recency criterion focusing on the extent to which Czech scholars draw on the latest developments in disciplinary research by examining references dated less than ten years prior to the publication of the text included in the corpus. Finally, the frequency of self-citation was considered as indicative of the self-promotional effort that Czech linguists invest in making their own research visible.

The second aspect of the interpersonal dimension of academic discourse examined in this study is the use of personal and impersonal structures for the build-up of authorial presence. In the last two decades this has become a widely debated issue, both in the works of discourse analysts scrutinizing different academic genres and disciplines (for example, Swales 1990, Swales 2004, Gosden 1993, Kuo 1999, Hyland 2001, Hyland 2002a, Harwood 2005) and in more cross-culturally oriented research which compares the writing of native and non-native speakers (for example, Tang and John 1999, Hyland 2002b, Charles 2006, Mur-Dueñas 2007, Samraj 2008, Vassileva 1998). The aim of the quantitative analysis was to find out the frequency of use of author-reference pronouns in the texts by the Czech authors. The corpus was searched for the target author-reference pronouns *I/me/my* and *we/us/our* using the freeware Antconc concordance programme. The concordance lists were checked manually to exclude occurrences of target structures in citations and examples and the raw data were normalized to frequencies per 10,000 words to allow for comparison with data reported by previous studies. The qualitative analysis examines the functions of impersonal structures and personal pronouns in relation to the generic structure of the research article – Introduction, Methods, Results and Discussion (IMRD) – as suggested by Swales (1990, 2004). The functional taxonomy of authorial roles expressed by author-reference pronouns draws on the classifications suggested by Tang and John (1999), Hewings and Hewings (2002) and Harwood (2005). It considers five major authorial roles, which can be seen as reflecting a continuum from the lowest to the highest degree of authority:

(1) Representative – the least authoritative role which positions the author as a member of a larger community; typically expressed by the plural first-person pronoun *we*
(2) Discourse-organizer – guides the reader through the text by outlining discourse structure and indicating intra-textual connections and transition points in the discourse
(3) Recounter of the research process – comments on data and research procedures
(4) Opinion-holder – an authoritative role associated with expressing attitudes and elaborating arguments

(5) Originator – the most authoritative and face-threatening role, related to putting forward claims, commenting on findings and highlighting the author's contribution to the field

It is important to stress that authorial roles are not defined only on the basis of the author-reference pronouns used; rather they are seen as a function of the structures in which the pronouns occur and are affected by the semantics of the verb phrase and the larger co-text.

## 2.4   Findings and discussion

The claim to be verified by this investigation is that English-medium academic texts published by Czech scholars over the last decade show features that differ considerably from traditional Czech academic writing conventions. Before turning to the analysis of citation practices and authorial presence, it is worth mentioning briefly some changes concerning topic presentation and discourse organization. The tendency towards the use of article headings indicating a general subject area expressed by noun phrases with modifying prepositions persists but seems to be in decline. Whereas Čmejrková and Daneš's findings (1997, p. 51) report that in 1990 such titles represented up to 50 per cent of the titles in volume 10 of the journal *Prague Studies in Mathematical Linguistics*, in my corpus there are only two instances of headings that follow this pattern (that is, 13 per cent). As to rhetorical structure, all texts included in the corpus broadly follow the IMRD model of standard Anglophone-centre academic articles and use numbered subsection headings to indicate discourse structure and facilitate text surveyability. They open with a clear statement of the topic under investigation, while the Introduction or Methods section often includes a precise formulation of the hypotheses the author undertakes to verify. This shows that Czech authors, under pressure to comply with the expectations of an international audience, have adopted the generic conventions of Anglo-American academic discourse to a large extent.

### 2.4.1   Citation practices

In order to examine how Czech authors use citation to position themselves with regard to the local and international linguistics discourse communities, the amount of citation and the geolinguistic context of the bibliographical references in all articles were examined. The average number of bibliographical references per article in the corpus (26 items per reference list) was found to be considerably lower than that reported by Hewings et al. (2010, p. 107) for their EMI 2 corpus comprising English-medium journal articles published in international contexts by authors affiliated to Anglophone-centre institutions in the UK and US (48 items per reference list). The difference is particularly striking in the case of articles by Czech authors published in national English-medium journals, which suggests that the authors assume that their readership is acquainted with the main theoretical tenets and methodology to which they refer. This is not surprising, since five of the articles deal with theme-rheme articulation – a traditional topic of Czech linguistics research.

The results of the analysis of the reference lists with regard to language, publication type, recency and occurrence of self-citation are summarized in Table 2.3 (totals are broken down by language and publication type). Obviously, English-language references dominate: they account for 88 per cent of all bibliographical references, 25 per cent of which refer to Czech authors' English-medium publications. In accordance with the traditional orientation of the Czech academic community, reference to publications in other languages comprises five references to German sources, one to a publication in Russian and one to a publication in French. The low representation of Czech and other language sources confirms the powerful role of English as the main language of academic communication (Hewings et al. 2010, Lillis and Curry 2010), which is also evidenced by the fact that all integral citations (Swales 1990) found in the corpus are in English, while works in other languages are incorporated non-integrally. By backgrounding the non-Anglophone origin of the authors, English-language quotations represent them as legitimate members of the English-speaking international academic discourse community (Hewings et al. 2010). The occurrence of self-citations (average 2.3 per article, ranging from 0 to 9) does not reach the rate established by Hyland (2003) for self-citations in a larger corpus of applied linguistics research articles published in leading journals (3.2). This suggests that Czech authors are faithful to the preference for the expression of authorial modesty in the Czech academic literacy (Čmejrková et al. 1999, Cahmonikolasová 2005) and thus differ from their Anglo-American counterparts in the degree of self-promotion they invest in their texts to highlight their contribution to disciplinary knowledge and build up their reputation and credibility.

As to the representation of the different publication types, reference to books and chapters in books is the most prominent (78 per cent), while reference to research articles seems to be underrepresented in comparison with Hewings et al.'s (2010) findings, which report

*Table 2.3*  Bibliographic references in English-medium works of Czech linguists according to language, publication type and recency

| Sub-corpora | Bibl. ref. No | Language | | | | Publication type | | | Recent sources | Self-citation |
|---|---|---|---|---|---|---|---|---|---|---|
| | | English | CzEng | Czech | Other | RA | B(Ch) | Other | | |
| 40+ | 84 | 43 | 15 | 21 | 5 | 17 | 67 | 0 | 10 | 12 |
| Group | | 51% | 18% | 25% | 6% | 20% | 80% | 0% | 12% | |
| 25+ | 95 | 53 | 33 | 7 | 2 | 10 | 77 | 8 | 25 | 5 |
| Group | | 56% | 35% | 7% | 2% | 11% | 81% | 8% | 26% | |
| 15+ | 105 | 75 | 20 | 10 | 0 | 26 | 75 | 4 | 53 | 13 |
| Group | | 72% | 19% | 9% | 0% | 25% | 72% | 3% | 50% | |
| 5+ | 108 | 87 | 20 | 1 | 0 | 15 | 88 | 5 | 42 | 4 |
| Group | | 81% | 18% | 1% | 0% | 14% | 82% | 4% | 39% | |
| Total | 392 | 258 | 88 | 39 | 7 | 68 | 307 | 17 | 130 | 34 |
| | | 66% | 22% | 10% | 2% | 18% | 78% | 4% | 33% | |

approximately 50 per cent of references to research articles in all corpora they investigated, including articles published in national and international journals by non-Anglophone and Anglophone writers. On the one hand, this reduced prominence of referencing to journal articles reflects the high proportion of publications in national journals included in my corpus; on the other hand, it reflects the semiperipheral status of Czech universities, whose subscriptions to international journals are dependent on their oscillating budgets (Bennett, Introduction to this volume). This concurs with the relatively low proportion of reference to recent publications (33 per cent), especially when taking into account that reference to Czech scholars' on-going research and self-citations constitutes a considerable proportion of the recent items.

A comparison of the distribution of bibliographical references across the four sub-corpora shows that variation reflects the academic experience of the authors. The average number of bibliographical references used by authors with extensive experience as academics (40+Group and 25+Group) is lower; however, it is in these two sub-corpora that the majority of references to publications in Czech and all references to publications in other languages occur. The stronger association of these authors with the Czech and the Central European academic discourse conventions is in consonance with the lower number of recent references in their works, as most of them tend to draw on recognized theoretical frameworks and methodologies. In the 40+Group sub-corpus references to Czech-language publications prevail slightly over English-medium publications by Czech authors; however, in the 25+Group sub-corpus the references to English-medium works by Czech authors are considerably more numerous. This shows clearly the dominant position of English in academic knowledge exchange and a shift in orientation on the part of Czech authors towards a wider, international readership, even with works published in a local context. Self-citations are relatively frequent in the 40+Group sub-corpus, thus reflecting the well-established reputation of these authors in the field and the continuity of their contribution to disciplinary knowledge. The rare instances of self-citation in the 25+Group sub-corpus may be seen as compliance with the objectivity and impersonality requirements of the scientific paradigm, the avoidance of self-promotion and the existence of fewer opportunities for self-citation in the humanities and social sciences, where issues are related to a wider academic context and thus are not necessarily immediately related to prior developments (Hyland 2003).

The increase in the number of bibliographical references in the 15+Group and 5+Group sub-corpora correlates with a decline in references to Czech-language publications and an absence of references to sources in other languages. While obviously affected by the globalization of academia, the scholars comprised in these groups consistently promote the work of their Czech colleagues by referring to their English-medium publications (20 per cent of all references in the two sub-corpora). The proportion of reference to research articles and recent sources is relatively high, especially in the 15+Group. This indicates the perceived impact and prestige of knowledge transmitted in particular through English-medium international journals, and the endeavour of Czech linguists to partake in the discussion on current issues and make their research relevant to the international academic community. The tendency to relate to central values and the competitive global context seems to motivate a greater self-promotional effort as expressed by a higher frequency of self-citation.

The frequency analysis of bibliographical references in the corpus has shown that in their English-medium texts Czech linguists are gradually turning from a more local to a more international readership and trying to represent themselves as legitimate members of the global academic discourse community. This tendency is particularly prominent in the texts of younger scholars. The assimilation of central values such as a preference for English-language bibliographical references, however, is combined with a strong association with the local tradition as expressed by systematic referencing to the research of members of the Czech linguistics community.

## 2.4.2   Authorial presence

When considering the construal of authorial presence, Anglophone-centre academic writing style manuals typically advise the avoidance of personal forms and recommend the use of passive voice, abstract rhetors (Hyland 1998, p. 172) and other impersonal constructions. However, Bennett's (2009) survey has evidenced some variation concerning the use of personal and impersonal forms as some authors consider personal pronouns acceptable in the humanities and social sciences or even acknowledge the apparent emergence of alternatives to the scientific paradigm which allow some subjectivity and reference to personal experience (Cottrell 2003). This ongoing change in Anglo-American writing conventions is also indicated by L. Flowerdew (2012), who points out that 'contrary to advice given in some style guides to maintain an objective, impersonal style, the pronoun system is exploited by writers of RAs for maintaining the writer-reader relationship and allowing the writer an authorial voice'. It follows that when using English as a lingua franca for academic publications, Czech authors, together with multilingual writers from other cultural contexts, must not only resolve the tension between their original academic writing tradition and the Anglo-American one, but also accommodate themselves to changes currently taking place in the Anglophone academic literacy.

The results of an analysis of the use of personal and impersonal structures for the construal of authorial presence in the corpus indicate that Czech authors show a clear preference for the use of impersonal forms. This is in agreement with the Central European tradition of backgrounding authorial presence and, quite importantly, concurs with the preference for objectivity and impersonality associated with the scientific paradigm.

The most prominent impersonal constructions in the corpus are passive voice, *it*-clauses followed by extraposed *that*-clauses and *it*-clauses with an adjective followed by extraposed *to*-clauses, and the use of abstract rhetors, such as discourse and research nouns. While avoiding explicit reference to the author, the use of these structures allows writers to organize the text, make claims, develop their argument and indicate their views and positions. Discourse nouns such as abstract rhetors are frequent in abstracts and introductions, where they occur in statements of research topic and claims of its relevance to current research, and when announcing the purpose of the study, which is often associated with the establishing and occupying of niche moves (1).

(1) *The paper argues for the inclusion of one more candidate for the status of a potential FSP indicator – typography or punctuation – to cover cases where FSP-relevant intonation is marked by typographical devices, such as italics, boldface, small capitals etc., in written text.*

*It*-clauses (see Hewings and Hewings 2002) are typically used as emphatics to draw the reader's attention to a point (2) and indicate deductions/ conclusions that should be reached (3). Taking into consideration the preference of Czech authors for authorial modesty (Chamonikolasová 2005, Čmějrková and Daneš 1997), it may seem surprising that the hedging function of *it*-clauses is not so prominent in the corpus. However, this may be interpreted as a sign of accommodation on the part of Czech authors writing for an international audience in order to achieve the more assertive style of argumentation typical of Anglo-American literacy.

(2) *It should be emphasized that neither macrostructures nor scripts are interpreted as static structures or fixed courses of action.*
(3) *When the three most frequent paratactic contrastive DMs in the German corpus, i.e.* however, but *and* nevertheless *are counted together, they are seen to represent more than two thirds of all paratactic markers found in the corpus; it follows that German novice writers tend to use rather excessively a limited repertoire of contrastive markers they know well and thus are able to use appropriately.*

As with Anglo-American academic discourse, passive structures are used to describe methodologies and procedures which are thus represented as objective, arguably, as Vassileva (1998, p. 170) claims, under the influence of the practice in hard sciences. In introductions, passive voice and introductory-*it* structures are used to withhold explicit reference to the author while indicating his/her alignment with previous research, (re) defining basic terms and concepts and outlining the approach adopted in the study

(4) *Before progressing with an analysis of conversational humour in quasi-conversation, it is necessary to contextualize this type of conversation with respect to fictional (non-authentic, scripted) conversation. The two categories are believed to be sufficiently distinct so as to warrant a terminological and analytical distinction, thereby reflecting the radically different ways in which the two types of conversation approach textual authenticity and authorship. It is held that the role of discourse mode is subsidiary to*

*authenticity of the textual segments that make up dialogic interaction. In other words, the approach adopted here shows that the spoken mode is not distinctive for conversations, which can also be cast in the written form.*

While impersonal structures are used to background the author, the main function of first-person pronouns is to highlight authorial presence and promote the writer's contribution to disciplinary knowledge (Harwood 2005). The results of a quantitative analysis of the occurrence of author-reference pronouns as summarized in Table 2.4 clearly show that Czech authors use both singular and plural first-person pronouns, although there is considerable variation in the rate of self-mentions across the different texts.

The average frequency of author-reference pronouns per paper is 14.2 (that is, 26.5 per 10,000 words, ranging from 3 to 39). This rate is lower than the rate of 32.00 per 10,000 words reported by Hyland (2001), who analysed self-mentions in a corpus of 30 research articles published in the 1997 and 1998 issues of *Applied Linguistics*. In addition, whereas in Hyland's (2001) data the rate of singular author pronouns per paper is slightly higher than the rate of plural author pronouns (17.2 and 15.0 respectively), in my corpus the overall average occurrence of *we/ us/our* (10.1) exceeds considerably the average occurrence of *I/me/my* (4.1). There is just one text in which there are no occurrences of plural first-person pronouns; however, five authors have not used the singular first-person pronouns for self-reference.

The use of first-person pronouns varies considerably across the different groups of scholars, although it clearly indicates that Czech authors are affected by the tendency in Anglo-American academic writing towards an increased use of personal forms. The subject forms *I* and *we*, conveying the highest writer visibility, are the most frequent, as when

*Table 2.4*   Frequency of author-reference pronouns in English-medium works of Czech linguists (normalized per 10,000 words)

| Group | Personal pronouns | | | | | | |
|---|---|---|---|---|---|---|---|
| | I | Me | My | We | Us | Our | Total |
| *40+ Group* | 3.64 | 0.61 | 6.06 | 16.36 | 1.82 | 10.91 | 39.39 |
| *25+ Group* | 7.77 | 1.29 | 11.65 | 1.29 | 0.65 | 1.29 | 23.95 |
| *15+ Group* | 0.37 | 0.75 | 0 | 16.82 | 1.50 | 0.37 | 22.06 |
| *5+ Group* | 3.72 | 0.93 | 0 | 11.63 | 4.65 | 3.26 | 24.19 |
| **Total** | **3.37** | **0.87** | **3.49** | **12.34** | **2.24** | **3.49** | **25.81** |

occurring in thematic position in the clause, author-reference devices identify the writer as the source of knowledge, opinion or attitudes expressed and thus enable him/her to control the social interaction with the reader and the academic discourse community (see Gosden 1993, Hyland 2005). The object forms of author-reference pronouns occur considerably less frequently; they are commonly part of the discourse-organizing structures *let me* and *let us*, indicating transition points in discourse, which in the case of the inclusive plural form *us* have the potential to create reader involvement. While the overall rate of singular and plural possessive forms *my* and *our* is the same (3.49), there is considerable variation across the individual groups of scholars. The singular possessive form *my* occurs with relatively high frequency in the texts of four authors, two from the 40+Group and two from the 25+Group. These occurrences, which have the potential 'to promote the writer's contribution by associating them closely with their work' (Hyland 2001, p. 223), mostly refer to the research process (*my analysis, my hypothesis, my findings*) or hedge the views of the author in the discussion (*my opinion, my view*). The occurrences of the plural possessive form *our* comprise its exclusive use referring to the researchers themselves and instances of inclusive use, which may refer to the researchers and the readers, to the discourse community as the holder of shared disciplinary knowledge, and broad generalizations to humans in general.

The most prominent use of singular first-person pronouns is found in the texts by more experienced scholars (40+Group and 25+Group). The function of the singular first-person pronouns in their texts is clearly self-promotional and positions the author as opinion-holder and originator who highlights the novelty and newsworthiness of his/her contribution to the field or indicates a difference between the author's view and that of his/her peers (5).

(5) *In my understanding of the notion of phatic communication I do not support Malinovski's claim that 'language here is not dependent upon what happens at the moment, it seems to be even deprived of any context of situation. [...]' (1999:302). In this article I will try to justify the claim that phatic communication cannot be dissociated from the context of communication. My hypothesis is that phatic communication is the product of the contextual specifications in the process of communication.*

However, in agreement with the Czech academic tradition, authors' statements of claims and purposes are often hedged by modals and lexical verbs expressing tentativeness and humility (6). This use of personal structures often has the additional function of outlining discourse structure.

(6) *Since the procedures with the infiltration of loanwords are well described in literature, I would like to focus on the contact-induced communicative strategies first and sub-categorize them into the following sub-types.*

Some Czech authors use personal pronouns to discuss the terminology adopted for the purposes of the current study, thus taking responsibility for making choices that reconsider existing concepts and approaches (7).

(7) *In this article, I use the terms 'dialogue' and 'dialogic' to describe the situation when a speech event is constituted by different interacting voices, i.e. when more than one (real or fictional) speaker is involved.*

Although scarce, self-citations combined with self-reference occur in introductions to convey the continual engagement of the author with disciplinary knowledge and to underscore the author's credentials by reference to participation in published research, which is one of the strongest demonstrations of one's membership in the disciplinary discourse community (Hyland 2003). This self-promotional function of personal pronouns is also present in the texts of younger scholars, indicating assimilation into the more competitive style of interaction that exists in the Anglophone-centre discourse community (8).

(8) *In recent publications (Adam 2005, 2006), I presented the idea of higher levels of text functioning as distributional macrofields; it seems that such a macro-structural approach may reveal – among other things – essential syntactic-stylistic characteristics of a text.*

The 15+Group sub-corpus differs significantly from the other sub-corpora in showing the lowest rate of first-person singular pronouns. The preferences of the authors included in this group are split, two of them opting for the exclusive *we* and two for impersonal constructions. This suggests that the approach that Czech linguists adopt when resolving the tension between the Czech academic tradition and the Anglo-American literacy is rather idiosyncratic.

Occurrences of first-person plural pronouns appear in all but one text by a Czech linguist; they are rather frequent and comprise instances of both exclusive (92 occurrences) and inclusive (42 occurrences) use.

There are no instances of combination of singular and plural exclusive self-reference. In this respect Czech linguists align with Spanish scholars in the field of business management (Mur-Dueñas 2007); however, they differ from the practice of using the *'I'* and *'we'* perspective simultaneously in the same research article, as reported by Vassileva (1998, 2000) for all the five languages she investigated (that is, English, German, French, Russian and Bulgarian).

The exclusive plural pronoun *we* appears systematically as a self-reference device in texts by four Czech linguists representing different groups, namely the 40+Group, the 15+Group and the 5+Group. Most frequently the editorial *we* positions the writer as recounter of the research process, specifying terminology and describing the procedure adopted in the current investigation and aligning with existing frameworks and approaches (9).

(9) *Following Quirk et al. (1985: 566 ff) we shall distinguish between adjuncts, i.e. obligatory or optional adverbials syntactically integrated in the superordinate clause, and disjuncts, subjuncts and conjuncts syntactically non-integrated in the sentence structure, expressing the attitude of the speaker. Disjuncts (3a) express the speakers' comments on the content or style of what they are saying while wide-orientation subjuncts (3b) specify the point of view applied. We shall use the term conjuncts (3c) to refer to participial adverbials which have a textual function: they are used by the speaker to indicate the organization of the text.*

The role of originator – stating claims and results in the discussion and conclusions sections, thus giving high prominence to the author as the agent of the research process by allowing him/her to report objective data in a personal way – may also be expressed by exclusive *we* (9). In this, Czech linguists seem to differ from authors in other Slavonic languages: Vassileva (1998, p. 177) reports that the employment of the *'we'* perspective in conclusive statements in articles by Russian and Bulgarian authors is low.

(10) *Generally, it appears that paragraph length results from an interplay of a whole range of diverse factors. In our analysis we have pursued several of them more systematically. In particular, we have scrutinized paragraphing in various register corpora. We have shown that in terms of utterances as well as in terms of main clauses, the journalism paragraphs were extremely short, academic ones long, the fiction paragraphs in between.*

The choice between the authorial *we* and impersonality may be affected by the audience the author intends to address, since the occurrence of exclusive *we* is associated primarily with research articles published in national journals (three out of the four cases in my corpus). This is also supported by the fact that one of the authors who has opted for an impersonal stance in his/her text, which is taken from a book published by an international publisher, uses consistently the authorial plural in an earlier research article published in a national journal. The use of the authorial plural reflects interference from the Czech academic writing style, where, similarly to the practice in most Central European academic literacies (for example, Slovak, Polish, Russian, German), the exclusive *we* is a conventional means of expressing authorial modesty. This is often considered 'one of the most common mistakes in English academic texts written by native speakers of Czech' (Chamonikolasova 2005, p. 82). It is a question for future research, however, whether this kind of cross-cultural variation could lead to a greater flexibility of international norms and the acceptance of rhetorical strategies and stylistic choices stemming from alternative literacies.

The rate of inclusive author pronouns (5.2 per 10,000 words) is low compared to the 37.4 per 10,000 words reported by Dontcheva-Navratilova (2013) in a corpus of 12 research articles by native speakers of English published in the journal *Applied Linguistics* in the period 2000–2010. They usually occur in the introductions to describe shared disciplinary knowledge and achieve greater reader involvement in the argumentation (6). An important difference between the use of the inclusive *we* in the texts of Czech linguists and Anglophone-centre writers is that the Czech authors practically do not use the persuasive potential of the 'shifting' signifier of *we*, which may have 'many potential scopes of reference even within a single discourse' (Wales 1996, p. 62).

(11)  *Crime news represents a genre which is particularly suitable for realizing the above mentioned social functions. It meets a number of criteria of newsworthiness, whether we turn to the traditional classification of news values formulated by Galtung and Ruge (1965) or later classifications by, for example, Harcup and O'Neill (2001) or Brighton and Foy (2007), which better reflect the situation in the modern media sphere.*

Since inclusive author pronouns enhance dialogicality, their infrequent use makes the research articles written by Czech linguists rather low on interactiveness. These findings suggest that despite the making of some adjustments to Anglo-American writing conventions, when writing in English Czech authors tend to transfer into their English-language academic texts some features of the generally more monologic Czech academic discourse, which is marked by a preference for backgrounded authorial presence (Čmejrková and Daneš 1997, Chamonikolasová 2005). The analysis of the construal of authorial presence in English-medium academic texts by Czech linguists shows that when attempting to resolve the tension between Czech and Anglo-American academic writing conventions, Czech writers most frequently opt for impersonality – a strategy that is in conformity with the scientific paradigm and the Czech tradition of backgrounding the author. Under pressure from the Anglophone centre, however, some Czech authors tend to use the whole spectrum of function of self-reference personal pronouns to convey a higher degree of author visibility and engage in interaction with the reader. The choice of authorial *we* typical of the Czech and Central European literacies seems to be restricted primarily to publications in national journals addressing a local audience.

When summarizing the results of this investigation into citation practices and authorial presence in English-medium publications by Czech linguists, it is obvious that in their efforts to represent themselves as legitimate members of the global academic discourse community, Czech authors have changed their citation practices and now show a strong preference for English-language bibliographical references. The mere occurrence of personal forms in my corpus also shows that under pressure of the necessity to publish in English in the context of globalized academia, Czech authors make efforts to accommodate themselves to the predominant Anglo-American academic literacy. Logically enough, however, their English-language academic discourse bears traces of their original academic literacy, which results in a preference for impersonal stance, reduced personal attribution by the use of exclusive *we*, tentativeness, a lower degree of commitment to claims conveyed by modal expressions and a lower degree of dialogicality.

## 2.5 Pedagogical implications

This investigation into citation practices and the construal of authorial presence in English-medium publications by Czech scholars who teach linguistics at Czech universities has evidenced that, when striving to publish for an international audience, they make strategic choices in order to resolve the tension between the Czech and the Anglo-American academic writing conventions. The resulting changes in their academic discourse are likely to be reflected in their teaching of academic English at Czech universities and thus transmitted to new generations of Czech linguists who are undergoing their socialization into the academic discourse community during their university studies. This may gradually result in a substantial shift in the academic writing conventions governing the English-medium discourse of Czech scholars, and eventually of the Czech-language academic literacy.

An important pedagogical implication of this and similar studies is that the exposure of university students to their local and the global Anglophone academic literacy should be combined with explicit instruction concerning the differences between the national and Anglo-American discourse conventions. This would raise the students' awareness of existing cross-cultural variation and of the linguistic and rhetorical choices they have at their disposal to construct their discursive identities. In addition, careful monitoring of novice students' written performance could reveal to what extent the tension between the local and the foreign academic literacies have affected their academic discourse. In the Czech context, previous corpus-based research (Dontcheva-Navratilova 2012a, Dontcheva-Navratilova 2012b, Povolná 2012a, Povolná 2012b, Vogel 2008) has evidenced that while clearly showing awareness of Anglo-American academic discourse conventions, the choices of Czech novice writers reflect the insufficient development of their rhetorical skills and interference from the Czech academic literacy. These include significant underuse and restricted scope of text-organizing devices (some of which are overused to the detriment of other, more appropriate ones), a lower degree of dialogicality and a reluctance on the part of Czech students to adopt a position of authority and show clear commitment to claims as expressed by a lower rate of personal pronouns which are confined primarily to the expression of less powerful authorial roles. However, discourse-based studies are not sufficient to explain the motivation for the choices of both novice writers and experienced scholars. They should be complemented by emic, interview- and questionnaire-based investigations, which have the potential to disclose how changes in the local and global academic literacies affect individual preferences. As the results of such a questionnaire-based study (Dontcheva-Navratilova and Povolna 2014) indicate, the tendency to background authorial presence and the notable variance in devices for the construal of authorial presence in Czech students' texts reflects the somewhat contradictory instructions received from thesis supervisors and in academic writing courses, where novices were advised to use impersonal structures, authorial *we*, and a combination of singular and plural author-reference pronouns. These findings suggest that not only students but also experienced multilingual writers would benefit from studying and editing their own academic texts, an approach akin to the 'on-line' genre analysis procedure advocated by Flowerdew (1993) for highlighting discipline-, genre- and culture-specific academic conventions.

In conclusion, the results of this study have evidenced that under the pressure of the Anglophone centre the English-medium discourse of Czech linguists is undergoing substantial change giving rise to 'hybridizing forms' which reflect the tension deriving from intercultural clashes (Gotti 2012). However, a wider-scope diachronic analysis of citation practices and devices used for the construal of authorial presence is necessary to reveal the gradual changes in the development of Czech English-medium academic discourse. Further insights may be gathered from a comparative analysis of Czech-medium and English-medium texts by Czech scholars, which could be indicative of the impact of the internationalization of academia on Czech academic discourse intended for the local audience. Within the context of the globalized academic world, the knowledge gathered from such investigations together with the findings of interview-based studies of the strategic choices made by scholars writing for publication can clearly contribute to a better understanding of the reasons for tendencies in the development of national academic literacies and the Anglophone-centre discourse conventions.

# 3

# Academic Discourse Practices in Greece: Exploring the 'International Conference of Greek Linguistics'

*Dimitra Vladimirou*

## 3.1 Introduction

In the past few years we have witnessed a proliferation of cross-cultural and cross-disciplinary studies of academic discourses. These studies, embedded in a view of language as a socially constructed practice, foreground the interpersonal dimension of academic texts, focusing on the examination of linguistic features and rhetorical practices, such as modality/ hedging, personal pronouns and citations, among others, and utilizing a range of methodological frameworks, such as corpus-based studies, discourse analytic and ethnographically based explorations.

This body of research has offered a detailed mapping of academic discourses in various languages and cultures, or 'academic tribes and their territories' (Becher 1989), to use a spatial metaphor, often raising questions about the social construction of knowledge, and about the ways in which power relations are played out in the academic market-place. However, they do not seem to place the discussion in the context of globalized superdiverse spaces, or to explore further the theoretical, methodological implications that emerge for the study of academic discourses.

This study constitutes an attempt to shift the focus to the exploration of rhetorical practices, as these are embedded in localities and in the international sphere of academic communication; in other words they are placed within an academic indexical field (see Eckert 2008) of discourses. This chapter borrows a number of theoretical tools from sociolinguistic research and social geography and attempts to explore the 'International Conference of Greek Linguistics'[1] as a semiperipheral space of academic discourse practices. I will focus on the language choices, citation practices and person reference choices by means of first-person plural and first-person singular, viewing the above as key elements that contribute to the social construction of knowledge. The aim of the chapter is to explore further the interplay between the international and the local dimensions of academic discourse practices of authors in the semiperiphery and to offer insights on the definition and delineation of semiperipheral spaces.

Specifically the questions that I will attempt to address are:

1. How is knowledge constructed in a space that stands between local and international spaces of academic production and publication?
2. How is locality and internationality played out in the indexical field of the semiperiphery?
3. What are the links between 'the local' and 'the international' as reflected in the writings of Greek-speaking linguists?

This chapter will begin with an overview of previous studies in the field and the theoretical background of the study. Section 3.3 will give an account of the corpus design and the methodology used; Section 3.4 will present the analysis of the results and Section 3.5 will end with some concluding remarks.

## 3.2 Academic discourses: the centre and the semiperiphery

In recent years the focus of much of the research into academic discourse has shifted to the study of academic writing in languages other than English. Most of these studies initially took the form of contrastive studies between writing in English and other languages, some of them inspired by Kaplan's (1966) contrastive rhetoric approach (see Connor 1999), which examined how cultural conventions can be transferred to second language writing, and therefore drew attention to the link between rhetorical conventions and writing and foregrounded a view of language as a cultural phenomenon. Thus, rhetorical practices and the instantiations of these practices through linguistic features prevalent in local national cultures and the central Anglo-American culture has become the focus of analysis, an approach clearly articulated in Duszak's (1997) edited collection *Culture and Styles of Academic Discourse*. For example, Mauranen (1993) discusses metatext in Finnish and English in the context of reader-responsible and writer-responsible cultures; Taylor and Chen (1991) and, more recently, Kim Loi and Evans (2010) compare organizational patterns in Chinese and English; Clyne

(1987) looks at culture and discourse structure in German and English and Vassileva (1998) offers a contrastive analysis of hedging between Bulgarian and English academic writing. More recent work is also interested in academic voices (for example, Fløttum et al. 2006), knowledge claims (for example, Dahl 2008) and diachronic investigations of academic rhetoric (for example, Shaw and Vassileva 2009). Amongst the above, personal pronouns and citation practices have attracted considerable attention as significant resources for knowledge construction (see Myers 1990 for an initial exploration of knowledge claims in scientific discourse). The above body of research offers very useful insights from a typological perspective and unravels the degree of variation across what Holliday (1999) refers to as 'large cultures'; however, more critical approaches addressing the politics of academic communication and knowledge production and circulation are rarely found in the literature.

To fill this gap, Lillis and Curry (2010) position academic discourse practices within specific geolinguistic spaces and foreground the politics of location as one of the main dimensions relevant to the study of academic discourses, reflected also in the title of the monograph *Academic Writing in a Global Context* (see also Canagarajah 2002). Drawing on conceptual tools from sociolinguistic research, and taking an explicitly critical stance, they examine academic discourse practices not as stable processes produced within specific national contexts, but rather as 'texts' that are the result of complex interplay between network building and the processes of globalization.

Lillis and Curry (2010) problematize and unpack the notions 'local' and 'global', as well as 'national' and 'international', by asking questions, such as 'what counts as local and/ or international knowledge' and 'what is the currency of this knowledge in various academic contexts?' Instead of exploring these as fixed categories they reveal the connections between various localities and the international context.

The discussions presented above are particularly relevant to the present study, which seeks to explore the interplay between the local and the international in an 'academic event' that interestingly claims to be both and positions itself between an international and a local context.

## 3.3   Data sources and procedures

The data presented and analysed in this chapter are part of a more extended study on academic discourse on the semiperiphery focusing on the Greek context. The 'International Conference on Greek Linguistics' is the main site used for this study. The starting point of the data collection was the conference website, which provided information on the trajectory of the event from 1993 until the present. Data sources included mission statements, information on the location in which the conference took place, information on the programme, languages used, plenary speakers and conference proceedings.

The methodological procedure followed two steps. Information on the various locations of the event and authors' language choices (whether they chose to present and publish in English or in Greek) was used in order to map out how the event developed as a semiotic practice situated within 'TimeSpace', to borrow Wallerstein's (1997, 2001) term. This part of the analysis examined all the data available on line, which ranged from 2005 until the latest 2013 conference, excluding the 2007 Ioannina event, which had no functioning website. The working languages of the event are English and Greek. The language used in the title and abstract of each chapter, as indicated in the programme was used as an indicator of the language choice of the author(s).

The second part of the analysis presented in this chapter draws on papers collected from the 2011 conference proceedings, following the conference organized at the Democritus University of Thrace, Komotini, Greece. The corpus consists of 20 papers written in Greek.

This part of the analysis follows a more strictly textual approach that leads us to a detailed examination of knowledge construction through authors' rhetorical practices, specifically citation choices, and the use of personal reference. Following Lillis et al. (2010), all bibliographical references appearing at the end of each paper were examined and coded according to their language used; the two main categories encountered were English and Greek and a third category included other languages.

The use of person reference has been extensively explored in the academic discourse literature. (for example, Fløttum et al. 2006, Harwood 2005a, Harwood 2005b, Harwood 2006, Hyland 2000, Hyland 2005b, Vassileva 2000). Following Vladimirou (2008, 2014), the present investigation includes plural person reference functioning in subject position and in possessives. Since the dataset examined for this study is in Greek I have included here a short summary of how person reference is linguistically encoded in Modern Greek.

### 3.3.1 Person in Modern Greek

Modern Greek is a zero-subject language in which 'we' is marked morphologically in the suffix of the verb (Holton et al. 2002, p. 199). According to Siewierska's (2004) categorization, this type of person reference belongs to the category of dependent person markers. The distinction between inclusive and exclusive pronouns is not formally marked in Greek (see Pavlidou 2012, 2008). The function of first- and second-person pronouns in a subject position when these are present in the sentence has traditionally been categorized as emphatic (Holton et al. 2002). However, Pavlidou (2012), who examines naturally occurring conversational data on the freestanding first-person plural pronoun, shows that *εμείς*('we') can perform a range of functions; these go beyond marking collective self-reference, such as marking 'the newness of the collective subject (...), the exclusion of others (...) and the speaker's disalignment with the addressee' (Pavlidou 2012, p. 43). The above point is particularly relevant to the analysis presented in this chapter, since part of the discussion examines the construction of collectivities across local and international contexts.

## 3.4   Analysis

### 3.4.1   Conferences as indexical fields in a globalized world

As Blommaert (2010, p. 63) suggests, one of the main challenges faced by researchers today is the traditional theorizing of cultures as belonging to specific territories, in other words the attribution of 'spatiality' to culture. This first section of the analysis will attempt to map out how space, time and language choice interact and produce 'globalized localities' (Blommaert 2007) and how these ideas can be applied to a specific social event, namely, the 'International Conference of Greek Linguistics'. Blommaert (2007, p. 5) reminds us that every social event develops simultaneously in space and time and that this semiotized TimeSpace is 'social, cultural, political, ideological, in short *historical*' (Blommaert 2007, p. 5) (emphasis in the original).

Table 3.1 presents the language choices of authors as these develop diachronically from 2005 until 2013, and shows how these develop depending on the location of the event. The final quantitative results demonstrate a clear preference for English, in other words for the international language of publication, or the widespread scale.

However, a more careful look at the data reveals a series of movements across centre and semiperipheral contexts, an approximation of which are depicted in Figure 3.1.

As Blommaert (2010, p. 6) puts it: 'Movement of people across space is (...) never a move across empty spaces. The spaces are always someone's space, and they are filled with norms, expectations, conceptions of what counts as proper and normal (indexical) language use and what does not count as such. Mobility, sociolinguistically speaking, is therefore, a trajectory'. Figure 3.1 depicts the trajectory of language choices

*Table 3.1* The International Conference of Greek Linguistics: location and language choice

| Conference Location | English | Greek |
| --- | --- | --- |
| Rhodes 2013 | 111 | 103 |
| Komotini 2011 | 56 | 65 |
| Chicago 2009 | 103 | 8 |
| Ioannina | no data | no data |
| York 2007 | 80 | 23 |
| Rethimno 2005 | 93 | 78 |
| Total | 443 | 277 |

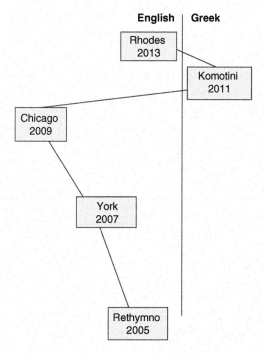

*Figure 3.1* The International Conference of Greek Linguistics: language choice and SpaceTime

starting from the semiperipheral local space of Rethymno, in Greece, in which the preference for papers in English is slightly higher than those in Greek, moving on to two centre locations in the UK and the US, in which English clearly predominates (especially in the case of Chicago in which we have only eight papers in Greek and 103 in English). When the conference takes place in centre contexts, authors demonstrate a tendency to position their work within the international sphere of the academic marketplace, thus, they choose the language that functions as the high currency. Interestingly, when the social event shifts location and is situated again in the semiperiphery of Greece, the local gains ground. In the last two examples, authors seem to invoke a stronger local identity.

This movement between higher and lower scales (English and Greek as language choices) observed between central and semiperipheral contexts allows us to imagine social events such as academic conferences as indexical fields. As Eckert (2008, p. 453) suggests, an indexical field is 'a constellation of ideologically related meanings, any one of which can be activated in the situated use of a variable. The field is fluid, and each new activation has the potential to change the field by building on ideological connections'.

The data analysed demonstrate the inequalities of the system with English constituting the language with the most normative value. But the most interesting observation is that we seem to be witnessing a return to the local which is also encoded in the rhetorical practices that we shall be examining in the sections that follow.

### 3.4.2  Analysis of selected papers from the proceedings of the Komotini 2011 conference

The next two sections of the analysis explore a corpus of 20 papers presented in 2011 at the Komotini conference[2] and published in 2012 in Greek. These sections present a more detailed analysis of texts by Greek-speaking authors and the rhetorical practices prevalent in this complex geolinguistic space.

### 3.4.2.1  *Language choice and bibliographical references*

Citations and bibliographical references are both conventional academic discourse practices. In his 1986 paper 'Citation Analysis and Discourse Analysis', Swales was one of the first who brought together two different approaches (from bibliometrics and applied linguistics) to citation analysis, and a few years later White (2004) revisited the study of citations by adding insights from information science. The study of citations from a social constructionist perspective is not new. Yet, as Lillis et al. (2010) suggest, two contextual dimensions have not been emphasized enough in the literature: language and geographical location. These two emerge as key aspects in the present study, which foregrounds the geolinguistic dimension of rhetorical practices in a semiperipheral context.

Following Lillis et al. (2010), the main questions addressed in this part of the analysis relate to the influence of English as an academic lingua franca in the works that get cited. Viewing citations as reflections of the knowledge that gets to be accepted, this analysis seeks to reveal the extent to which 'local' and/or 'international' knowledge is circulated in the dataset examined (Table 3.2).

In total 622 bibliographical references were examined. Although the results presented here are drawn from a small corpus of 20 articles, they provide an indication of the kinds of knowledge that gets accepted and cited. The overall results seem to map out the 'International Conference of Greek Linguistics', as indeed, a semiperipheral space in which both English-medium and Greek-medium knowledge circulate almost to the same degree, although English still slightly prevails. If we compare the above findings to Lillis et al. (2010), and specifically to the citation choices made by psychologists publishing in English-medium national journals (from four national contexts: Slovakia, Hungary, Spain and Portugal), we notice that only 51 per cent of references are in English as opposed to 81.2 per cent found in the Lillis et al. 2010 corpus. Additionally, Greek-medium references constitute 40 per cent of all references, and 8 per cent appear in other local academic languages, such as Italian, German, French and Albanian in the dataset examined here. This finding is again contrary to the 15.6 per cent local national language and 3.2 per cent other languages observed in the Lillis et al. (2010) corpus. Epistemological differences between linguistics and psychology, as well as the different genres compared, appear as explanatory factors for the variation observed. Standing as a discipline between the hard and soft sciences, linguistics seems to invite more contributions in the local language, whereas psychology embraces a more positivist epistemology which perhaps relates to a higher degree to the use of English.

Overall, the findings concur with the image of the semiperiphery sketched in the previous section of the analysis. Both English and Greek predominate, but locality seems to hold a dominant position in the choices of authors.

*Table 3.2* Person reference choices of Greek-speaking linguists: 'I' versus 'we'

| No of articles: 20 | Greek | English | Other local languages | Total |
| --- | --- | --- | --- | --- |
| Raw figures | 252 | 320 | 50 | 622 |
| Percentages | 40% | 51% | 8% | |

The next section of the analysis deals with personal reference choices in the dataset, starting with a comparative quantitative analysis of first-person singular versus first-person plural, following a qualitative analysis of how 'we' is used as a resource for the construction of the 'local' and the 'international'.

### 3.4.2.2   *Personal reference choices: I versus we*

The overall findings of the distribution of first-person singular and first-person plural reveal that Greek-speaking authors adhere to some degree to a personalized way of writing. In fact, the interpersonal dimension of academic writing has been explored extensively in the literature (see Hyland 2000). These results are also in line with previous studies of person reference in Greek academic discourse (for example, Vladimirou 2008) (specifically the discipline of linguistics), which suggest that Greek-speaking authors show a tendency to use less the first person plural and to opt for the so-called 'we for I' or 'editorial we' (see next section). Although the use of first-person plural can have a cline of authorial visibility depending on whether it is used to describe one's methodological choices, as a signposting device or in order to make a strong claim, we may assume that *I* carries a more self-promotional tenor. The Greek-speaking authors whose work is examined here seem to follow the claim-making patterns observed in the Greek context, including a high tendency to use the 'we for I'- whose functions will be analysed in the following section.

*'We' for 'I' (exclusive).*   According to Vladimirou (2014), this type of pronominal reference may be defined as the writer's use of 'we' in order to refer exclusively to himself/herself. Previous studies of academic discourse have identified this type of 'we': for example, Rounds (1987) and Fortanet (2004) in oral academic discourse; Kuo (1999) in his study of scientific journals; Martin and Burgess (2004) and Fløttum et al. (2006) in journal articles; Coffin and Mayor (2004) in international students' essays, and more recently, Hewings and Coffin (2007) in electronic discussions and essays. One of the main functions of 'we for I' is the avoidance of an egoistical *I* (see Quirk et al. 1985, pp. 350–1) and the creation of a balance between being too personal or too impersonal (Wales 1996). The following examples illustrate some of the rhetorical possibilities of 'we for I':

(1) Αξίζει να σημειώσ**ουμε** ότι ακόμη και σήμερα αρκετές περιοχές της Θράκης παραμένουν γλωσσικά αχαρτογράφητες (ΒΑΖ)

It is worthwhile for **us** to note (+ **we**) that even today some of the areas of Thrace remain linguistically unknown.

(2) Αν και αναγνωρίζ**ουμε** τη σημασία των πιο πάνω διακρίσεων στη βάση ενός συνεχούς, στην παρούσα εργασία θα προσπαθήσουμε να επικεντρω**θούμε** στα κριτήρια της διάκρισης των ονοματικών δομών ως λέξης και μη λέξης (ή ως πολυλεκτικού συνθέτου και μη) ελέγχοντας όλα τα γλωσσικά επίπεδα, όπως -επιπλέον της μορφολογίας και σύνταξης- τα επίπεδα σημασίας και χρήσης (...)

Even though **we** recognize the importance of the above distinctions on the basis of a continuum, in the present paper **we** will attempt to focus on the criteria of distinction of nominal structures (...)

Both Example 1 and the first 'we' in Example 2 are cases of claim-making. In the first the author is making a clarification, whereas in the second the author differentiates his/her position from work previously done in their area of investigation. Even though the above claims appear to be unmitigated, the choice of plural person reference itself encapsulates some degree of mitigation, compared to the use of first person singular which highlights the contribution of the author, reflects a view of research and science as individually rather than collectively constructed and has a promotional function that is often observed in international contexts of publication (see also Hyland 2000).

*'We' as Greek speakers.* The author whose work we are examining in example 3 below uses a range of first person plural types, including 'we for I' and 'we' inclusive of the author and the audience (for example in cases such as 'we see below'). In Example 3 the author opts for an inclusive 'we', referring to Greek speakers, which results in the construction of a strictly defined national collectivity and which could only be sketched out in smaller, semiperipheral academic contexts:

(3) αντίθετα **μας** φαίνεται μάλλον αντιγραμματική η πιο κάτω πρόταση. Μπορ**ούμε** να π**ούμε** (...) ---*ενώ* δεν μπορ**ούμε** να π**ούμε** (...) *αλλά* μπορ**ούμε** να παρεμβάλ**ουμε** άρθρο (...) σε δομές που θεωρούνται instead the following sentence rather seems to **us** ungrammatical (...) **we** can say (...) But **we** cannot say (...) but **we** can insert an article in structures that are considered (...) CHR

The use of this type of 'we' not only delineates a specified collectivity (Greek speakers) but also ties in with the process of claim-making and specifically the approach proposed in this chapter, namely a semantic approach to the notion of the lexical unit. In other words, the author claims that we need to consider what 'we' or 'Greek speakers' can say and what seems to a 'Greek speaker' ungrammatical. This is a strategy that I – as a Greek speaker – would not use in the present chapter, since my audience extends the space of the Greek semiperiphery.

*Addressing the local academic community: 'we Greek linguists'.*   In 4 and 5 we observe another rhetorical strategy that can occur in semiperipheral rather than 'international' contexts of publication. The topic of discussion here refers to number of terminological distinctions and the translation of terms from English to Greek. The author moves from an *I* ('I think) that reflects her contribution/thoughts on how the issue should be resolved to a 'we' that semantically refers to the Greek community of linguists. The claim presented here, thus, responds to the concerns of the specific academic community, which is constructed as a collectivity, placing emphasis again on the local, but linking it to the international.

(4) Επίσης, θέλοντας να αποδώσ**ουμε** την εξωτερική *διγλωσσία*, θα έπρεπε να καταφύγ**ουμε** στο παράδοξο και ακατανόητο «εξωτερική διμορφία/διυφία». Και μόνο γι' αυτούς τους λόγους οι όροι «διμορφία/διυφία» είναι μάλλον ακατάλληλοι. Ως τούτου η επιλογή θα έπρεπε, **νομίζω**, να εστιαστεί στους όρους *διγλωσσία, κοινωνική διγλωσσία* και *διπλογλωσσία*. Ο «φυσικός» συνειρμός της λέξης «διγλωσσία» με την συνύπαρξη δύο διαφορετικών γλωσσών (bilingualism) **μάς** επιβάλλει, νομίζω, να **κρατήσουμε** για το bilingualism τον όρο «διγλωσσία», οπότε η «κοινωνική διγλωσσία» και η «διπλογλωσσία» φαίνονται προς το παρόν οι πιο κατάλληλοι όροι.
Also, in **our** attempt to define external diglossia, we would have to resort to the incomprehensible/ problematic dimorphia. For these reasons, the terms dimorphia, are probably not appropriate. Therefore, the choice would have to focus, **I think**, on the terms '*διγλωσσία, κοινωνική διγλωσσία* και *διπλογλωσσία*'. The natural connotation of the word '*διγλωσσία*' with the coexistence of two related languages makes us keep the term '*διγλωσσία*', to mean bilingualism, therefore, '*κοινωνική διγλωσσία*' και η '*διπλογλωσσία*' are the most appropriate terms.

(5) Στο σημείο αυτό **θεωρώ** πως υπάρχουν δύο περιοριστικές παράμετροι που είτε **μας** εμποδίζουν να χρησιμοποιήσουμε τον όρο κοινωνική διγλωσσία (λ.χ. για την ελληνιστική κοινή) είτε **μας** αναγκάζουν να τον χρησιμοποιήσ**ουμε** με σαφείς περιορισμούς.
At this point **I think** there are two limiting dimensions which either do not allow **us** to use the term κοινωνική διγλωσσία (for example for Common Hellenistic), or they make us use it with strict limitations.

### 3.4.2.3 Scale shifts between the international and the local

A similar strategy is observed in Examples 6 and 7 in which the authors make explicit links between the local and the international. The claim-making process here is embedded in the concerns of the international community of linguists and their application to the Greek context. These shifts between the local and the global, the macro and the micro, or in other words the construction of various centres in the writings of Greek-speaking linguists emerges as a characteristic of semiperipheral writing and point again towards an image of the 'The International Conference of Greek Linguistics' as an indexical polycentral space.

(6) <u>Τοποθετώντας το ζήτημα σε διεθνές επίπεδο</u>, θεωρο**ύμε** καλό να αναφέρο**υμε** τον προβληματισμό του Truchot (2002, pp. 17–19) σχετικά με τη θέση και τις λειτουργίες των γλωσσών σήμερα που το μόρφωμα εθνικό-κράτος τείνει να ξεπεραστεί και να θεωρηθεί αρχαϊκό μπροστά στα νέα σχήματα που επιβάλλει σταδιακά η παγκοσμιοποίηση της αγοράς. (CHR)
<u>Placing the issue on an international level</u> we think that we need to refer to the issue raised by Truchot (2002, pp. 17–19) in relation to the position and the functions of languages, since nowadays the construct nation state tends to be considered archaic in relation to new constructs imposed by the globalization of the marketplace.

(7) <u>Η αναφορά στον Fishman</u> και την εξωτερική διγλωσσία **μάς** οδηγεί απευθείας στο δεύτερο σημείο που χρειάζεται διευκρίνιση, την απόδοση του όρου στη νέα ελληνική. (KAR)
<u>The reference to Fishman</u> and the external diglossia leads **us** straight to the second point that needs clarification, which term to use in Greek.

## 3.5 Concluding remarks

The present chapter has attempted to explore the 'International Conference of Greek Linguistics' as a semiperipheral space of knowledge construction and production. The first part of the analysis presented an image of the specific social event, as it developed diachronically across various centre and peripheral spaces, focusing on the distribution of language choices. This representation follows the trajectory of language choices, which, as expected, correlate with the location of the conference and confirm the 'symbolic value' of English as the language of internationally accepted, and often valued as high-quality academic discourse. Interestingly enough, though, authors also seem to move more towards local normative choices. The results obtained from a closer examination of 20 selected papers by Greek-speaking authors also point towards the idea that the local seems to hold a central place on the semiperiphery. The citation practices of Greek-speaking authors paint a very balanced image between locally produced knowledge in Greek and internationally accepted knowledge in English. Authors also seem to invoke a strong local identity by using the first person plural in order to construct collectivities inclusive of Greek speakers or Greek-speaking linguists. They address the concerns of the Greek community of linguists, but at the same time they often situate their work within/ or link their work to the international higher scale.

In line with the focus of this book I have attempted to offer an image of an academic social event as an indexical space situated on the semiperiphery and operating across central and peripheral spaces, filled with attributes or in our case, language choices and rhetorical strategies, which have symbolic and often material value. We have seen how movement takes place across lower and higher scales and we have tried to pin down the workings of these globalized, 'transcending localities' (Blommaert et al. 2005, p. 198). Although the exact hierarchical relations between scales is not easy to predict, we need to remember that 'scales are not neutral terms, they attribute meaning, value, structure and characteristics to the processes they are a part of' (Blommaert et al. 2005, p. 202). A more ethnographically oriented study, which examines the voices of authors who participate in social events such as conferences, could provide a more comprehensive image of the semiperiphery and its workings in translocal spaces.

## Notes

1. See the 2009 statement of purpose of the International Conference of Greek Linguistics: 'ICGL is a biennial meeting, held every two years since 1993, that focuses on all aspects of the linguistic study and analysis of Greek, from Ancient up through Modern Greek, though with greater emphasis on the later stages of the language.

   ICGL 2009 will feature papers on a wide variety of topics relevant to Greek linguistics, broadly construed, thus covering a range of subfields within linguistics, including applied linguistics, computational linguistics, conversational analysis, corpus linguistics, dialectology, discourse analysis, historical linguistics, language description, morphology, neurolinguistics, phonetics, phonology, pragmatics, psycholinguistics, semantics, sociolinguistics, and syntax, among others, and focusing on any period in the history of the language'.

2. In 2011, 56 papers were presented and published in the Proceedings in English and 65 in Greek.

# 4
# Teaching Academic Writing for the Global World in Poland: The ELF Perspective

*Anna Gonerko-Frej*

## 4.1 Introduction

The struggles Polish students of English have with academic writing are rarely analysed in the context of the battleground of different cultures within the paradigm of contrastive rhetoric or linguistic imperialism. Adjusting to the demands of a different model of writing, students often channel their efforts into the adoption of foreign norms, losing sight of their main goals. Research findings in the field of English as a Lingua Franca (ELF) may help redirect the attention of both students and teachers towards effective global communication, accommodating various cultural expressions and helping to re-establish the main goals of written texts.

The specific difficulties of Polish students trying to express their ideas in English writing are usually described in terms of inadequate foreign language skills, rated on the scale of conformity to a model, provided by either British or American course books or examination bodies. The students' written output is typically discussed in terms of structural or lexical failures, evaluated according to some 'native speaker' criteria, described in 'native speaker' terms. There have been very few attempts to see some aspects of writing as an expression of the local culture, with strong local roots. Duszak's contrastive studies of Polish and English written academic discourse (1994, 1997b, 1998) are rare examples of the description of the specificity of Polish rhetoric as conditioned by the national system of education and socializing into the Polish culture.

I will try to present the difficulties of Polish students against the background of Polish education culture and traditional values, arguing for the change of models in the days of global English and presenting some results of an ethnographic study of students of English at the University of Szczecin.

## 4.2   Polish academic culture

Although the Polish system of education has undergone many changes in the post-communist era, it still largely emphasizes rote learning and imitation. In a system where self-expression is often stifled or punished as immature or naive, pupils quickly learn that imitation is the only technique that will lead to good marks and appreciation. This is even clearer in the EFL class, where the mythical native speaker is the (unrealistic) model, so success can only be measured by the degree of the faithfulness of imitation.

Polish pupils' inventiveness is directed to the creation of 'cribsheets'[1], as only the regurgitation of the approved texts can lead them to success (the moral problems connected with a wide-scale cheating have still not been resolved). Scollon (2000) offers a helpful perspective with his description of 'Confucian and Socratic models' in different educational contexts; Poland seems largely reminiscent of the 'Confucian' style, where 'training in virtue meant passing on the best of [Chinese] tradition, which took precedence over thinking for oneself' (Scollon 2000, p. 16), and the teacher's role is to provide best models for imitation.

> Rather than a midwife who helps give birth to a truth that lies within (Socratic tradition), he is a messenger who transmits the wisdom of the ancients. Instead of invoking an internal authority, he has been seen as providing his students with an external authority (...).
>
> (Scollon 2000, pp. 19–20)

The 'regurgitator model' finds expression in the famous maxim of the Polish student – the so-called 'three zet method': *zakuj, zdaj, zapomnij* (learn by heart, pass [the exam] and forget). The idea is to give back what you 'swallowed', preferably intact, undistorted by your own mind. Although this may seem an unfair generalization, it is still common practice, and a concern of academic teachers in Poland. Trying to convince the students of the value of critical thinking is a hard task in Polish academia; I strongly believe this is one of the reasons Polish primary- and secondary-school pupils do really well in international tests but Polish students fail in comparison with their peers elsewhere.[2] Whether this is still the heritage of the communist system, forcing submission, remains a question to study. Still, the students' demand to be provided with writing models that can be faithfully imitated may be seen as part of the local culture.

Writing skills do not get much emphasis in the Polish education system. Pupils in primary and secondary schools are usually asked to submit occasional compositions in their Polish class once or twice a month; other subjects rarely involve written assignments. Even at the tertiary level, Polish tradition favours oral examination, in the form of individual meetings with the tutor. The constantly expanding presence of English instruction in the Polish education sector (since 1989) has brought some explanatory training in writing skills to Polish schools. In fact, the explicit guidelines for writing are often first introduced by the English language course books. This may be partly due to the Polish tradition of exposing the student to good models rather than providing step-by-step instruction, as discussed earlier.

### 4.2.1 The hierarchy of publications

The official Polish system of evaluating academic output is based on the different categories of publications. Category A (the highest) contains Impact Factor journals, listed in the Journal Citation Reports (JCR). This means that publications in English are almost exclusively the ones that can score top points. Although this reflects the power of English as the academic lingua franca and the incentive towards gaining international recognition, it is also a matter of ideological choice, effectively stigmatizing national language and culture, which are frequently rejected by local researchers. To be accepted by international journals, the academics need to conform to British or American writing traditions, giving up the national cultural characteristics. Even if this is self-imposed hegemony of English rather than linguistic imperialism, relegating national language and culture to a lower position and changing it to the norms of McLanguage (Snell-Hornby 1999) remains controversial. The immediate association of higher academic quality with one, specific linguistic code creates a danger of 'linguicism', or discrimination based on language (Phillipson 1992, pp. 54–55).

The local discourse in the native language, often openly discriminated against, appears to be yielding to the power of the global 'killer language' (Pakir 1991, cit. Mühlhäusler 1996).

Despite some purist attitudes to language use in Poland, it must be acknowledged that Polish academic discourse is changing as a result of the prevalence of English. Modern academic Polish is said to imitate English when it comes to text formatting, level of interactiveness and style, leading to a more 'feuilletonic', easily accessible, essay-like, style of writing.

(Duszak and Lewkowicz 2008, p. 110)

In her numerous studies of the cultural 'load' of languages, Wierzbicka (2010, p. 5) describes English as a transmitter of the so-called 'Anglo-culture' and warns that this language is not a 'cultural tabula rasa, a blank slate', even though its global role is often linked with the suggestion that 'English (...) unlike other languages is "neutral" – a purely functional, international language that is free from the baggage of any particular history and tradition'. This claim must be refuted: 'rather than denying the existence of the cultural baggage embedded in Anglo-English, I believe it is important to explore the content of that baggage' (Wierzbicka 2010, p. 6). Different cultures cannot express themselves in the same way in one language; this would lead to 'misguided universalism'. The different treatment of emotions in Polish and English writing can serve as a good example. While the 'Anglo-culture' 'identifies emotion primarily with irrationality, subjectivity, the chaotic and other negative characteristics. (...) One of the most pervasive cultural assumptions is that it is antithetical to reason or rationality'; in Polish 'national ethos, *serce* (heart) is opposed to the scientist's *szkiełko i oko* (magnifying glass and eye) as a source of "live truth" versus the domain of "dead truths", and this opposition has retained an important place in the Polish ethnotheory'. (Wierzbicka 1991, p. 54). Hence, restraining the students' flow of emotional expressions in academic writing is high on the agenda of the writing instructors in Poland.

### 4.2.2   Prescriptivism

Phillipson's (1992) discussion of the imposition of British or American norms in language education as a manifestation of 'linguistic imperialism' has helped to raise awareness of the cultural 'baggage' of language. After the collapse of the communist system in 1989, Poland became a market for British EFL publishers (Longman, OUP), examination boards (UCLES) and material providers; the subsequent creation of teacher training colleges, generously supported by the British Council, also contributed significantly to the absolute dominance of British English in educational institutions across the country. To satisfy the new demand for about 20,000 English language teachers (Komorowska 2012), the newly created educational institutions were opened across the country and quickly grew in numbers (up to 60 in the years 2000). The model of English promoted in all those colleges, as well as in most English departments at Polish universities, was rather uniform. I discuss the cultural implications of the post-communist developments on the ELT business in Poland elsewhere (Gonerko-Frej 2011, 2013).

In her empirical studies of EFL writing in Poland, Reichelt et al. (2005a, 2005b, 2012) gives an overview of the history of English in Poland and her perception of the Poles' attitudes toward English. She observes:

> Most students choose English as their FL, and generally, motivation for learning English, including learning to write in English, is high. There is a perception that written English skills are important, primarily for making and maintaining foreign business contacts.
>
> (Reichelt et al. 2012, p. 33)

My own experience as a teacher at both secondary and university level rather shows that writing skills have been mostly perceived as tools for passing exams, either British ones (UCLES, IELTS, and so on) or Polish ones modelled on British norms (such as the secondary school-leaving exam, *matura*, or the so-called Practical English exam for students of English).

The early years of the new post-communist era in Poland were also the time of the development of the field of intercultural education studies. The significance of cultural understanding in foreign language studies became the focus of research in the 1990s (Byram 1989, Byram and Morgan 1994, Byram and Fleming 1998, Gonerko-Frej 2007, Kramsch 1993, 1998, 2001). Without resorting to the extreme version of the Sapir-Whorf theory of linguistic relativism, numerous publications demonstrated the need for awareness of the cultural dimension in the language teaching process. Unfortunately, the writing skill as such did not receive special attention from scholars, though, as all language skills, it was largely exposed to cultural influences, another seemingly innocent transmitter of foreign values and norms. In her book, 'Listening to the World', Fox (1994) shows how much the so-called 'good writing' is

> based on assumptions and habits of mind that are derived from western culture, and that this way of thinking and communicating is considered the most sophisticated, intelligent, and efficient by only a fraction of the world's peoples.
>
> (Fox 1994, p. xxi)

That is to say, Anglocentric writing models push culturally different modes of expression to the margins of 'inappropriateness'.

The prescriptivism of the teaching of academic writing in English has meant that students that try to retain their identities and internalized mother-tongue conventions in their second-language writing are penalized. Their work is often downgraded and classified as sloppy, undisciplined and inadequate. As Canagarajah points out:

> To be academically literate in English, second language students have to acquire not only certain linguistic skills, but also preferred values, discourse conventions (...) In writing in English to the academy, periphery scholars face the need to take on an identity and subjectivity constituted by these discourses
>
> (Canagarajah 1999, p. 147).

### 4.2.3   Contrastive rhetoric and the Polish 'polot'

Cultural aspects of writing were the focus of Kaplan's pioneering studies in the 1960s, and his attempt to illustrate different rhetorical patterns in various parts of the world (Kaplan 1966) became the inspiration for the development of contrastive rhetoric (CR) (Connor 1996, Čmejrková 1996, Duszak 1998, Kubota and Lehner 2004, Petrić 2005). The five types of paragraph development identified by Kaplan correspond to culturally determined rhetorical tendencies. The famous 'doodles' (as he himself called them later) on the one hand established the validity of different models of writing, but, on the other, launched new stereotypes, leading to gross oversimplifications and unjustified generalizations.

In Kaplan's model, the Polish rhetorical pattern is represented by the so-called *Russian* line – with an irregular pattern of numerous turns and deviations from the path. This is translatable into a writing style that often loses focus, diverting the reader from the main line of argumentation with frequent digressions and a substantial amount of irrelevant material. Whether this description adequately portrays the peculiarities of the 'Polish style' is definitely debatable and would need to be supported with research data. Still, the tendency to interrupt the simple progression of ideas with some 'witty' comments often is considered a mark of the 'writing talent' and a broad, open mind. 'Good writing' in Polish schools is intriguing, impressive, sophisticated; and this is impossible without 'a flair for writing', or rather – a *polot*. The Polish word *polot* has no good equivalent in English. Eva

Hoffman, who established her career as a writer in America, believes it gives Polish writing a distinctive character. When she recounts her Polish writing classes in her famous book, *Lost in Translation* (1989), she recalls,

> What counts in a written composition – whether it's about our last school excursion or a poem by Mickiewicz – is a certain extravagance of style and feeling. The best complement that a school exercise can receive is that it has *polot* – a word that combines the meanings of dash, inspiration and flying. *Polot* is what everyone wants to have in personality as well. Being correct and dull is a horrid misfortune.
>
> (Hoffman 1989, p. 71)

*Polot*, appreciated and desirable in Polish writing, is stifled and criticized in the Anglophone writing tradition. What in Poland is considered a mark of talent, in English is discredited as bad style. The development of CR marked a first step towards acknowledging the existence of other writing styles and became an important element of intercultural education.

If written linguistic expression is largely conditioned by culture, common experience should lead to similarities in rhetorical patterns. Indeed, a number of studies on Slavic languages point to some shared characteristics of academic writing style. When Čmejrková compares Czech and English academic writing (1996), she makes references to Central and Eastern European traditions, influenced by the Russian and Teutonic intellectual styles (p. 140). Her description of the 'culture-specific characteristics of Czech discourse', with its 'vagueness, associativeness, parallelism, and the interplay of meanings' (p. 145) could also be applied to Polish style. The Polish reader can truly appreciate the Czech writer, who 'does not write simply, plainly, precisely or in a straightforward manner.' (p. 145). Similarly, when Čmejrková compares the reader's responsibility, she states that 'Czech readers have been trained to read between the lines and to infer the sense that is text immanent. The sense of the text is something that should be sought for and not explicitly formulated' (p. 145). A potential Polish reader is well familiar with that role, thus often finding it difficult to adopt different criteria when writing in English. Whereas the Anglo-American norms require the writer to lead the reader 'by the hand' through the meanders of his/her reasoning, Eastern European writing advises leaving the reaction and interpretation to the reader, providing only the stimulus.

The pedagogical implications of contrastive rhetoric are nowadays more often linked with negative than positive effects. Overgeneralizations have led to essentializing and easy stereotyping, directing attention away from regular language problems, which are also an important part of native speaker's experience. The 'initial enthusiasm often led to simplistic pedagogical practices and prescriptive teaching, which tended to present the Anglo-American writing pattern as superior to others' (Leki 1991 quoted in Petrić 2005, pp. 213–214). However, what is important is that Kaplan put the cultural aspects of writing into focus and inspired further studies on the cultural conditioning of writing, initiating an important area of research, crucial for cross-cultural understanding.

### 4.2.4 Deference to the Anglo-Saxon model

Enforcing the monocultural model of writing in foreign language teaching often leads to uniformity and imitation. In her study of the influence of a short writing course on Russian students' essays, Petrić (2005) demonstrates the emerging uniformity of form and content:

> In about half of the essays (52.6 per cent), these changes can be directly traced to the students' adherence to the sample essay used in the course, ranging from direct imitation of the original to some variation in the syntactical and lexical expression of the TS.
>
> (Petrić, 2005, p. 225)

That is to say, after being introduced to the problem of cultural differences in writing styles, it seems the students decided that imitating the sample texts provided by the teacher would be the only safe and successful option.

In Poland, the most popular writing handbooks among students and often teachers are those that provide the long lists of linking words or 'useful phrases'. Hence, students' essays abound with 'firstly', 'secondly', 'moreover', 'furthermore' or 'however', regardless of whether they fit the context or not. Writing involves mostly ticking off the words provided, underlining the topic sentence, counting the words (procedure unknown before the British books and exams expansion) and paragraphs. Concern for the ideas and reasoning is of lower importance. The meaningless introductory statements, followed by the assigned number of paragraphs, built around a topic sentence (with supporting examples) and a repetitive conclusion do not have much in common with the expression of student's original ideas.

> But just as for the teaching of writing formats in the FL classroom, language issues can give students the false impression that writing well in the FL involves simply learning the appropriate vocabulary and grammar and overlaying it upon English composition formats.
>
> (Reichelt et al. 2012, p. 27)

The analysis of foreign students' troubles with writing analytical papers or dissertations at the University of Michigan led Fox (1994, p. xx) to see how 'factors of culture, education, gender, status, personality and willingness to be "obedient to the system" (...) affect the writing of the multicultural student population'. To counteract the urge to imitate, Kubota and Lehner (2004, p. 46) advocate a critical pedagogy of English:

> Rather than avoiding the teaching of the standard forms of the target language, critical linguistic actions encourage students to learn the standard language critically, to use it to critique its complicity with domination and subordination, and to subvert the normative linguistic code. (...) Pluralisation of target language and cultural codes needs to be achieved through critical scrutiny of how the norm regulates and limits possibilities for marginalised people, and how oppositional voices can create new possibilities.
>
> (Kubota and Lehner 2004, p. 46)

The normativity of English writing models, thoroughly described in language teaching materials and rigorously checked at language examinations, paves the way for the uncritical imitation and adoption of foreign frames by the students. In an education culture that is largely characterized by rote learning, the original expression of ideas is typically restrained; writing in a foreign language blocks it more. The students get so absorbed in following the formal guidelines that less care and attention is given to the successful transmission of ideas (as obviously more difficult). Students' efforts are absorbed by ticking off linking phrases from lists, underlining topic sentences and trying to build ideas around them. The fear of inadequacy brings another temptation: copying from texts written by native speakers. This practice is often considered more of a good learning strategy than a dishonest act of plagiarism.

## 4.3   Problems with English academic writing among students at the University of Szczecin

In response to the constant criticism of the written output of students of English at the University of Szczecin, I decided to research the cultural underpinnings of the problem, asking the students for their perceptions of the issue. The questionnaire, consisting of 15 open-ended questions, was distributed to 101 students in June 2013 (55 from Year 1; 46 from Year 2). The students were informed that one of the important aims of the study was to improve the teaching of writing in the department, so most were motivated enough to give quite extensive answers.

Asked to identify the place (stage of their educational career) where they had received their major writing instruction, the students often emphasized (26 per cent) that they were introduced to the explicit teaching of writing for the first time at university. As they all had to do some writing at school, this was often done without any clear guidelines or preparation, students were just expected to use (imitate?) the texts to which they were exposed (in the spirit of the 'Confucian'-style education model described above). Those who pointed to their secondary school mostly added they had 'very little', 'not much', 'very general' preparation for writing and few writing tasks.

What is interesting is that almost 25 per cent of those students said they learned about writing in their English as a foreign language class, and applied that knowledge to their Polish writing assignments. Private English lessons are a staple element of the Polish education culture and were also mentioned, though not all respondents would openly admit they had private tuition: for some pupils this would classify them as weak and in need of 'special attention', though others might have wanted to boast of the privileged, elite tutoring, which is available only to the well-off. Some of the comments were: *'At my school I hardly had any writing tasks in Polish'*; *'I never studied how to write essays in Polish as thoroughly as in English'*.

Asked about the perceived differences between English and Polish written discourse, only 9 per cent believed there were none. Others emphasized various points, with clearly distinguishable categories such as 'form', 'structure', 'rules' (for example, *'Polish discourses don't have that many rules'*; *'English writing is more concise and obeys strict rules'*; *'English writing is more logical and organized'*). The English style of writing is often perceived by the students as more 'strict', schematic, and thus also limiting for the author (for example, *'The English writing is more strict, rigid, less free for the imagination'*; *'It sounds more formal and it feels like a scheme which you just need to fill with necessary information'*). Only one respondent saw the formal limitations as general elements of academic style, not linked to a particular culture: (*'Polish and English have very similar and strict rules of writing, with which we should comply. In both kinds the register is very important, use of certain phrases. Our creativity and opinions are not required nor wanted'*).

A number of responses referred to the greater importance of clear goals and reader-awareness in English writing (for example, *'English texts pay more attention to the logical development of ideas'*; *'In English, the reader is most important'*; *'English writing is more straightforward and focuses strictly on the topic'*; *'English writing is more focused on the goal, there are less off-topics'*; *'Writing in English is more concise. One has to be clear and do not use "hot water"'*[3] [sic]). For a number of students the logical flow of ideas emphasized in English writing is interpreted as a call for 'simplicity', in sharp contrast to the Polish style with which they are familiar (for example, *'Polish writing is expanded and complex, the English puts emphasis on strict forms and simplicity'*; *'It [English writing] is more straightforward and focuses strictly on the topic'*; *'In Polish writing form is more important than content, what is appreciated is complex nature. In English the clear transmission of information counts, which surprised me'*). The proverbial 'baroque' quality of Polish writing was also emphasized (*'English writing is not as flowery as the Polish text'*; *'In Polish one has to show off, even if what one writes is not understandable'*).

When asked to compare the school writing tasks in English and Polish, the students struck the familiar notes again. Writing in English was described as much more focused on form than content (for example, *'There is emphasis on structure, clearly defined scheme. with all deviations from it regarded as unnecessary, strange'*; *'English writing requires more familiarity with structures, grammar schemes'*; *'You write according to the pattern, watching the linking and coherence'*). The right to 'freedom of expression' was emphasized in comments on English writing (for example, *'I don't have to guess what the author wanted to say but I can interpret it myself'*; [English writing offers] *'a chance to give your opinion'* / *'to rethink some issues, opinions'*).

The students' contrastive comments on the Polish writing most often pointed to the different content, as their Polish writing was typically *'based on books we read'*, *'written about assigned texts'*, *'mainly about analysing pieces of poetry or literature'*, *'so much longer and based on literature'*, *'mostly involve descriptions'*.

Asked to comment on the perceived differences of focus in English and Polish writing, the students confirmed the opinions expressed in their previous answers: the primary importance of form over content, clarity ('simplicity') or the importance of the reader (for example, *'The best writers in English are those who use simple ideas, their thoughts are clear, you focus more on the reader'*; *'In English – mostly grammar, in Polish – content'*; *'English writing focuses on general meaning and the message, as opposed to listing as many details as possible in Polish'*; *'In Polish there is no thesis statement, no topic sentences'*).

Although some students were not ready to discuss the 'models' they used in writing (*'I don't know the models'*), most mentioned British and American (*'There is a choice of British and American'*), with the majority (over 50 per cent) favouring the British option. The pressure to adjust was felt by some and not by others, hence there were no conclusive results (*'No pressure to adhere to any models, mine is British'*; *'My choice is British'*; *'There is pressure to write in British model'*; *'Most teachers use British models'*; *'I am for British model'*).

The most frequently identified areas of difficulty in writing in English for the students were: grammar (42); vocabulary (22); punctuation (15); collocations (9); spelling (6); cohesion (finding synonyms and avoiding repetition) (5). The division into paragraphs was frequently mentioned (in over 25 per cent of the answers); one of the students saw it as an almost existential dilemma (*'To divide the main body into paragraphs or not to'*). The students also found it difficult to *'write a topic sentence'* or *'a good thesis statement'* (19), and some referred to the time restriction (6) and word limit (9). Another problem was register (*'formal'*, *'academic'*, *'proper'*, *'correct'*, *'not too casual'*). The students also expressed their concern for the interference of Polish, listing problems such as *'borrowing forms and phrases from Polish'*, *'writing similarly as in Polish'*, *'writing sentences close to Polish grammar and construction'*, *'directly translating from Polish to English'*, *'thinking in Polish'*, *'using commas the same way I do in Polish'*.

To sum up, then, the results of the questionnaire confirmed most of the observations discussed earlier. Due to the limited exposure to writing instruction in schools, and very limited variety of topics, the students view writing in English as much more codified and rigid. They are conscious of two different models in operation, though no one described them as the expression of a different culture. The clear preference for the 'British' model was of no surprise. Further study of the students' perception of different writing norms is needed, to allow for more definitive conclusions. As the questionnaire used consisted only of open-ended question, the motivation to provide answers might have been lower; a more structured questionnaire, with a set of ready answers, could either support or invalidate some of the results presented. It would also be interesting to find out how an introduction to contrastive rhetoric would alter the students' perceptions.

## 4.4 Conclusion: the ELF model

Writing in English is now a common academic practice for contemporary scholars, as English is the language of international journals. Blackwell and Martin (2011, p. 2) consider this as *'clearly unfair'* (original emphasis) and predict that the situation may change in the future: 'as China's economic power grows, it is quite possible that in a few decades everyone will have to write in Chinese'. However, the unprecedented scale of the spread of English over the last few decades and research into its possible future development (Graddol 1997, 2006) suggest that such change may not be imminent. Consequently, if English is to be used for global communication among equals, it needs to accommodate various cultural norms:

> The question is how the bias of this medium in favor of Anglo-Saxon content can be mitigated.(...) English should be taught in a critical vein, emphasizing that the adoption of English need not at all entail the acceptance of American or British conceptions and practices.
>
> (de Swaan 2004, p. 144)

Non-native English-speaking scholars may be encouraged to find their own voice by an awareness of the English as a Lingua Franca (ELF) debate. Questioning the ownership of English in our global world (Widdowson 1987) may help to build the self-confidence necessary to harness a foreign language to one's own purposes, make it a vehicle for one's original ideas, coloured and enriched by various cultural values and traditions.

Fifteen years after Duszak (1998) expressed her concern at the neglect of discourse analysis in Poland (leading to the field becoming a fully fledged area of linguistic studies, largely thanks to Duszak herself), a similar 'caution' can be made about studies in English as a Lingua Franca. Mainstream linguistic research in Poland marginalizes if not discredits the quickly developing research on ELF, also avoiding the political and ideological discussion about the spread of English within the framework of linguistic imperialism (Phillipson 1992). This may be due to the country's historical past, as it fought for a long time for a place in the international arena alongside the idealized 'western countries', with all their attributes of wealth and power, which largely expressed themselves through English. In his thorough study into the sociolinguistics of English in Poland after 1989, Przygonski (2012, p. 80) emphasizes the 'post-communist fixation on everything that is Western (and especially of English or American origin)', and explains how 'Poles tended to mythologize the prosperity and affluence of the Western world, despite the communist propaganda of the day, and envied their citizens accessibility to a wide variety of products – both everyday and luxurious ones'. The fear of ELF is largely due to suspicion of an attempt to deprive the people of their hard-won privileges, to leave them with 'a broken weapon'; as Prodromou (2008, p. 250) argues, 'a reduced form of ELF does not condemn L2-users to voicelessness, but risks bringing them stuttering onto the world stage of ELF, i.e. with reduced linguistic capital'.

The largely misinterpreted work of the major ELF scholars (Jenkins 2000, 2007, 2009, Mauranen 2012, 2013, Mauranen and Ranta, eds, 2009, Seidlhofer 2011) is often resisted and criticized in Poland as of question-able academic value (Dziubalska 2013, Scheuer 2010, Sobkowiak 2008). Jenkins (2007) comments on the emotional reactions to ELF in Poland and the Polish reverence for native-like performance, arguing that it is 'the local forces rather than imperialism that are "sustaining the local hegemony of English"' (Jenkins 2007, p. 232). Although Jenkins analyses the phonology of English, the attitudes of Poles, 'for whom perfection is to sound like a native speaker' (p. 214) are shown as 'the traditional Polish perspective', in which the dominant perception of non-native qualities is as deficient, wrong and simply undesirable (Jenkins 2007, p. 214).

Research into ELF, though developing fast outside Poland, still needs to fight its way into the academic 'power base' of English studies. The sixth ELF conference in Rome (September 2013) had only one partici-pant from Polish academic centres (the author). However, the slow awak-ening to the new reality of English is becoming a part of the education of many students of English (future teachers), eagerly joining courses on World Englishes or ELF (for example, at the University of Szczecin). Reshaping the attitudes of English language professionals with the ELF approach may help to replace the well- and long-established monocen-tric and monolithic positions toward English

Academic writing for the global world also needs to revise its list of key features that ensure successful communication. At the University of Helsinki, Anna Mauranen initiated the ELFA (English as a Lingua Franca in Academic Settings) corpus project, to research the global use of English among scholars; in 2008, the project completed the compila-tion of a 1,000,000-word corpus of spoken academic ELF. The Written

ELF in Academic Settings (WrELFA) project has made global writing the focus of scholarly activity. The new corpus facilitates studies of the written medium and inquires into the elements constituting a globally 'good text'. At a recent ELF conference in Rome, Mauranen (2013) emphasized:

> Our understanding of what makes 'a good text' is a matter of acquired taste, acquired in the process of socialization into our cultures, a matter of internalized values. A 'good text' in times of global English should be described in terms of intelligibility and effectiveness. This can in no way be interpreted as 'lowering the standards'; ELF is not an 'easier English', with 'less to worry about' but a matter of what works globally.
>
> (Mauranen 2013)

As Mauranen concluded, one of the tasks in ELF research is to discover globally effective rhetoric. This should not be interpreted as 'near-native competence', 'native idiomaticity' or native-like rhetoric.

Do the ideas of ELF scholars find reflection in the world of academic publishing? The editors of the *Journal of English as a Lingua Franca*, make their policy clear in the first issue: 'We see no need to insist on conformity to native-speaker idiomatic usage for its own sake as long as the points being made are accessible and coherent' (Seidlhofer, Jenkins and Mauranen, 2011, p. 2). One can only hope that other editors of worldwide publications will follow suit, and allow non-native writers to express their ideas in a globally shared language that can accommodate a rich variety of cultures, without the risk of being found inadequate by native speaker proof-reader.

In the globalizing world, even McDonald's provides local variations in the menu, while Procter and Gamble adjust the ingredients of a global washing powder to the habits of local users and the same brand names cater for local preferences of style. Glocalized needs are well analysed by market specialists. It is time the authors of English texts stopped worrying about a native speaker's 'pat on the back', and instead concentrated on the message and worked on their own style, cultivating English in service of the global community.

Awareness of ELF offers a liberating change, empowering the students to express their voice in a global language. The focus of writing instruction of an ELF-conscious teacher can move to things that matter most – effectively conveying the message rather than painfully underlining the topic sentence in every successive paragraph.

## Notes

1. *ściąga* in Polish; Polish pupils are invariably surprised by the lack of good English equivalent, suggesting lack of the equivalent practice in British or American schools.
2. The most recent test results from the OECD's Programme for International Student Assessment (Pisa) show that Poland is ranked 14th for reading, ahead of the US, Sweden, France and Germany – and well ahead of the UK, at 25th (Hicks 2012), while in science and maths, Polish students are now well ahead of Americans according to some international assessments (Ripley 2013). In contrast, Polish universities constantly occupy very low places in any international ranking of universities; in the Shanghai Ranking (2013) only the Jagiellonian University and University of Warsaw get into the first 500 (ranked 301 and 400), while Webometrics World Rank gives the University of Warsaw 271st place and Jagiellonian University 311th position. (Webometrics 2013)
3. This is a curious combination of different idiomatic expressions: 'hot air' is described in Polish as 'pouring water'.

# Part II
# Communities in Conflict

# 5
# Centre–Periphery Relations in the Spanish Context: Temporal and Cross-Disciplinary Variation

*Sally Burgess*

## 5.1 Introduction

The unequal relations between countries which we experience as the centre–periphery divide have been a major preoccupation for an increasing number of scholars of academic publication, among them Bennett (2011c), Canagarajah (1996, 2002), Duszak (2006), Englander (2011), Lillis and Curry (2010, 2013), Salager-Meyer (2008, 2013), and Uzuner (2008), who provides a review of the literature. Green (1994) sees notions of centre and periphery as constructed discursively and, therefore, as Terra-Figari (2009, p. 9) suggests, as variable not only across temporal and geopolitical boundaries but also in terms of how they are perceived by scholars in the disciplines. For those working in what Becher (1989) characterized as 'urban disciplines' (for example, molecular biology), the perception of the centre as being located in North America, Northern Europe and the UK is likely to be particularly vivid. Even hard science scholars working in economically privileged situations in Kachru's (1985) inner-circle, experience their professional lives as being constrained and influenced by centre–periphery relations, locating themselves on the periphery, and their British, North American and Northern European counterparts at the centre. Connell and Wood (2002), for example, have recorded Australian scientists' descriptions of professional life, noting that they experience it as conditioned by centre–periphery relations. They further observe that the scientists themselves are implicated in the reproduction of centre–periphery discourses and that their efforts to maintain connections with centre science actually contribute to feelings of isolation and frustration. Many of those whose contact and communication with scholars working in the centre is mediated through a language other than their first language experience that isolation and frustration in a more extreme form. For some, however, particularly those in the social sciences and humanities, the feeling is not so much one of isolation and frustration but of resentment. The acceptance on the part of research evaluation agencies of core ideologies and research publication practices is changing the ways in which work is done in their disciplines. These changes are not always welcome.

Just as core–periphery relations are perceived and constructed by subjects, so too are disciplinary communities, communities that, as already noted, were characterized by Becher (1989) as 'urban' and 'rural'. Fry (2004) provides a synthesis of Becher's seminal work. Research workers in urban disciplinary communities such as physics typically adopt, authorize and reward rapid and frequent publication by means of research articles and letters produced by tight-knit, highly competitive teams focusing on discovery and explanation. The organs of publication are journals owned and produced by large international publishing houses with headquarters in core nations. Knowledge production in these disciplines is fully globalized and the lingua franca of research publication is English. Productivity is equated with impact, which is measured by the number of citations publications accrue. Rural disciplines such as history, on the other hand, tend to be individualistic and loosely structured, with a holistic approach to research, the focus of which is complication. In rural disciplines, writing for publication is a slower process and, consequently, a smaller volume of work is produced – if indeed volume is measured by the quantity of individual publications rather than their length or complexity. The prototypical research genres are books, monographs and book chapters and these are often published by smaller locally based publishing houses including university publishing services. In these 'niche disciplines' (Ammon 2008a) authors may continue to write and publish in languages other than English. In many rural disciplinary communities, even a relatively small number of publications regarded as being of intellectual, literary or aesthetic merit would once have been sufficient to guarantee a successful academic career. If, largely because the publications themselves are less accessible (Bishop 2012), the work produced by these scholars failed to garner as many citations as the typical research article in the urban disciplines, this mattered less than recognition of the work as the product of scholarship and erudition.

In Spain, the focus of this chapter, the globalization of knowledge production has meant that increasing pressures are being brought to bear on researchers to embrace fully the research publishing practices of the urban disciplines and the core nations. This has meant that some of the publishing practices and values of local Spanish disciplinary communities are under threat. In the first part of the chapter, I discuss Spain's status as a semiperipheral nation, and examine how Spanish researchers and Spanish research publications have been affected by changes to research evaluation policies and procedures. I then compare the responses to the research evaluation criteria of specific disciplinary communities in Spain. Finally, I focus on pockets of resistance that still exist in some branches of the humanities and social sciences.

## 5.2 Spain: a semiperipheral country par excellence

The relations between groups cannot, of course, be reduced to a simple centre–periphery dichotomy. The complex network of structural, geopolitical, cultural and linguistic factors that position a group is such that some countries are best characterized as semiperipheral. Spain is a case in point. Once the eighth largest of the world's economies in terms of GDP, Spain was formerly categorized by some commentators as a core nation (see, for example, Kentor 2008). Magone (2009), on the other hand, argues that structural weaknesses in the Spanish economic system mean that it was never either truly core, in terms of the global economy, or, strictly speaking, peripheral. Wherever Spain once stood in relation to the core, few would doubt that it currently finds itself on the economic semiperiphery. This semiperipheral situation has particular impacts on research, research writing and research publication. Research and education spending are among the many casualties of the austerity measures put in place by the Popular Party government in response to the crisis and the demands of core nations such as Germany. Cutbacks in these areas now push research carried out in Spain across a range of disciplines into the same semiperipheral position as the Spanish economy. Unlike centre contexts such as the UK, there has never been more than limited private research funding (Archontakis 2008) available to Spanish researchers, even in fields that, in core contexts, would readily attract investment from private enterprise. Public research spending, while never generous, is now all but drying up. Even the elite research-only institution, the Spanish Council for Scientific Research (CSIC), faces funding cutbacks that pose a threat to many of its departments and staff members. This has led to a much-reported 'brain drain' (see, for example, Cuenca 2013), with younger research scientists being lured to the US, the UK or other Northern European countries, in search of employment security and a brighter professional future. The proliferation of associations of Spanish scientists living outside Spain testifies to this phenomenon.

The universities have seen ceilings put on staffing, which have led to increased teaching loads in departments with large student numbers, and a growing lack of professional stability for those who work on undersubscribed degree courses. Retiring academic staff members are often not replaced, which means that those remaining are obliged to take on more and more teaching and administrative work. In departments that offer courses taught to students across a range of degrees (for example, mathematics, physics, English and Spanish language), staff now find themselves teaching on two or more degree courses and dealing with large cohorts of students. Reduced teaching commitments, job security and, in some but not all cases, salary increments are available only to those who can demonstrate research activity to the satisfaction of the Spanish National Commission for the Evaluation of Research Activity (CNEAI). This effectively creates a vicious circle in which those university staff members who have not succeeded in demonstrating that they are active and productive researchers are penalized with heavy teaching loads or left vulnerable to the threat of department closures and redundancies. It goes without saying that neither circumstance is likely to foster increased research activity and output. Humanities and social sciences departments are particularly hard hit.

## 5.3   The consequences of research evaluation policy

An added burden is the greater emphasis now placed by the CNEAI on publication in ISI journals and proof of impact of one's work in terms of citations. This burden falls far more heavily on scholars in the humanities and social sciences than it does on their counterparts in the hard sciences, where a greater number of citations per paper is the norm. Price (1970), cited in Macdonald (1994, p. 25), makes a distinction between disciplines that echoes Becher's (1989) urban–rural dichotomy reviewed above. He suggests that, whereas some disciplines grow from the 'skin', with frequent citation of recent work, others grow from the 'body', requiring considerable time for scholars to accommodate contributions to their field. Where less time is needed to absorb new knowledge, there will be more citations of recent research. Sixty to seventy per cent of references in physics and biochemistry journal articles in Price's survey were to recent publications, while in the social sciences the figure was 40 per cent and in the humanities less than 10 per cent. In a much more recent survey, Harzing (2010) found that the average article in the social sciences and humanities is cited less than once a year. One's chances of being cited at all are thus far greater in the hard sciences than they are in softer disciplines. Add to this the phenomenon Whitehand (2005) refers to as 'Anglophone squint', namely the tendency of humanities and social sciences scholars from the core to cite other centre scholars more frequently than they do those in the periphery or semiperiphery, and the situation of the Spanish humanities or social sciences scholar with regard to the evaluation of research productivity is particularly delicate.

There are also consequences of the evaluation criteria for the research publications themselves. One such is the gradual ceding of ground to the journal article by the book chapter, the book and the monograph. A recent survey (Giménez-Toledo 2012) of the output of humanities and social sciences scholars at the CSIC indicates that although 26 per cent of their publications were in book chapters, by 2010 as many 21 per cent were to be found in journals. Books now make up only 6 per cent with the remaining 47 per cent taken up by conference proceedings. Both Giménez-Toledo (2012) and Las Heras-Navarro (2013) exhort scholars in the humanities and social sciences not to abandon the book and book chapter as publication modes. In a bid to put a brake on the shift to journal article publication, Giménez-Toledo et al. (2013) have also arrived at a ranking of both Spanish and international academic book publishers in the humanities and social sciences to parallel the ranking of journals in terms of impact factor. The publisher ranking is intended in part to offer proof of status in response to the CNEAI policy of giving little or no credit to book chapter publications unless their authors can demonstrate that the volume is published by a prestigious publishing house and has a high-status editor, and that their contribution has been peer reviewed (*Boletín Oficial del Estado*, 21 November 2013).

Locally published Spanish-medium journals may also begin to suffer. In the social sciences, although the number of Spanish-language journals included in ISSN data base was 75 per cent higher in 2011 than it was in 2001, these journals still only made up 4.4 per cent of the total; there are only four Spanish social sciences journals in the second quarter and none in the first (Ramos-Torre and Callejo-Gallego 2013). Thus, although Spanish is second only to English as the most frequently used language of research publication, what Ramos-Torre and Callejo-Gallego (2013) term 'the Anglo-Americanization' of research impact indices drastically reduces, they argue, the importance of Spanish publications, particularly those that use Spanish exclusively as the research publication language. It is these journals that are likely to see a decline in numbers as researchers themselves begin to absorb and respond to the new demands of the CNEAI. The editor of one of the higher status 'small journals' in the field of English and North American studies observes that this decline is already taking place in his field (M. Brito, personal communication, 6 February, 2014). One strategy is to switch to English or to a multilingual policy. The higher-status multilingual or English-language journals published in Spain look set to survive. Bocanegra-Valle (2014) notes that in her survey of contributors to *Ibérica*, the journal of the pan-European languages for specific purposes group AELFE (Asociación Europea de Lenguas para Fines Espécifica), the vast majority supported the continuation of the journal's multilingual publications policy. Through adoption of such a policy, *Ibérica* has been able to attract high status international contributors, and after an exhaustive review of its editorial and peer review procedures, it now has an impact factor, thus ensuring a continued supply of good-quality submissions from scholars both within and beyond the geographical boundaries of the Iberian Peninsula. That said, the 'peripheral' journals (Canagarajah 2002) that hold out against the push to switch to English-only or English and other languages provide an important vehicle for scholars to publish their work, particularly where the logical audience is a local community of practitioners or fellow researchers concerned with similar issues, as Salager-Meyer (2014) points out in a recent paper. As has been observed (Rey-Rocha and Martin-Sempere 1999), if researchers begin to turn away from the local journals in favour of international publications, or if the local journals adopt a multilingual or English-only policy that ultimately attracts more and more international contributions, there may be implications for research agendas, with researchers turning away from topics of local concern to address issues that are likely to appeal to an international/centre rather than a local/semiperipheral readership. In their survey, Rey-Rocha and Martin-Sempere (1999) found that domestic publication dropped by between 5 and 21 per cent in the period covered and only increased in the case of researchers working at privately funded research institutes. Furthermore, they found that the institutions in which scholars were already subject to research productivity evaluation were those in which the greatest shift away from domestic publication had occurred. They also note that the more scholars in a particular discipline turn away from the local journals in favour of the international index-covered journals, the smaller the sample of submissions the local journal editors have to choose from for inclusion in their journals. If the quality of the journal cannot be maintained because of the limited options available to editors, this in turn makes it less and less attractive as a vehicle for publication of results and encourages researchers to tailor their studies to the needs and expectations of the metropolis in order to get the merit-bearing publications they need for tenure and professional promotion.

It has also been noted (Burgess 1997, 2002) that addressing a smaller, local audience requires different rhetorical practices to those used when addressing a large, anonymous, international audience – an audience which is often perceived as residing at the centre, since the journals themselves are owned by centre corporations. In a corpus-based study, Burgess (1997, 2002) found variations in rhetorical structure of research-article introductions in linguistics that she argued reflected writers' responses to the size and perceived knowledge base of the audience, as well as the writers' actual and imagined social and academic relations with potential members of that audience. Drawing on the work of Scollon (1993), Burgess maintained that where writers believed themselves to be in a stable relationship with their notional audience, the topic of the paper could be introduced early in the introduction, often in an initial sentence stating the purpose of the study. This was the preferred practice of established members of this community writing in Spanish and addressing the relatively stable, identifiable local readership of Spanish linguistics journals. Burgess (1997, 2002) argues that this relatively small community shares a clearly established research agenda. In contrast, Spanish English language and linguistics scholars, whose papers made up two further sub-corpora in Burgess's (1997, 2002) study, typically published their work in general English Studies journals addressing a wide range of topics and concerns in linguistics, both applied and theoretical, philology, literary theory, literary criticism and cultural studies. Although their readership was in all likelihood made up of people these writers actually knew or would come to know through conference participation, thesis defences, competitive tenure examinations and so on, it was also possible that a reader might have little or no knowledge of the specific topic the writer addressed. This put writers in a position where they chose first to attend to stabilizing the epistemological relationship with the audience by means of lengthy introductory sections made up of topic generalizations (Swales 1990) or exhaustive reviews of the literature. The research niche creation move identified by Swales (1990) where researchers identify omissions or gaps in the literature, was often dispensed with because, as Burgess (1997, 2002) noted, there is little point in rhetorically carving out a niche for one's work when the reader is wholly unfamiliar with the territory and unlikely to challenge any claims made to it.

The shift from local 'small journals' to the international 'big journals' involves researchers not only in a change of language of research publication but in adjusting their socio-pragmatic and rhetorical practices to make them acceptable to this larger audience. Spanish scholars in the humanities and social sciences accustomed to publishing in small local journals acquire and employ a repertoire of rhetorical strategies not all of which are applicable or appropriate when they come to write for an international audience. Instead, they are faced with developing the ability to address simultaneously the three concentric circles of audience that Myers (1989) posits for the research article, a task which typically involves a delicate balance between recognition of the value of previous research and strategically hedged criticism. As several authors (for example, Burgess and Fagan 2002, Moreno and Suárez 2008) observe, this is something Spanish authors can find challenging.

## 5.4   Sites of acceptance and resistance

While the changes in research evaluation policies and procedures are a source of great concern for some, this is not the case of all research workers in Spain. Research chemists, for example, appear to offer little resistance (Mur-Dueñas et al. 2012), doing whatever is necessary to get their work into high-ranking international journals with impact factors without, apparently, questioning the injustices of the ranking system. For the Spanish researchers in the hard and medical sciences responding to a recent online questionnaire-based survey (Moreno et al. 2013), preparing an article for publication typically involved writing in English with or without the support of authors' editors, preferably those with specific expertise in their field (Burgess et al. 2013, Lorés-Sanz et al. 2012). Others have also found that support from English-speaking co-authors (see Fernández-Quijada et al. 2013) is sought especially in disciplines where members of international teams typically write up their research collaboratively.

Analysis of data from the survey mentioned above (Burgess et al. 2014) showed that where the quality of the writing itself was as important as the content, and where scholars did not have sufficient command of English, translation was the preferred publication strategy. In some cases, these scholars noted that acquiring competence in English for academic purposes involved a large time and financial commitment, sapping resources that might well have been used for research activity. If language professionals such as translators and authors' editors are employed, the publication process is not only a lengthy but also a very costly one, all the more so when the costs are likely to be borne by the scholars themselves given cuts in research funding. Lack of funds available for translation is one of the reasons some Spanish scholars ultimately choose not to publish in English (Burgess et al. 2014). It also accounts for the use by Spanish scholars of unpaid editors such as family members and friends rather than appropriately trained translators and editors with discipline-specific expertise. Lillis and Curry (2010) have reported on this practice, one which Burgess and Fagan (2006) also found to be quite common in the Spanish population they surveyed, even before the period in which the recession began to bite.

While some researchers accept the demand for publication in centre journals as a *fait accompli,* others find it a hurdle – one that is occasionally insurmountable. A third group adopt a position in which they challenge the very premise on which the dominance of Anglo-American research publication rests, namely that it is of superior scientific merit.

It is with this group that I will concern myself in what remains of this chapter. As has already been noted, it is scholars in the humanities and social sciences who have been confronted with the most far-reaching demands for changes to their publication practices and which, in some cases (for example, Hispanic studies), have a strong claim to centre status and thus perceive themselves as contesting these policies from a position of power. These scholars raise questions about the justice and good sense of applying research evaluation criteria initially developed for the experimental sciences to the very different practices of humanities researchers.

## 5.5   Humanities research in the Spanish context

Celebrated annually since 2011, the *Conferencia sobre calidad de revistas de ciencias sociales y humanidades* (CRECS) has drawn attention to the history of the commercialization of scholarly publishing and the power of big business in controlling access to research and, more recently, the nature of research genres themselves. Cronin (2013), a keynote speaker at their most recent meeting, looks at the new formats and platforms for digital research articles developed by Elsevier and Wiley-Blackwell. It seems likely that scholars in the urban disciplines, already accustomed to the quick-fire genres and rapid turn-around in hard science publishing, will find these new publishing modes far more palatable than their colleagues in the humanities who tend to hold out against innovations of this kind.

Spanish historians are a case in point. In the survey the findings of which were reviewed above, these scholars were found to contest the status of English as a language of research publication and see the implicit privileging of journal articles as a by-product of the application of the publishing practices of the metropolis, already so dominant in the sciences, to disciplines with very different epistemologies (Burgess et al. 2014). Like the researchers asked to rank academic publishers in the survey conducted by Giménez-Toledo et al. (2013), the historians regard Spanish publications as superior (Burgess et al. 2014). Their resentment of the policies adopted by the national evaluation agency is as much a defence of a different notion of where the centre might be said to lie as it is a determination not to succumb to the 'butler syndrome' described by Bennett (forthcoming). These scholars publish far more in Spanish than they do in English and are comfortable with the fact (Burgess et al. 2014).

Aside from the desire to address and cater for the needs of a local audience, the status of Spanish as an international language would also account for this reluctance to abandon it as a medium of research publication. Across a range of measures such as the number of speakers, the number of territories in which it is spoken, the number of people studying it as foreign language and the number of UN committees using it as a working language, Spanish is in second or third position after Chinese and English (Otero 1995). The historians in Burgess et al. (2014) seemed to resent greatly the implication that, despite its strength as a world language, Spanish is only a world language in the semiperiphery and periphery. While it is hard to imagine that it will overtake English in the near future as the major language of research publication, there is definitely a rear guard action to promote and celebrate its use beyond the borders of Spanish-speaking countries. There is also evidence that these efforts are bearing fruit. Spanish research output in the humanities and social sciences increased in the period 2001 to 2011, though the number of publications in English did not (van Weijen 2012). Where Spanish is the object of study, or documentation in Spanish is the primary source material, Spanish is anything but peripheral as a language of research publication for Spain-based scholars.

The status of a language of research publication is not only a product of the peripheral, semiperipheral or core status of the places in the world in which that language is spoken. English is of course a particular case in point, since it is used as a first language, an official and second language and a foreign language in the centre and on the periphery and semiperiphery but retains its position as 'a global science creole' (Ribeiro and Escobar 2008, p. 3). Languages other than English may acquire core status as media of academic communication because the countries where the languages are used have become core countries in a particular discipline. Ribeiro and Escobar (2008, p. 13) quote Kuwayama's (2004) observation that anthropologists in Britain, the US and France, despite differences in approach, form a united front and act as a core unit with 'collective power such that other countries, including those in the rest of Europe are relegated to the periphery'. French in anthropology would therefore have prestige alongside English as a language of academic publication. Similarly, historians who follow the *Annales* School will favour French as a language of research publication, while those working in renaissance history of art are likely to look to Italian. In the survey we have referred to above (Burgess et al. 2014), Spanish historians were found to publish in a far wider range of languages other than English than their colleagues in other disciplines, among them Modern Greek and Hungarian. Faced with the task of improving their skills in these languages, some of the Spanish historians in the survey were reluctant to sacrifice time and effort to acquiring a command of English, particularly in such areas where the English-speaking countries were not seen as core locations for work in their sub-disciplines. Similarly, some Spanish historians in the same survey (Burgess et al. 2014) see time, effort and economic resources devoted to the study of English for research publication purposes as depriving the study of Latin of the attention it merits, a trend with epistemological consequences for their discipline. One historian commented that if fewer and fewer historians are able to study primary source materials in Latin, the study of periods of Spanish history earlier than the 18th century may become unsustainable.

One cannot help but wonder how long historians and other humanities scholars will be able to maintain this resistance to the norms of the research evaluation agencies. There are some indications that historians are already beginning to look at publication in English more positively. In the survey on which we have drawn heavily here (Burgess et al. 2014), many of the historians expressed just as much enthusiasm for the possibility of taking part in training courses in English for research publication purposes as their colleagues in other fields. Of course, what may be reflected in the results reported in Burgess et al. (2014) are the opinions and views of two distinct groups of scholars: on the one hand the disaffected *Annalistes* or pre-history scholars who have determined to hold out against the onslaught of core/urban/hard science norms and practices and on the other hand the less conservative post-structuralist and feminist historians who embrace these new trends, if not with enthusiasm, the at least with curiosity and a willingness to forge connections with scholars in the core. In an earlier study of the publishing practices of scholars at the University of La Laguna conducted between 2003 and 2005 (see Burgess and Fagan 2006) the forging of connections emerged as an important step in the research trajectory of scholars participating in unstructured interviews. These Spanish researchers often attributed their first experience of publishing success to skilful mentoring they received from scholars with whom they had often maintained contact for several years after returning home from periods spent abroad. It has, of course, become more difficult to fund attachments or study visits to foreign universities, but it is likely that digitally mediated mentoring will take on a similar level of importance for the next generation of scholars, perhaps eliminating or ameliorating the sense of isolation Connell and Wood (2002) found to be so prevalent among the Australian scientists in their study.

## 5.6   Conclusion

In conclusion, research publication in the humanities and social sciences in Spain has reached a watershed, where tensions between semi-peripheral practices and the imposed demands of core science place the Spanish humanities or social sciences scholar in what is sometimes an unenviable position. Pressures are being exerted on the research evaluation agencies to adjust their criteria for assessing research productivity to the current realities of publication in these disciplines, and there is some evidence that this message is getting through. Nevertheless, the agencies are unlikely to waver on the issue of quality and peer-evaluation of research. The scholars, for their part, have a good chance of defending their right to publish in their first language and in other languages that they deem appropriate vehicles for their work as long as they are able to establish the quality credentials of their publications, especially through the recognition of their peers. It would seem that one way in which they might successfully achieve this is through adopting newer modes of digital open-access publication.

# 6
# Portuguese Academics' Attitudes to English as the Academic Lingua Franca: A Case-Study

*Rita Queiroz de Barros*

## 6.1 Introduction

Set in the southwestern and less affluent extreme of the European continent, and facing the consequences of a serious economic crisis since 2011, Portugal is no doubt part of the semiperiphery of the world systems. Following Sousa Santos's understanding of this nation in such terms on mainly geopolitical and economic grounds (1985), Nunes and Gonçalves (2001) and Bennett (2011c) have convincingly shown that this is also the case with regards to scientific/academic production.

This surfaces both in Portugal's marginal share of the internationally acknowledged academic production and in its role as a transmitter of centre-produced knowledge to more off-centred communities (such as the African Lusophone countries like Angola and Cape Verde, and also Brazil, which, despite a long history as an independent nation with a celebrated culture and flourishing economy, still prefers Portuguese over English in academic contexts). Portugal's semiperipheral status is furthermore shown by the fast but still ongoing establishment of a meritocratic culture in research and higher education institutions: although internationalization has been a major concern of Portuguese research policy for the last couple of decades, to the extent that funding is by now entirely dependent on the quality and outreach of publications, the so-called publish-or-perish dictum is still somewhat milder there than in other western countries.

As a consequence of the sustained strategy of internationalization mentioned above, and since the selection of English has proved to be a decisive step in the conquest of global visibility, Portuguese research communities are not only being encouraged to use English for academic purposes more often, but also are actively choosing to do so. English is thus a working language for at least some Portuguese researchers these days, and it is gaining ground as a teaching medium.

As has happened in other traditionally non-Anglophone European settings (see Ammon ed. 2001, Ammon and McConnell 2002, Coleman 2006, Duszak and Lewkowicz 2008, Ljosland 2007, Polo and Varela 2009), the growing use of English for academic purposes in Portugal has already attracted the attention of researchers. In fact, Portugal has been mentioned not only in large-scale investigations of European reach (such as Lillis and Curry 2006, Lillis and Curry 2010, Mollin 2006), but also in particular studies by Bennett (2010a, 2010b, 2011a, 2012b). Against the background of a 'broader project' meant to examine 'Portuguese academic writing practices from the perspective of Translation Studies' (Bennett 2010a, p. 194), this author surveyed the attitudes of Portuguese researchers towards the hegemony of English within their professional activity and also 'their habits as regards the production of academic texts in English' (p. 195). The respondents in her sample were collected from lists of members of Portuguese research centres or from client lists from translation services that had appeared in some Portuguese universities at the time of her research, and included researchers from various disciplines, especially the Humanities and Economics.

Despite this interest in the use of and opinions about English as the academic lingua franca in Portugal, no systematic analysis has so far been conducted into the attitudes to English among the staff of a higher education institution in Portugal. The case study described in this chapter is a first attempt to fill this gap and intends to attune further the received understanding of an inexorable spread of English in academic circles. In particular, it aims to assess and discuss the attitudes of the staff of the Faculty of Letters of the University of Lisbon towards English as the language of academia in Portugal, for both teaching and publication.

## 6.2   Attitudes: concept and relevance

The concept of attitude, which was imported from social psychology, is variously defined in the literature. Yet many authors share the conviction that it combines three components (Dittmar 1976, Gardner 1985, Garrett 2010, Lambert et al. 1960): cognition, since attitudes depend on belief structures; affect, because they 'involve feelings about the attitude object', thereby developing 'favourability or unfavourability' towards it (Garrett 2010, p. 23); and finally behaviour, as attitudes predispose subjects to act in certain ways.

Despite its triadic conception, this description basically divides the concept of attitude into two types of constituents: the triggers of a certain behaviour, dependent on both cognition and affect; and the action resulting from it. These are thus the two issues that will be borne in mind in the present study, the purpose of which is, first, to determine Portuguese academics' linguistic behaviour (that is, the extent to which they effectively use English) and, second, to investigate the motives prompting them to choose either English or Portuguese in their work.

Though such approaches have been central to sociolinguistics ever since Labov's groundbreaking work on Martha's Vineyard (1963), and crucial in historical linguistics because 'prestige and stigma afforded by speech communities to specific language features' (Garrett 2010, p. 19) very often motivate language change, their true significance for the study of academic English lies elsewhere: attitude is an important factor in 'language restoration, preservation, decay and death' (Baker 1992, p. 9). And English is, curiously enough, a living testimony of this fact. Its survival after the Norman conquest in medieval times and its later restoration and growth as a prestigious language in England resulted from the unfavourable attitudes towards the competing languages used in that speech community, namely French and Latin. Of course the sociolinguistic situation of late medieval England is too different from that of early 21st century Portugal to allow for direct comparisons. But this lesson from history proves that attitudes do matter in the course of languages and makes us wonder about the alleged inescapable growth of English as the language of the academia.

Furthermore, the growing use of English in academic discourse has already been shown to be rather controversial. Attitudes to English as the language of academic discourse reported in the literature range from more or less enthusiastic acceptance to emotive disapproval. Acceptance is a conclusion that may be drawn from the 'dramatically increasing numbers of academics whose first language is not English but who publish in English' (Hyland 2006, quoted in Römer 2009, p. 89). Strong reluctance, however, has been manifested in Germany (Mocikat et al. 2005), France (Lévy-Leblond and Oustinoff 2007) and Israel (Hovel 2012).

Elsewhere, responses tend to be more ambivalent. For example, in Spain local languages rather than English have been proven to be favoured, at least in the University of Santiago de Compostela (Polo and Varela 2009, p. 1); Duszak and Lewkowicz (2008) report hesitation among Polish academics with regard to their choice of language for publication; and the Portuguese researchers questioned in Bennett's study identified both advantages and disadvantages in the use of English

(2010a, p. 197). This is certainly the reason why the European Science Foundation has already explicitly addressed the issue of the dominance of English in a Forum for Early Career Researchers in 2011 (Maynooth, 9–11 June) on the subject of 'Changing Publication Cultures in the Humanities' (conclusions can be accessed in http://www.esf.org).

This controversy is certainly not eccentric. In fact, even if one is willing to accept that an academic lingua franca is desirable, and that languages of communication are to be distinguished from languages of identity, as asserted by House (2003), it cannot be ignored that the addition of a foreign working language to the academics' repertoire entails the loss of prestigious functional domains by local standard languages. As Joseph insists (1987, pp. 79–80), 'science and technology are key standard language domains' and 'the use of a (...) standard as a vehicle of instruction (and not just as a subject of instruction) in its nation's universities has undeniable symbolic value'. And in fact not only does my personal experience reveal that many students resent not having (more) references in Portuguese in their recommended reading, which they know jeopardizes their ability to use their own language in academic contexts, but various authors have also unambiguously stated the dangers that this procedure entails. For example, Coleman (2006, p. 10) claims that 'the Englishization of European Higher Education represents an extension of the global threat to minority languages', while Ljosland (2007, p. 408) concludes that 'the situation in [Norwegian] academia shows signs of heading towards diglossia', adding that 'a diglossic state in academia may ... be a first step towards developing diglossia in other areas of society in the future'.

Against this background, there are naturally no foregone conclusions as far as Portuguese academics' attitudes are concerned. English is certainly gaining ground, since the internationalization target of Portuguese research policy has meant the imposition of English in certain contexts. But there is both acceptance of and resistance to this linguistic practice. This last reaction is perhaps to be expected in a speech community whose language ranks eighth in the world as regard the number of native speakers (250 million, expected to reach c. 300 million in five or ten years) and is explicitly protected by a national Constitution.[1] Indeed, this negative reaction found explicit expression in a manifesto published in 2011 by three Portuguese-speaking and three Spanish-speaking scientists (Pais Ribeiro et al. 2011), in which the authors attribute the pressure of publishing in English to the interests of the publishing industry and maintain that researchers should publish at least 30 per cent of their texts in their native language.

## 6.3 Methodology

### 6.3.1 Sampling Portuguese academics: the Faculty of Letters of the University of Lisbon

Though not statistically representative of the Portuguese academics working in their homeland, the Faculty of Letters of the University of Lisbon (henceforward FLUL) is certainly worth investigating.

Founded in 1912, FLUL has 259 lecturers and/or researchers working within its various departments in different areas of the humanities (History and Archaeology, Philosophy, Romance Studies, English and German Studies, Classics, and Linguistics) and a similar number of collaborators in its research centres. No language policy has been assumed so far, and the acceptance of English as the academic lingua franca is uncertain. Academics working within the humanities are generally known to be more reluctant to use English than their colleagues in the hard sciences (Ammon 2008b, Duszjak and Lewkowicz 2008, p. 113, Ljosland 2007, p. 396), a tendency which may be exacerbated in Portugal since the rhetorical characteristics of the local academic discourse are substantially different from those of English and are particularly cherished within these areas (Bennett 2010a). On the other hand, however, FLUL has achieved a considerable degree of internationalization in research, and most of its lecturers are used to dealing with international students coming to Lisbon via multiple exchange programmes (275 in 2012/2013).

### 6.3.2 Data collection and treatment

Data for this study was collected by two means. The first involved a self-administered questionnaire, written in Portuguese and sent by email in July 2012 to all researchers affiliated to three research centres in FLUL, who were asked to enter their answers in the same document and send it back by September of that same year. The definite version of the questionnaire was completed after a pilot study presented in Barros (2009). It contained 28 questions, 23 of which were closed or had preset answers or scales.

These questions were ordered according to the general principles recommended in the literature (Bradburn et al. 2004), according to which fact-based questions should be presented in the first place and opinion-based questions left to the end. The questions were thus divided into three sections, covering: (i) basic academic and demographic variables (area of research, highest academic degree, age, native language, self-assessed competence in English); (ii) language choice in research, teaching and bibliographic resources (both used and recommended); and (iii) opinions on the use of English as academic language and higher education teaching medium in Portugal.

The choice of a self-administered questionnaire resulted from its adequacy as an information-eliciting tool within the study but also from well-known advantages of this methodology: its capacity to reach a numerous sample in a very short time, low cost, avoidance of interviewer bias, and higher response rate (Bradburn et al. 2004, p. 103). Though the first three expectations were met, the fourth and most important one was not: the questionnaire was sent to 425 lecturers or researchers and only 40 of them answered it; as 5 of these were not native speakers of Portuguese but foreigners working in Portugal, only 35 could be considered, that is, 9 per cent of the sample contacted. Though the response rate to this type of procedure is usually not very high (around 25 per cent, according to Polo and Varela, 2009, p. 155), this was a disturbingly low number, revealing either a lack of interest in the issue or the tremendous workload academics are facing these days.

The distribution of responses across research areas is uneven: 22 were sent by academics working within English Studies, 2 in German Studies, 7 in Romance (Portuguese, French and Spanish) Studies, 1 in Linguistics, 1 in Theology, 1 in Psychology and 1 in Museology (the last three are working within different projects on Portuguese literature and culture, hence their presence in the sample). Despite including various areas, there is in this sample an obvious overrepresentation of English studies researchers, which has to be borne in mind in the analysis of the answers. Such imbalance is not to be observed in the age groups of the informants (28 per cent are 35 or under, 42 per cent between 36 and 50, and 30 per cent 51 or over), which is a fair representation of FLUL's faculty, since the economic situation of the country is preventing the renewal of the staff and driving young researchers abroad.

Given the limitations of the data collected by the questionnaire, another source of information was used. This was a database compiled by the library of FLUL at the request of the Faculty's board, including all publications of its staff from 2000 to 2009, which was kindly put at my disposal.[2] Though it presents evidence only of the action component of attitudes, and allows conclusions to be drawn only with regard to the choice of language for research, this database has proved a very rich source of information. After the exclusion of translated works, editions of canonical and other texts, dictionaries and entries by foreign researchers, it comprises 5,160 entries (one per published item) by 342 lecturers or researchers, covering a period of almost a decade. So, although this was collected from a much larger sample than the questionnaire, thereby deviating from the ideal methodology, this was the source of information I used to study textual production in FLUL.

The publications database covers all areas investigated in FLUL's research centres: History and Archeology (1533), Philosophy (252), Romance Studies (1461), English Studies (497), German Studies (176), Classics (470) and Linguistics (743), which are the traditional areas pursued at FLUL, and also the more recent area of Media Studies (29). The proportion of their contributions is presented in Figure 6.1.

The proportion assumed by these research areas once again offers a fair reflection of the constitution of the Faculty's staff. Since the data collected from the questionnaire did not allow for any statistical treatment, the information from both the questionnaire and the database was submitted to basic quantitative treatment centred on raw and relative frequencies and meant to identify tendencies. The results will be presented in the order initially planned, beginning with factual information concerning the language(s) of publishing, teaching and bibliographic resources (both used and recommended), before moving on to opinions on the use of English as an academic language in Portugal.

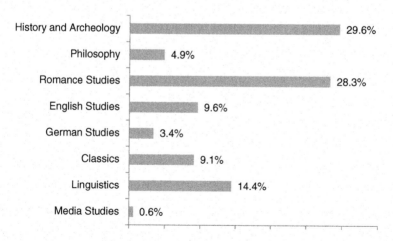

*Figure 6.1* Publications in the database of Faculty of Letters, University of Lisbon, by area (%) (2000–2009)

## 6.4   Results

### 6.4.1   Language(s) used in publications

The analysis of the academics' choice of language for publishing purposes relies on the database mentioned in the previous section. The first observation worth mentioning about of the 5,160 entries is that a total of 10 different languages were used in publishing from 2000 to 2009: Portuguese, English, French, Spanish, German, Italian, Romanian, Galician, Polish and Catalan (9 out of the total of 5,160 items were published in bilingual editions – 8 in Portuguese and English, and 1 in Portuguese and Spanish; they were ignored in the remaining analysis). Despite such dispersal, the frequency of use of the various languages is substantially different, as shown by Table 6.1.

This table confirms that, despite the presence of eight other main and minor European languages, only Portuguese and English have a noticeable presence in publishing, while all others, including French and Spanish, have a negligible share thereof. The data presented in Table 6.1 additionally show the overwhelming predominance of Portuguese, which is used in no less than 80 per cent of the written production of FLUL's researchers, and leaves a modest stake of 15 per cent to English.

As to the relevance of research areas for language choice, data prove that the responsibility for English language publishing is shared by all of them, though again in various proportions. Figure 6.2 summarizes this information.

Apart from the natural presence of English Studies, this chart reveals that Linguistics is the strongest producer of publishing in English at

*Table 6.1*   Publications in the database of Faculty of Letters, University of Lisbon, by language (2000–2009)

| Language | Absolute frequency | Relative frequency (%) |
| --- | --- | --- |
| Portuguese | 4102 | 79.6 |
| English | 795 | 15.4 |
| French | 106 | 2.1 |
| Spanish | 84 | 1.6 |
| German | 34 | 0.7 |
| Italian | 22 | 0.4 |
| Romanian | 4 | 0.1 |
| Galician | 3 | 0.1 |
| Polish | 2 | 0.0 |
| Catalan | 1 | 0.0 |
| TOTAL | 5152 | 100 |

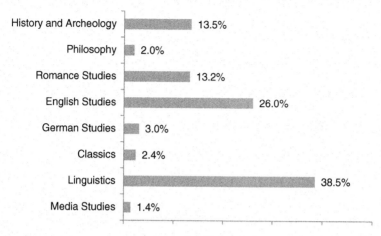

*Figure 6.2* Publications in English in the database of Faculty of Letters, University of Lisbon, by area (%) (2000–2009)

FLUL. It suggests therefore a stronger tendency for the use of English among the researchers working within this area. This conclusion is supported by the observation of the use of the various languages per research area, summarized in Figure 6.3. This chart, which ignores all languages used in less than 1 per cent of the publications within each research area, confirms that Anglicization is limited to Linguistics, English Studies and possibly Media Studies, and that within English Studies, its proportion is probably lower than might be expected (42 per cent English as opposed to 58 per cent in Portuguese).

Given the modest total number of publications in English (15 per cent, as seen above), it is reasonable to expect that many lecturers and researchers could not have published in English in the period considered. Excel filtering and sorting tools, namely the partial totals, allowed me to conclude that of the 342 authors included in the database, only 161 (47 per cent) have written at least one of their works in English.

Finally, and since recourse to English in academic texts is a tendency allegedly growing every year, attention was given to the publishing dates of those works in English. This procedure has revealed a sustained but modest increase in the use of this language, as the year 2001 contributed with 7 per cent of the works written in English and 2009 with 12 per cent; the peak was reached in 2007, when 20 per cent of those references were published.

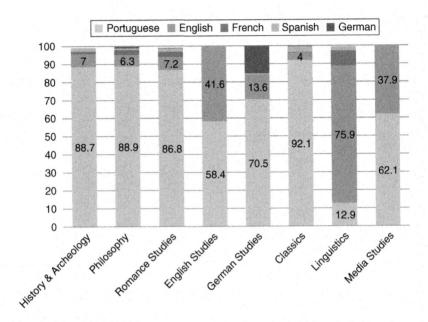

*Figure 6.3*   Publications in database of Faculty of Letters, University of Lisbon, by area and language (%) (2000–2009)

### 6.4.2   Proficiency, preferences and attitudes

The results presented in this section are drawn from the analysis of the 35 questionnaires described in the previous section. Information on publishing was ignored, since the database made it redundant.

The first piece of information taken from the answers to the questionnaire concerns self-assessed proficiency in English. Respondents were asked to assess their active and passive proficiency in both the written and oral modes as very good, adequate or poor. The results are as found in Table 6.2.

Though such confidence was to be expected from a sample dominated by lecturers and researchers working within English Studies, it should be stressed that (i) some lecturers working within this area also confessed to a merely adequate proficiency in active writing and speaking (1 and 4 respondents, respectively) and (ii) some researchers in other areas claimed very good skills at all levels.

As to information on the use of English in teaching, 48 per cent (12/25) of the respondents who are also lecturers claim to use it. However, only one of them works outside English Studies (Museology). So, although the frequency seems relevant, the overrepresentation of

*Table 6.2* Self-assessed proficiency in English among staff of Faculty of Letters, University of Lisbon

|  | Written Mode | | Oral Mode | |
|  | Passive | Active | Passive | Active |
| --- | --- | --- | --- | --- |
| Very Good | 97% | 89% | 94% | 83% |
| Adequate | 3% | 11% | 6% | 17% |
| Poor | – | – | – | – |

English Studies in the sample does not allow for any generalization. These classes involve both graduate and post-graduate courses and those lecturers who have used English in their teaching consider they do it with a reasonable frequency.

The next issue considered in the questionnaire was the weight of English language bibliography in research and reading lists recommended to students. In the first case, 86 per cent (30/35) have claimed that the academic literature they have used in the last three years is 'best described as written mostly in English', while only 9 per cent (3/35) have considered it to be 'mostly in another language', namely in Portuguese (2) and German (1), and 6 per cent (2/35) described it as 'in various and equally represented languages'. Furthermore, it should be stressed that a total of 62 per cent (8/13) of the lecturers and researchers not working within English Studies stated they used a bibliography written mostly in English, which certainly confirms the greater outreach of English language academic production worldwide.

The situation is similar with recommended reading. Though the presence of items in English was considered 'negligible' by one of the lecturers (which is certainly worth noticing), the weight of references in English is very significant. In fact, when asked to choose the best option to describe them, 68 per cent (17/25) chose the phrase 'prevailing and irreplaceable', 8 per cent 'prevailing but replaceable' (2/25) and 20 per cent (5/25) considered them as important as references in other languages. So, despite the shortcomings of the sample, this weight of English language literature seems revealing, especially if we bear in mind that two lecturers working within Romance Studies, one in Museology and one in Psychology, claimed that references in English were irreplaceable within their classes.

In the opinions section of the questionnaire, respondents were asked to agree or disagree with five statements and to explain their response. Results relating to the closed part of the answer are presented in

Table 6.3, in which the 'agree' and 'disagree' possibilities are joined by a 'don't know' column; this was not in the questionnaire but was added by some of them.

These results show that there is no unanimity regarding any of the issues raised (hence the addition of the 'don't know' column), though some tendencies can be identified. In the first place, most academics in the sample (63 per cent) responded favourably to the spread of English as the language of research. This reaction is invariably justified with the advantages of internationalization and of increased visibility that this entails, to which the question of international cooperation and progress is sometimes added. However, more than one respondent explained that it was not their wish to see a spread of English as the language of academic publishing, but that it was an inevitability that could not be resisted. Those who considered that the spread of English in this context was not desirable justified their choice insisting that every language should have and keep an academic register (most respondents), pointing to the risk of thought limitations due to the use of a single and most often foreign linguistic system (1 respondent) and mentioning the threat it entails to Portuguese (1 respondent). Two of the younger respondents further claimed that publications should always be bilingual, with both a Portuguese and an English version.

Despite this tendency to deem the spread of English as the language of academic publishing desirable, most respondents (63 per cent) believe that Portuguese academics do not prefer to publish in English. Low proficiency in English, costs involved in translating or revising by native speakers of English and extra work are the motives usually

*Table 6.3* Opinions among staff of Faculty of Letters, University of Lisbon, about English as the academic lingua franca

| | Agree | Dis-agree | Don't know |
|---|---|---|---|
| The spread of English as the language of academic publishing is desirable. | 63% | 37% | – |
| Most researchers in Portugal prefer to publish in English. | 29% | 63% | 9% |
| The spread of English as the teaching medium in higher education is desirable. | 54% | 43% | 3% |
| In the short term it is impossible to turn English into the teaching language in higher education in Portugal. | 60% | 34% | 6% |
| The spread of English in the academic world threatens the status of Portuguese as a language of culture. | 60% | 34% | 6% |

invoked for this preference, but two respondents believe that such rejection is due instead to nationalistic feelings and to the conviction that it hinders their research capacities.

Opinions about the desirability of the use of English as the teaching medium in higher education are less consistent. Fifty-four per cent of the lecturers answering the questionnaire support this possibility and justify their choice by stating that it enables Portuguese students to enter international academia and access state-of-the-art knowledge, prepares them for the demands of a global labour market, mitigates the difficulties faced by international students in Portuguese universities and attracts foreign scholars to national higher education institutions. Some of these informants suggest, however, that there should be an only partial switch into English, limited to some of the more general courses.

The 43 per cent of the respondents who resist the use of English as a teaching language argue that this procedure would increase an already noticeable interference of English in Portuguese, that it is an unreasonable practice in many of the subjects taught or that Portuguese should be used in Portuguese universities for ideological reasons, especially in Humanities courses. However, one of them confesses to feeling that it is an inevitable change, bound to take place in a near future.

As to the feasibility of this switch, 60 per cent of the academics in the sample agree that it is impossible in the short term in Portugal. In most of the cases, this is justified by the allegedly low proficiency in English of Portuguese academics, though the same problem is identified in students by the same and other respondents. Others point to the economic situation of the country, implying the same appreciation (the need for teachers of English, especially for their staff, which universities cannot afford). Informants disagreeing with the impossibility raised in the statement insist that the use of English as a teaching medium in higher education is already taking place in Portugal, which means that it is feasible.

The last statement respondents were asked to consider ('The spread of English in the academic world threatens the status of Portuguese as a language of culture') was probably the most controversial (see Figure 6.4).

Though there is considerable variation in the respondents' opinions, only 34 per cent of them do not fear that the increased use of English as the global language of academia will threaten the status of Portuguese as a language of culture. They explain this conviction in various ways, arguing (i) that an academic language is not a language of culture, which one of them explicitly associates with a national literature; (ii) that only the academic community is involved in its use, which is not

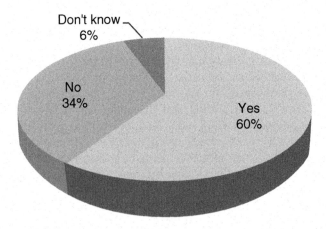

*Figure 6.4*  Opinions of staff at the Faculty of Letters, University of Lisbon, in response to the question: does the spread of English in the academic world pose a threat to the status of Portuguese as a language of culture

enough to annihilate a language of culture; or (iii) that language contact is always valuable, so that Portuguese would certainly benefit from the resulting interaction with English.

Neither the age of the respondents nor their research area seemed to interfere with the opinions stated.

## 6.5  Discussion and conclusions

As stated above, the specific purposes of this study were twofold: (i) to determine Portuguese academics' behaviour as far as English is concerned (that is, the extent to which they effectively use this language in their work); and (ii) to investigate the motives prompting them to choose or reject this language.

The results presented in the previous section make it very clear that the effective use of English is far from prevalent within publishing, representing a mere 15 per cent. The Anglicization of FLUL's academic production is therefore far below not only that of European non-peripheral countries such as Sweden (Gunnarsson 2001), Switzerland (Murray and Dingwall 2001), Norway (Ljosland 2007) or France (Truchot 1990), but also of neighbouring Spain (57 per cent in the Humanities School of the University of Santiago de Compostela according to Polo and Varela 2009, p. 156). This conclusion also shows a much lower recourse to English at FLUL than among Bennett's respondents (of whom 80 per cent claimed to have published in English), thereby confirming, once again, the lesser degree of Anglicization among the Humanities.

Results also show that an undeniable multilingualism among the FLUL faculty's written production does not compensate for an overwhelming domination of Portuguese, used in 80 per cent of the whole volume of publications. This situation is once again very different from that of Spain (Polo and Varela 2009, p. 156), and may be the result of a strong monolingual tradition in Portugal. The single research area effectively escaping the dominion of Portuguese is Linguistics (even more so than English Studies), which may be a consequence of its closer affinity to the hard sciences. Language choice at FLUL therefore confirms, once again, that the humanities are more reluctant to use English in academic writing (as Ammon 2008b, or Bennett 2010a among others).

However, as Bennett concluded (2010a, pp. 207–208), the dominion of Portuguese seems to be bound to change in a near future. In fact, according to the answers received, most bibliographic references used by researchers, lecturers and their students are in English, which confirms not only the stronger visibility of academic publications in that language, but especially the continuous contact with English texts. Additionally, the attitudes expressed are never radically opposed to the use of English as the language of academia in Portugal, with one single exception. Responses to the questionnaire reveal instead a very pragmatic approach to the language issue at stake: academics prove to be very aware of the outreach awarded by the use of English in the dissemination of research and higher education teaching, and are conscious of the importance of this for the survival of both individuals and institutions in this competitive century. Such pragmatism is also revealed by the suggestions given for the incorporation of English into Portuguese higher education teaching, either as a teaching medium in part of the courses or as an autonomous curricular unit.

Combined with the very low rate of effective usage of English in publishing and teaching, this acute awareness of its importance is of course the sign of a community in conflict – not for nationalistic concerns, as might happen in an outer-circle speech community, but because of a perceived lack of proficiency in English among Portuguese academics and students (this is mentioned by various respondents, despite a high confidence rate in their own command of the language). The extent of this conflict is certainly best assessed if we recall that, despite the recognition of the benefits of the use of English as the academic lingua franca, more than half of the authors in the database have never published in this language (thereby confirming that especially older researchers in Southern Europe are only 'narrowly-proficient' in English, Swales 2004).[3]

So, although Swales's Tyrannosaurus Rex (Swales 1997) has not yet swallowed Portuguese academia, it has certainly managed to drag it into conscious conflict.

## Notes

1. Constitution of the Portuguese Republic, Article 9: 'The following are fundamental duties of the Portuguese state: (...) (f) To ensure the teaching and permanent enhancement of the Portuguese language, to defend its use and to promote its international diffusion'.
2. I would like to thank Pedro Estácio and Isabel Rebolho for their invaluable help in this regard.
3. Notice, however, that Portugal is now included in the group of the countries considered to have a high proficiency rate in English, according to an international report published in November 2013 and based on data collected from a sample of 750,000 adults from 60 countries: http://www.ef.com/__/~/media/efcom/epi/2014/full-reports/ef-epi-2013-report-master.pdf. Accessed 10 Jan 2014.

# 7

# Changing Research Writing Practices in Romania: Perceptions and Attitudes

*Mirela Bardi and Laura-Mihaela Muresan*

## 7.1 Introduction

Although underpinned by well-intentioned reform efforts, Romanian academic culture is currently in a state of flux, which has had a disturbing effect upon the communities and practitioners involved. Accession to the European Union has brought the need for harmonization of academic practices, and has increased awareness of how things are done in other academic environments. As a result, Romanian scholars have been expected to cope with repeated reform attempts, some of which have been abandoned halfway through implementation.

The public discourse on education is very well aligned to the principles of a student-centred approach to teaching and learning. However, the classroom reality is much more diverse, with traditional teaching methods coexisting with attempts at analysing and evaluating knowledge and fostering increased interaction and collaboration in the classroom. Equally, diverse practices coexist with respect to conducting and reporting research, which features more and more strongly as a main career advancement criterion. Nevertheless, research activity and publication in international peer-reviewed journals tends to be 'encouraged' more by mandate (legislation, promotion criteria) than by support through a collective search for worthwhile topics, resources and international exposure. Hence, we would claim that Romanian academic culture is trying to find an identity for itself at the interface of genuine individual dedication and the need to fulfil promotion criteria that require a stronger international presence.

Research evidence (Muresan and Pérez-Llantada 2014) suggests that Romanian researchers do make efforts to familiarize themselves with internationally accepted research practices and to develop their writing expertise. In many cases they look up to other European and international education realities without any grudges or resentments, possibly due to a need for 'belonging' after many years of isolation. But there is also a sense of frustration among economics researchers that their chances of getting published are seriously diminished by the fact that their research is undertaken in an economy that lacks international significance.

One of the key issues in exploring such a complex reality is whether the adoption of centre-style research practices is merely a formal exercise designed to fulfil criteria leading to promotion, or if it is truly accepted, learned and internalized as a more rigorous way of doing research. If this latter situation is the case, then evidence should become apparent – albeit after a lengthy period of time – at various levels in the education system: in classroom teaching and learning, training of PhD students and supervision practices.

This study aims to give a voice to researchers at the Bucharest University of Economics, and by doing so, to explore the significance and implications of writing in English for 'off-network' researchers (Swales 1987, p. 43), trying to understand the obstacles they encounter and the ways they adapt their research dissemination practices to the challenge of publishing in international English-language journals. The outcomes of the study can inform the design of suitable support for academics who aim to disseminate their research in high-profile publications.

## 7.2  Background

In response to Ministry of Education statement of expectations issued in 2005, that academic staff should publish in international West European and American journals, the Bucharest University of Economic Studies set up a staff development programme at MA level designed to support academics' efforts to strengthen their international presence. The programme aims to enhance academic skills – teaching, research and educational management – as well as academic communication in English. The majority of the course participants are academics of various specializations within the wider field of economics, who have an interest in research methodology and dissemination writing as well as in innovative approaches to teaching, learning and evaluation (Muresan 2009). While individual priorities may differ, a common denominator is the participants' genuine interest in their professional development and their desire to deepen their understanding of international requirements and discourse practices, as well as to refine complex sets of skills (Bardi and Muresan 2012). The existence of this programme is worth mentioning as evidence of institutional response to ministry guidelines, on the one hand, and to individual academics' attempts to increase their international visibility, on the other. This is nevertheless an isolated initiative, as no other Romanian university runs similar programmes. Unique as it may be, such a programme brings evidence of Romanian universities' attempts to harmonize their practices with international ones.

Two issues deserve attention in relation to English language publication practices of Romanian researchers: one is the challenge of writing articles in a language other than their mother tongue (that is, in English) and the other is attempting publication in high-profile Anglophone journals. Many international journals are indexed in international databases, but the quality varies and the challenges of publishing well-researched, well-structured articles written in accurate and fluent English vary as well. Many Romanian journals, some of which are indexed internationally, require submission in English. However, few Romanian researchers choose to take the challenge of publishing in high-profile Anglophone journals, for reasons which are still to be explored. Unfolding research (Bardi, ongoing) has shown that one reason is researchers' perception of their own limitations regarding both research and linguistic abilities. Another reason is the apparent inaccessibility of those journals, which are considered unapproachable from the start, and few people venture to target them.

*Targeting one of the top quality Anglophone journals was a personal challenge. I could have satisfied evaluation criteria by publishing in an internationally indexed but less reputable journal. I wanted to learn from the experience of dealing with the reviewers' comments – I was simply curious.* (Interview 10)

While the challenges encountered by researchers who use English as an additional language have been extensively studied in many cultural contexts (for example, Buckingham 2008, Buckingham 2013, Duszak and Lewkowicz 2008, Flowerdew 1999b, Lillis and Curry 2006, Pérez-Llantada et al. 2011, Pérez-Llantada 2012), there is still room for voices of researchers from other parts of the world to be heard. In addition, research can usefully examine the attempts of such researchers to adapt their writing practices to the requirements of high profile English-medium journals. Our study aims to document, albeit on a small scale, the change of writing practices entailed by international publication endeavours through an integrated approach that compares the way researchers perceive such changes with textual production. This chapter is organized around key themes that emerged from the data, highlighting the skills and abilities involved in the complex multi-level task of writing for international publication, the balance between personal abilities and institutional support, issues related to isolation and parochialism, attitudes to the spread of English and the role of reviewers, and changing practices as evidenced by perceptions and textual production. Many of these issues are worth investigating through further research.

## 7.3   Investigating perceptions

We have combined survey, interview and textual data in order to build a comprehensive picture of perceptions about reporting research according to international journal standards and actual writing practices. Two main themes have guided the collection, analysis and interpretation of the data: challenges encountered by researchers and the possible change of practices generated by the attempt to access high-profile journals. The first issue has been investigated through responses to the final, open questions of a wide-ranging questionnaire, designed within the framework of a broader research project and aimed at capturing attitudes to the dominance of English as a research dissemination language (Muresan and Pérez-Llantada 2014).

As a lead-in to the current research, we shall briefly summarize some of the main findings discussed in the above study (Muresan and Pérez-Llantada 2014). The responses to the first part of the questionnaire, aimed at finding out what place was ascribed to English as compared to other languages in the academic context analysed, underlined the prevalence of English in the domain of written communication for research publication. At the same time, the findings confirmed the existence of an 'ecology of linguistic diversity' (Skutnabb-Kangas and Phillipson 2008) for research communication, reflected in the use of various languages in addition to English, such as Romanian – especially for research exchanges and dissemination in the local/national context – complemented by French, German, Italian and Spanish for accessing scholarly research and in spoken interaction with fellow academics and partner institutions, especially in bilateral relations. Several experienced researchers also pointed out in follow-up interviews that, until seven to eight years ago, their language choice had been in favour of French and/ or German for publishing research outcomes. Over the last few years, however, due to institutional pressures and a changing linguistic landscape in the world of research publishing, with English taking on a leading role even in non-Anglophone countries (Muresan 2013), they had had to switch to using English for research writing. The scholars' readiness to resort to communication in a foreign language is not surprising in Central-Eastern European academic contexts (as reported also by Medgyes and Kaplan 1992, with reference to Hungarian scholars).

The scholars' views on the peer-review process, and their experience of submitting articles for publication in international journals, reflected disbelief that editors would be sympathetic to the problems faced by non-Anglophone researchers. In line with this perception, almost two-thirds of the respondents agreed that articles should be reviewed by at least one non-native speaker. Further findings, based on responses to the attitude- and perception-oriented questions, revealed ambivalent attitudes to the predominance of English in research publication. While the majority of the 91 respondents agreed/completely agreed that the dominance of English represented an advantage for English native-speaking academics, only 40 per cent considered that this advantage was unfair. At the same time, two-thirds of the respondents felt more advantaged than disadvantaged in their academic work by the dominance of English for research purposes. This finding was reinforced by the belief of an overwhelming majority of respondents (irrespective of their self-perceived level of language proficiency) that there was a need for one international language of research (Muresan and Pérez-Llantada 2014).

To gain further insights into the researchers' perceptions and research writing practices, the survey-based data related to challenges of writing in English will be analysed and reported here. In addition, ten interviews were conducted with researchers who have published in high-profile journals, with a view toward understanding how these researchers adapted or changed their research and writing practices in order to comply with demanding requirements.

The research questions that guided the perception exploration part of our study were the following:

RQ1:   What are the main obstacles encountered by Romanian research-ers in the field of business and economics when communicating their research through the medium of English?

RQ2:   Are text drafting/revising practices changing as a result of pub-lishing in English-language journals?

The data shows that obstacles encountered by semiperipheral research-ers are various and pertain to several types of expertise. Linguistic abili-ties are just one such obstacle. Language communicates concepts that define disciplinary content and builds arguments meant to bring out the value of the contribution, thus making it publishable. Language, scientific content and structural patterns and conventions cannot be separated, as they contribute jointly to constructing a convincingly communicated piece of research. Equally, the educational circumstances in which researchers operate impinge on their publication success (Swales 2004, Salager-Meyer 2008). Therefore, themes that emerge from the data are diverse, and linguistic implications need to be discussed within the wider cultural and institutional framework. Those themes were identified through analysis of open-question responses in the questionnaire (challenges) and of interview transcripts (investigating change of practices). The textual analysis of 35 articles followed, in order to compare perceived changes with those implemented in textual practice. The discussion and conclusions section of articles published in internationally indexed journals were analysed looking for specific elements that were mentioned in the course of interviews as instances of changing practices.

## 7.4   Findings and discussion 1 – perceptions

This section reports on the questionnaire and interview findings.

### 7.4.1   Writing for publication – a complex, multi-level task

The results indicate the complexity of the challenges researchers encounter, the array of competencies they need and the institutional circumstances that may facilitate access to reputable journals.

The challenges mentioned by respondents have been grouped into several categories:

- Linguistic/Rhetorical/Structural
- Methodological and Discipline-related
- Institutional.

For data presentation purposes we have decided to merge linguistic challenges with rhetorical and structural awareness of conventions related to research articles as a specific genre, although it could be argued that the former are to do with mastery of English while the latter apply to writing in any language. In practice, competencies and circumstances related to all those categories are at work simultaneously and affect researchers' publication success in a measure that can only be established by further research. Table 7.1 offers a map of responses about the major challenges encountered by Romanian researchers in economics and business in the process of scholarly writing.

Levels of confidence in their ability to communicate fluently and subtly in English vary among respondents, from acknowledging the need

*Table 7.1*  Challenges faced by Romanian economics researchers writing in English (questionnaire data)

| | |
|---|---|
| **Linguistic/Rhetorical/ Structural challenges** | Preserving structural conventions and journal-specific ones<br>Building a clear, coherent argument<br>Using an impersonal, standardized style<br>Softening claims, hedging<br>Accurate communication of ideas<br>Coherence in expressing ideas<br>Specific terminology and appropriate definition of concepts, particularly in niche domains<br>Writing fluently<br>Developing an original, elegant and fluent style<br>Using synonyms to avoid repetition<br>Knowledge of idioms<br>Metaphoric and subtle expression<br>Avoiding redundant writing, repetition<br>Avoiding long, incomprehensible sentences<br>Writing straight into English<br>Getting professional support from language experts/translators |
| **Methodological/ Discipline – related challenges** | Limited methodological abilities<br>High complexity of econometric practices<br>Limited access to documentation |
| **System-related challenges** | Access to previous publications in the field – informational challenge<br>Need for training in the specific language of the field<br>Wider participation in international exchanges/ networks needed<br>Recognition of research results, integrating results in the literature.<br>Insufficient international visibility.<br>Biased attitude of international journal editors and reviewers<br>Need to participate in knowledge creation in the respective fields |

to improve their English language proficiency to expressing preference for writing in English rather than Romanian. However, the prevailing attitude indicates awareness that, despite high English proficiency, a certain level of linguistic sophistication easy to achieve by native speakers will always be missing. An understandable sense of frustration emerges (*'I cannot communicate all the nuances particularly when interpreting the results.'*), similar to the frustration of Spanish researchers communicated by Perez-Llantada et al. (2011). Insufficient syntactic and lexical resources seem to prevent both groups of researchers from finding the most appropriate phrasing for their ideas.

More proficient respondents prefer to draft their articles straight into English and to revise repeatedly, while others rely on assistance from professional translators. Collaboration with language experts is not always straightforward, and linguistic revision by language experts has not been entirely reliable, with reviewers requesting improvement of article structure after revision by language experts. Indeed, 'convenience editors' (Willey and Tanimoto 2013) may not necessarily be familiar with the conventions of scientific writing in a range of disciplines, and English language proficiency is not sufficient for effective editing of research texts. For both researchers and 'literacy brokers' (Lillis and Curry 2006), drafting and revision of research articles requires familiarity with research methodology and rhetorical/structural conventions apart from linguistic abilities.

Linguistic and discipline-related challenges appear to be merged. 46 per cent of the respondents to the questionnaire refer to the need for 'shared definition and understanding of concepts' which, one may argue, is both a linguistic challenge to do with breadth of lexical knowledge and a conceptual, discipline-related one, whereby concepts that emerged from centre-specific realities and contexts may be inappropriately defined and understood in peripheral areas. As one respondent put it: '*Language is a first step, but the challenge is more profound and is to do with conceptual and curricular differences.*'

The same opinion is put forward in the interviews. The main barriers to publication in scholarly journals are 'a mixture of philosophy, politics, language and resources' that include insufficient language abilities; inconsistent research and writing tradition; lack of focus in developing a research writing style (publishing in too many journals with different styles and requirements); promotion criteria based on quantity; lack of access to data bases and scarce documentation; and vanity/ quick rejection of feedback, which is perceived as failure rather than as a chance to improve.

Perceptions expressed by respondents support our argument that writing for publication in scholarly journals is a multi-level task, to do with linguistic abilities, current discipline knowledge, conceptual clarity and methodological competence. In the words of one respondent, 'content and form are strongly related' (Interview 2). It could be argued that many of these competencies depend on circumstances pertaining to the professional context of researchers who have higher chances of keeping current with developments in their fields if they have access to the latest resources, participate in conferences and network more intensively with international researchers. The mingling of personal and institutional circumstances comes out strongly from the data, in line with the vast literature that has stated the importance of location and environmental factors in publication success of off-centre researchers (Lillis and Curry 2006, Salager-Meyer 2008, Swales 2004).

Respondents are concerned about the relevance of their chosen topics for the international community and about the 'significance of their scientific contribution' (Interview 7). Although the word itself is not used, the respondents' understanding of the need for wider relevance and articulation of contribution indicates an attempt to avoid 'parochialism', which editors interviewed by Flowerdew (2001) indicate as a major weakness of semiperipheral research writing. Respondents who teach less well-established disciplines on recently introduced programmes of study are aware of the fact that insufficiently developed disciplines (for example public administration) generate a mismatch between topics that concern the periphery as opposed to the centre – research topics relevant for the Romanian context are no longer interesting for the centre.

Inadequate resources generate difficulties with conducting and disseminating research. Time itself is a valuable resource, but matters are complicated by limited access to databases (both as sources of literature and of data). Assembling a corpus of primary data for empirical quantitative research from several sources requires time that centre researchers can dedicate to planning and conducting their research (Interview 9). Equally, scarcity of access to the latest publications turn drafting the literature review section into a great challenge, the more so as reviewing previous literature helps with the formulation of hypotheses (Interviews 2, 3, 9).

*The literature review section is an obstacle difficult to overcome – we are not fully knowledgeable about recent literature and we do not engage with it critically. Reviewers of one of my articles objected to inappropriate evaluation of the literature. Linked to this, we usually cannot build a coherent argument.* (Interview 2)

*We cite the literature we can get hold of, not necessarily the most suitable.* (Interview 4)

While 'methodologies tend to become more complicated, particularly as regards econometrical modelling' (Interview 4), the local methodological approach is described as 'quite simplistic' in the sense of using, interpreting and designing a limited range of models. The result is research unable to challenge existing theory, or to contribute to it for that matter, and – in the absence of a large corpus of data – of little practical relevance. Although respondents identify cooperation with statisticians as their solution of choice for dealing with ever more sophisticated statistical tools, working in a multi-disciplinary team can pose several challenges, due to the need to make a clear link between 'figures and their meaning' (Interview 3). In order to properly integrate figures in the overall content, and to provide interpretation of their meaning, collaboration needs to run through the whole research and drafting process. Indeed, the practices described in the interview data consistently include interdisciplinary collaboration as a prevailing element. Generating and sharing ideas needs to involve all team members throughout. The same pattern is suggested as regards linguistic revision. Language experts, one category of 'literacy brokers' as described by Lillis and Curry (2006), are expected 'to contribute to structuring the information' (Interview 2) and to provide comments and feedback on the text as a whole (Interview 8).

*Valuable research cannot be individual any longer. Small teams whose members work together all along are needed. Writing an article and having it translated afterwards doesn't work anymore.* (Interview 1)

Several respondents are well aware of their training needs and have taken action to identify and attend suitable training in order to bridge the gap and prepare themselves for participation at conferences, after disconcerting experiences that generated an uncomfortable sense of inadequacy.

### 7.4.2   Isolation and parochialism

Isolation has been identified as a main obstacle to publication. Working outside the centre affects researchers' visibility in many ways, and prevents them from keeping up with progress in their disciplines, through lack of access to well-provided libraries (Hyland 2011), insufficient participation in research networks (Curry and Lillis 2010), lack of consultation with other researchers and absence of opportunities to encounter and use the language register of specific disciplines (Flowerdew 2007). Isolation can be associated with 'parochialism', a concept present in the literature (Flowerdew 2001) and also tackled by our respondents whose comments shed further light on the issue.

In Flowerdew's (2001) study of journal editors' attitudes to non-native speaker (NNS) contributions, parochialism, defined as 'failure to show the relevance of the study to the international community' (2001, p. 135) emerges as one of the substantive problems with NNS submissions. Contributions tend to be too localized, and they often deal with obscure topics that are irrelevant to a wider audience. Reasonable as the editors' objection may seem, it has encountered opposition, primarily to do with the possible exclusion of contributions that may bring out a reality inaccessible to centre researchers and /or a new cultural perspective on topics already accepted as salient. Flowerdew (2001, p. 122) warns about 'impoverishing in terms of creation of knowledge' while Swales (2004, p. 52) detects 'the skewing of international research agendas to those most likely to pass the gatekeeping'. Consequently, it may seem reasonable to argue that both off-centre researchers and editors are 'guilty' of parochialism, albeit in different ways. Indeed, an experienced researcher interviewed in this study detects parochialism in the behaviour of journal reviewers who seem to 'try to preserve the status of their own universities by preventing newcomers to accede to higher levels' (Interview 1). In addition, 'linguistic parochialism' is at play through quick detection of articles written by semiperiphery academics, who often lack the refined expression of a native speaker. Conversely, parochialism of article writers is identified in our data set in the same terms as journals reviewers do (Flowerdew 2001), that is reporting research on very specific realities, a damaging strategy to adopt in social sciences and particularly in economics (Interviews 1, 2, 5).

> *As people tend to speak convincingly about what they know best, many studies report about realities that are very specific to a domain or a country, thus reducing their chances of being accepted by journals that prefer wider-ranging articles.* (Interview 1)

Moreover, some Romanian researchers also manifest 'behavioural parochialism' – accepting the effortless solution and giving in to the hardships of publication in high profile journals. Discouragement, generated by very critical and demanding reviews ('If I had been the sole author, I might have given up.' – Interview 2), or excessive pride are possible causes of surrender. The data is unambiguous in associating such behaviour with the need to fulfil quantitative promotion criteria, which 'demanded large numbers of publications in order to compensate the lack of quality' (Interview 2).

> *The 'I want to publish somewhere easy and quick' attitude was generated by a quantitative approach to promotion which generated malformations – we had to publish a certain number of books and articles, no matter where.* (Interview 1)

Indeed, personal and institutional agendas are closely connected and they affect each other. A major issue in a discussion of factors

affecting international publication success of semiperipheral researchers is whether making their way to high-profile journals is a matter of
individual ability, or whether it requires institutional involvement and
assistance. If the focus on scholarly publication is a manifestation of
globalization of academia (Flowerdew, J. and Li 2009), then academic
institutions have a responsibility to support individuals' efforts. The data
bring evidence of system-related challenges, as perceived by researchers,
and the institutional support they need and expect. Not surprisingly,
researchers need institutional support in their attempts 'to participate
to the international dialogue in our fields', and to have their research
results recognized and 'integrated in the literature' (Questionnaire data).

All interviewees agree that it is the institution's role and duty to
provide support for research and to facilitate unfolding and dissemination of research proactively rather than reward achievements after they
have happened. Provision of documentation facilities through access
to journals and sources of data, support for conference participation
and sabbatical terms are some of the courses of action suggested by
respondents. Development of English communication skills is regarded
as a 'necessary, strategic investment for all universities' (Interview 9).
The same respondent made practical suggestions in terms of translating
such strategic measures into 'a process of initial training and targeted
continuous professional development' (Interview 9).

Interviewees (Interviews 1, 9) also raise the issue of evaluating academic performance in a way that reflects curricular and educational
realities, taking into account that teaching and research abilities do not
necessarily coexist in the same person. Currently, 'the same combination between the teaching and research components of an academic
career is applied to all university staff, ignoring the complementarity of
skills' (Interview 1).

### 7.4.3   Reinventing academic practices

Most respondents seem to feel the need for a change of attitudes and
practices. The data build a complex picture of interrelated issues, underpinned by the point that scholarly publication is a learning process, and
refinement of writing competence can only be achieved by engaging
in writing and submitting articles to reputable international journals.

*Scaling difficult heights is essential for reinventing our practices.* (Interview 1)

While attempts to overcome barriers are encouraged, there is scepti-
cism about the chances of succeeding. Too many factors beyond the

academics' control are involved – factors to do with university strategy, international criteria for establishing league tables, some of which are too difficult to achieve, and the elitist 'club-culture' of high-quality journals. The belief exists that access can be obtained only through co-authorship with a well-known name. Fears are expressed that a 'mercenary system' might evolve, whereby universities employ staff with a good publication record while neglecting the quality of educational processes. Moreover, journal metrics has not always proved relevant.

Publication in some well-quoted journals (although not in the Web of Science) with a stronger internationalization character has proved valuable for some respondents as it has entailed frequent citation and international partnerships. Nevertheless, steps forward on the path to acceptance by scholarly journals have been made, and the data provides many examples. The process has started with increased awareness of requirements and standards, while the overriding attitude is one of willingness to learn the rules of the game. In this sense, several of the respondents considered that reviewers' feedback – however disapproving – should be accepted and worked upon rather than perceived as a failure. In their view, careful reading of such feedback and resubmission represent a step forward as opposed to abandoning the process and choosing easy publication in a less rigorous journal. 'Avoid the easy solution' (Interviews 1, 2, 3, 5) is the kind of attitude that respondents seem to agree upon as the way forward towards a consistent overhaul of practices leading to a stronger international presence.

In the process of changing practices, the role of reviewers seems to be contradictory. They are perceived, in agreement with the literature, as 'obstacles on the path to publication' (Belcher 2007, p. 4), because of their own agenda in preserving the status of the academic environment to which they most often belong. Equally, reviews can become an obstacle when they are too demanding, and when fulfilling the requirements takes too much effort (Interview 9).

> *The reviewers' comments were harsh, but justified. I did pass all the barriers in the end, but I had to fight. If I had been the sole author, I might have given up.* (Interview 2)

Nevertheless, several respondents value the feedback received from reviewers and admit that it was 'relevant and useful' (Interview 3, 4, 10). Thus, reviewers seem to fulfil their role as 'facilitators in providing needed feedback to authors.' (Belcher 2007, p. 4).

Publication strategies have become more elaborate. Journal selection sometimes proceeds top-down, from high-class journals to lower-level ones, if rejected (Interview 3). Articles that undertake a review of the field are destined to local journals, as international ones prefer reports of empirical research. Awareness of journals' editorial priorities and agendas is one main lesson, sometimes learned the hard way after rejection because of the article's unsuitability to the priority field of the journal. Moreover, journals are seldom transparent about their editorial criteria – the recommendation is made in Interview 6 to journal editors to be more specific as regards structural and rhetorical criteria. Despite considerable publication expertise, researchers are often unsure about what to expect, and the process of publication can be utterly unpredictable (Interview 6). The presence of other East-European researchers in the targeted journal is often an indicator that encourages publication attempts.

### 7.4.4   Text drafting and editing practices

Researchers who have published in high-quality journals have learned valuable lessons from the process of drafting and revising articles. Some of the respondents seem to have learned from careful examination of how other researchers have written. Attention is given to the careful selection of topics: 'there are fads ... you either go with the trend or anticipate the next trend' (Interview 9). Equally, researchers give attention to selecting the most appropriate methodology for the topic under investigation, to contextualizing their topic and showing its relevance, to writing conclusions that show the implications of findings and to indicating limitations of research. The need to structure information and build a clear, convincing argument emerges as a main challenge from questionnaires and as a valuable lesson derived from publication endeavours by participants in the interviews. Researchers further identify specific aspects to do with text organization such as 'the structure of paragraphs', 'sequence and balance of ideas', 'rhythm and fluency of writing', 'considering several points of view, not only those that coincide with your own' (Interviews 2, 6). More insights indicate focus on meanings to do with the very essence and value of the work:

> *Based on the literature review, I try to build a conceptual framework for my research hypotheses and the model I want to test and improve. It is a necessary link between the reviewed literature and the specific aims of my study, something which has always been in the texts I wrote, somehow implicitly. Now I pay more attention to constructing a theoretical framework for my research.* (Interview 3)

This particular piece of data may be interpreted as evidence of the researchers' attempts to establish the value of their contribution by carefully integrating it in the field. If the challenges indicated by respondents mention researchers' desire 'to participate in the international dialogue in their field', and for their research 'to be integrated in the literature', the interview data quoted above may indicate that the process has already started, with researchers' realization of the need for closer integration of their own contribution into the respective field of study. Textual rhetorical features support such attempts, and discourse construction contributes to building the argument. It is an example in which 'content and form are related', as noticed in Interview 2, or an example of how texts should be regarded as 'the outcome of interactions among academics engaged in a web of professional and social associations' (Hyland 2011, p. 61).

Such a level of detail indicates increased awareness of internationally accepted practices and standards, as well as willingness to comply with them. Awareness is accompanied by specific text drafting and revision strategies that researchers employ to make their writing clearer and more readily acceptable. Avoiding 'lexical and informational redundancy' is a new practice linked with attempts to write more critically and to build stronger, clearer arguments (Interviews 1, 2, 5, 6). Refining expression by shortening sentences and focusing on transmission of meaning, ensuring that tables and graphs 'tell the story' and are not a simple addition to the text, are examples of specific practices generated by the need to adjust text production to international standards. Researchers also mention ongoing revision and monitoring of their own writing (including reading aloud), in order to avoid repetition and to make sure the rhythm is appropriate.

New practices include endeavours to expand linguistic knowledge, particularly as regards vocabulary. Discipline-specific, as well as more general, vocabulary has drawn researchers' attention. While reading, they write down new words and phrases they would like to use in their own writing.

*I do a sort of double reading: I read for content, but I also focus on the language and identify those phrases I do not usually use but I would like to use more often.* (Interview 3)

Indeed, article reading helps improvement of writing, as researchers identify the language features they would like to introduce in their own practice. Apart from vocabulary, attention is given to the style and rhetoric of articles. Making claims more carefully is one change introduced to their own writing, by some researchers who have noticed that many published articles use more tentative language when expressing claims.

*I am more careful about the claims I make, I am now less direct than I used to be. Other opinions may exist that do not coincide with my own.* (Interview 8)

It is worth noting that the researcher quoted above has attended the Master's programme in academic training established by the university in order to support its staff's efforts to achieve international visibility. In the analysis of articles conducted in class, attention was drawn to the need to use more tentative language and the need to regard knowledge as provisional. While the balance between the benefits of researchers' own efforts to improve linguistic and rhetorical ability and those of explicit tuition is an issue to be investigated through further research, one could justifiably wonder about the most appropriate pedagogical tools that could be developed to help researchers improve their research writing abilities. The dominant attitude in the data discussed in this study is that writing practice is the tool to improving writing, as pointed out in Interview 6 – the researcher made considerable progress when he started drafting his articles straight into English.

The spread of English as the lingua franca of academic communication (Mauranen 2012) does not seem to 'scare' our sample of semiperipheral researchers, who see the use of English as a vehicle for integration of their research into the literature of their respective disciplines. Many of them seem willing to make the required efforts to enhance English language proficiency and awareness of structural and rhetorical conventions. What is more, they warn centre researchers about the possible disadvantages of using their language only, in line with Flowerdew (1999b, p. 245) who writes about 'the cultural impoverishment brought about by the encroachment of English upon other languages'.

*In the long run, there may be a disadvantage for English native speakers who do not need at present to use other languages.* (Questionnaire data)

What they are not prepared to accept is a biased reviewers' attitude towards researchers from off-centre areas for reasons that have little connection with research quality. The participants to this study reject the perpetuation of the 'club-culture' that tends to bar access of newcomers (Questionnaire response) and the deliberate rejection of new contributors by reviewers preoccupied to preserve the status of their own universities in a highly competitive academic market (Interviews 1, 2, 6). Respondents are not directly critical of the rhetorical conventions at play, or of the need to report their research in a language other than their own, probably due to the perceived need to upgrade or 'reinvent' current local academic practices. Harmonizing research dissemination practices with internationally accepted standards seems to be regarded as a worthwhile learning experience which off-centre researchers are prepared to undertake, despite the considerable difficulties highlighted earlier in our analysis. Nevertheless, the researchers who participated in this study expect to be treated fairly, on grounds related to the quality of their work.

> *We need to become more coherent in the way we carry out and disseminate research, now we tend to grab various opportunities and are not concerned about focus or continuity. … I am ready to learn and to try harder provided we are all treated alike and are not rejected simply because we are outsiders.* (Interview 2)

## 7.5  Investigating textual practices

The data presented so far have highlighted perceptions about the challenges of writing and publishing in English, as well as about the change or adaptation of research writing practices in view of publication in scholarly journals. In order to compare perceived changes with actual text drafting practices, we compiled a corpus of 35 research articles published by Romanian academics in English-medium journals and analysed them looking for the specific textual features indicated by respondents when invited to reflect on the lessons they have learned from the process (text drafting and submission) of international publication. Several changes regarding drafting practices were mentioned in the interviews, many of which had to do with constructing a clearer argument, showing the relevance and implications of findings, indicating limitations of research and possible constraints encountered. As most of these rhetorical functions occur in the discussion and conclusions sections of research articles, we decided to analyse the communicative functions and language used to express them in those sections. The discussion and conclusion sections of the selected articles constitute a sub-corpus of 36,350 words. The texts were anonymized and all reference to the authors' institutional affiliation was removed.

The thematic areas covered by the selected articles belong to various business and economics related subfields, such as applied economics, economic forecasting, management research and practice, international comparative management, economics and finance, fiscal policy, business studies, and so on. The articles in the corpus have been published in 20 journals, 11 of which are published in Romania and nine in different other countries (Canada, the Czech Republic, Germany, Lithuania, Turkey, the US).

The first step in selecting the articles was that of inviting respondents to the questionnaire and participants in the interviews to indicate two of their research articles that best displayed the authors' writing abilities. More than half of the articles selected were thus suggested by specialty informants. Apart from the latter's own choices, more articles were selected for inclusion in the corpus, based on criteria such as:

• publication in the same or similar journals as those named by the respondents when giving them as reference/source for their own articles
• the authors' affiliation to a Romanian university of economics
• comparability of articles in terms of disciplinary subfields they belong to
• internal organization following the IMRD structuring principle, making sure all the articles selected had a concluding section
• year of publication (2008–2013, with the great majority published between 2010 and 2013)
• balance of authors represented in the corpus (making sure that there were not more than two articles per author or the same combination of co-authors) and number of articles per journal (one to three articles per journal).
   In addition to the above, there was also a degree of randomness.

## 7.6   Findings and discussion 2 – textual practices

Building on the genre-based approach to the analysis of research articles (Swales 1990 and 2004), we explored first the move-structure of the sections in this sub-corpus. Overall, the analysis reveals the presence of moves typical of discussions and conclusions, in line with those mentioned by Swales (2004, pp. 234–239), Swales and Feak (2008, pp. 268–278), Dudley-Evans (1994, pp. 219–228), Thompson (2005), Paltridge and Starfield (2007, pp. 145–154):

• consolidation of the research space, especially through mentioning of the initial aims of the study and/or brief contextualization of the study, highlighting the rationale for embarking on it

- reviewing of the research findings, often in relation to the methodological approach(es) and research instruments used
- suggestions regarding possible applications and implications of the research findings
- reference to limitations and/or constraints
- recommendations for further research directions.

At the same time, the findings confirm Swales' observation that 'despite a number of major studies devoted to this part-genre, it has to be conceded that at present the picture is rather blurred.' (Swales 2004, p. 235). On the one hand, in over half of the articles analysed the discussions are integrated as a subsection at the end of the Results section, most often without a special subheading. In some cases they are merged with the conclusions and labelled as 'Discussion and Conclusions'.

At the level of moves, for instance, the initial ones – consolidation of the research and review of the findings – can be found in all the texts, while some of the other moves – suggestions regarding applications/ implications, reference to limitations, recommendations for further research – display a more varied distribution across texts and subfields. Going a step further, to take a closer look at the internal organization of information inside the moves and the weighting given to various subcomponents, it appears that the internal structuring and the presence or absence of some of the elements could be considered as method-related or as subject-bound.

For instance, in the subfields of economics forecasting and finance, the discussion and conclusion sections of studies relying on statistical models include ample reference to the research methodology, as well as comparisons and evaluation of the findings in relation to the model used, as illustrated in the example below, from one of the research articles (RA) analysed:

*In summary, although a different conditional volatility model was found best suited for each series in terms of in-sample modeling, on an out-of-sample basis EGARCH clearly dominates the other models, ranking first in terms of forecasting performance in three cases and second in the fourth case. Thus, the MAPE statistic clearly identifies the EGARCH model as superior.* [RA6]

The studies in the subfields of public or business management, on the other hand, in most cases apply qualitative research methods, and tend to devote the discussion and concluding sections to implications for practice and recommendations to the virtual readership on how to change existing management practices, thus highlighting a stronger connection to the real world (as Swales and Feak 2008, pp. 269–270).

> *As we can see in this paper, the absorption of the ethical values should happen in different ways, depending on the environment and the organizational culture and the particular characteristics of the human resources. A balance between political and administrative level should exist.* [RA3]

As a next step we wanted to see if aspects the respondents identified as indicative of changing practices are reflected by the discussion and conclusion sections, at the level of linguistic features. Our analysis was guided by the ample in-depth analysis of various linguistic features reported in the EAP literature. The frequency of recurrent lexical patterns in research articles and EAP writing is one such area of analysis. Building on the taxonomy of 'lexical bundles' introduced by Biber et al. (1999), research focuses on, for instance, disciplinary variation (Cortes 2004, Hyland 2008), expertise-bound differences between published articles and student writing (Cortes 2004), genre and register related comparisons and contrasts in a university environment (Biber and Barbieri 2007). Several studies compare L1 and L2 use of frequently occurring word combinations in academic writing, with special reference to Chinese students (Chen and Baker 2010), or to the Swedish academic environment (Ädel and Erman 2012), among others.

Other researchers have taken Hyland's framework for the analysis of metadiscursivity markers (Hyland and Tse 2004, Hyland 2005b) as point of reference for investigating, for instance, the linguistic realization of author stance, comparing the use of hedging items and boosters by Anglo-American and Spanish academics across disciplinary fields – marketing, mechanical engineering and biology (Vázquez and Giner 2008, Vázquez and Giner 2009). Several studies combine qualitative and quantitative analysis to explore the interrelatedness between disciplinary specificity and linguistic choice, such as in the case of pure mathematics, with a special focus on markers of stance and engagement (McGrath and Kuteeva 2012).

Areas focused on in this study include:

- reference to limitations of the research and/or to constraints encountered
- balanced approach to one's own and others' points of view, including comparison, critique of own and other's research
- explicit reference to the research outcomes and the value of the contribution made to the field

- lexical features, such as discipline-specific vocabulary, discourse organizing and referential expressions
- rhetorical means, tentative language for expressing various nuances, author stance, and so on.

For the purpose of our study, we have used the AntConc concordancing software (Anthony 2012) – the automated extraction of recurrent 4-word clusters ('lexical bundles') with the n-gram option of AntConc, as well as the concordancing facility, combined with manual extraction of lexis relevant for the aspects mentioned above.

### 7.6.1 Reference to limitations of the research and/or to constraints encountered

For identifying explicit reference to limitations, we have used the concordancing option, introducing limit* as search item. Here are some examples from the research articles (RA) analysed:

*Another limitation of this study is* [RA12]

*There are limits to research as well* [RA15]

*The analysis is limited to a study of research in universities, without comparisons to other important actors in Romania* [RA15]

*The limitations of the research consist in the selection of the respondents, the lack of argued answers of respondents and, based on this, the weak interpretation of certain issues discussed in this paper.* [RA18]

*The objective evaluation of our scientific approach underlines a series of limitations, explained by being a pioneer in this type of research: the working assumptions have included only few aspects, with simple variables that didn't lead to more complex conclusions, while the dependencies between elements of the external environment, which generate the competitiveness of the organization and internal processes, have been insufficiently studied. However, these represent the main challenges for future studies.* [RA4]

*Another limitation of this study is that it was completed in the lack of comparable preceding research in Romania. The absence of resembling research papers did not allow comparing the findings of this study with similar content-related results.* [RA11]

As can be seen from the examples above, in most cases the authors also indicate the reasons for the limitation or constraint encountered. In addition, there is also implicit reference to limitations, combined with recommendations for further research, as shown in the example below:

> *The research can be further improved by including more indicators in the analysis and by creating more complex real and structural convergence indexes. A particular attention will be paid to the extension of the period of time analysed in order to consolidate the econometric model.* [RA5]

### 7.6.2   More communicative functions

Several other functions have been identified, examples of which are provided below:

i) Balanced approach to one's own and others' points of view, including comparison, critique of own and other's research

> *Nevertheless, caution should be used in the interpretation of these results, as a change in sample size, rolling window, forecast horizon, frequency of observations and other variables could greatly impact the above findings.* [RA6]

> *The procedures employed for the cointegration results offer contradictory results. While (...). At the same time (...) The lack of cointegration indicated by the Engle-Granger procedure may be due to the lower power of the test, as recognized in the literature.* [RA1]

ii) Explicit reference to the research outcomes and the value of the contribution made to the field / Highlighting the relevance and value of the research instrument selected for the analysis

> *The Real-Structural Convergence Matrix is a <u>very important</u> tool which allows <u>us</u> to <u>clearly</u> distinguish the CEE countries progress in the last decade.* [RA5] *(...) there have been identified <u>a series of useful elements</u> for improving the competitiveness of MNAR.* [RA4]

Such examples may be considered to indicate concern for argumentative, critical writing which is more likely to enable researchers to highlight the value of their work and to integrate it more appropriately in the relevant literature, as they say they wish to do.

### 7.6.3   Lexical features: discourse organization and referential expressions, discipline-specific vocabulary

The extraction of raw data with the help of the concordancing facility of AntConc, followed by manual selection of relevant expressions has revealed the existence of a variety of expressions typical of academic vocabulary, performing functions comparable to those in other academic corpora (such as Cortes 2004, Hyland 2005b) (Table 7.2).

*Table 7.2* Subcategories and examples of referential and discourse-organizing lexis in English-medium research articles by Romanian economics researchers

**Category: Referential expressions**

| Sub-category | Lexis | Examples from the corpus analysed |
| --- | --- | --- |
| Framing | *perspective* | from the perspective of, in this perspective, in a wider perspective, at sector or country-level |
| Method related | *estimat\** *(estimate, estimated, estimating, estimation)* [57 occurrences in 10 different texts] | The cointegration test confirms the OLS estimation, which showed that the reaction of the government to changes in public debt is not appropriate as far as the sign of the response is concerned. [RA32] The econometric estimation of the elasticities; Estimates of uncertainty; Estimation uncertainty; The estimated output; Estimation techniques / samples / model |

**Category: Discourse organizing**

| Subcategory | Lexis | Examples from the corpus analysed |
| --- | --- | --- |
| Framing | *considering* | considering that the |
| Framing | *given th\** | Given the current macroeconomic context characterized by a deep economic recession, a healthy and flexible fiscal policy plays an important role in overcoming these difficulties. [RA33] |
| Framing / method-related | *considering* | Considering that the required primary balance works as a fiscal rule, deviations of the current primary balance from the required one are calculated. [RA28] In the case of Bulgaria, considering the different orders of integration of the two variables implied by equation (7), the primary balance (the dependent variable), (...) is regressed on the second difference of public debt (...) [RA32] |
| Framing / method-related | *given th\** | In addition, given the low values of the variables implied by the public debt dynamic equation it was easier for Estonian government to run primary surpluses. [RA23] |
| Method related | *correlation* | the correlation between, negative correlation between, positive correlation between |

In addition, the extraction of 4-word n-grams has helped us identify further examples of 'lexical bundles' with *referential* and *discourse organizing* functions (following the taxonomy of Biber et al. 1999), that we have grouped into subcategories, as illustrated in Table 7.3.

*Table 7.3* Reference and discourse-organizing lexical bundles in English-medium research articles by Romanian economics researchers

**Category: Referential bundles**

| Subcategory | Examples from the research articles (RA) analysed |
| --- | --- |
| Framing | in this paper we..., in the case of, in the context of, in this context the, in accordance with the, in the face of, an indirect relationship between, of the social realm, corresponds to a change |
| Quantifying | a high level of, a greater degree of, for most of the, the rest of the, a decrease of the, an increase of the, annual values of both, surplus or an increase |
|  | *Statistical* |
|  | balance is regressed on, into intervals the annual (values), is regressed on the, leading variables for the, primary balance is estimated, primary balance is regressed |
| Time markers | at the same time, at the end of, after the end of, for the entire period, in the long run, in the short term |
| Place/direction markers | at the centre of, in the opposite direction, in the same direction, in the European Union, in Central and Eastern (Europe), pave the way towards |
| Text reference | in the previous section, are presented in table |
| Descriptive/ methodology related | in the same way, the nature of the, the realm in which, interval analysis we group, be tested in a |
| Subject-specific | a vulnerable fiscal policy, cost of public debt, debt to GDP ratio, deficit and public debt, the overall tax burden, liquidity and/or solvency (risk), of the indebtedness ratio, stock of public debt, the decision making process, of the stock market, public managers and the, to achieve fiscal sustainability |
|  | *Trend/change markers* |
|  | tax burden change of fiscal, change in public debt, change of fiscal revenues, changes in public debt, deviations from the fiscal, level of public debt, of corporate environmental performance, and the economic growth, public rate of growth, the dynamics of public |

**Category: Discourse organizing**

| Subcategory | Examples from the research articles (RA) analysed |
| --- | --- |
| Topic introduction | taking into account, the object under study, the results of the |

*(continued)*

*Table 7.3* Continued

Category: Discourse organizing

| Subcategory | Examples from the research articles (RA) analysed |
| --- | --- |
| Topic elaboration/ clarification | in the sense of, in the sense that, in terms of real, on the one hand, on the other hand, with respect to the, be explained by the |
| Contrast/ comparison | as well as the, as well as in, constant and equal to, more flexible fiscal policy, rate was higher than, the first difference of |
| Inferential | as a result of, as an effect of, from the fact that, on the basis of |
| Causality | causes the overall tax, due to the fact, the result of the, the results of the |
| Purpose | with a view to |

### 7.6.4 Tentative language and author stance

Table 7.4 includes examples of lexis embedded in expressions performing specific functions in the research articles analysed.

Further examples of lexical bundles expressing *author stance* were identified using the 4-word n-gram option of AntConc. As above, they were grouped into subcategories, using the taxonomy of Biber et al. (1999) (Table 7.5).

The findings of our text-based research are comparable, to a certain extent, to those characteristic of other research contexts (Cortes 2004, Vázquez and Giner 2008), especially in terms of discourse organizing and referential bundles. Fully aware that the corpus is too small to arrive at generalizations, we can conclude, however, that the RA sections analysed display generic and lexical features illustrating the preoccupation of Romanian academics of complying with the requirements of academic research writing. Further research therefore will attempt to extend the corpus, so as to have more scope for comparative analysis, both among subfields in the wider economics domain, and between our environment and other L1 contexts using English as a lingua franca for research publication purposes.

## 7.7 Conclusions

The data have shown the complex needs as well as the efforts undertaken by researchers on the semiperiphery in their attempt to become accepted members of the international research community in their

*Table 7.4* Examples of lexis expressing author stance in the discussion and conclusion sections of English-medium research articles by Romanian economics researchers

| Subcategory | Lexis | Examples |
| --- | --- | --- |
| epistemic-impersonal-probable-possible | *likely* | are likely to emerge<br>are also more likely to draw on<br>Nor are they likely to contest that<br>the most likely scenario |
| hedging | *seem* | The situation could seem intriguing in some cases but, at the same time, further studies will tell whether or not aspects related to Business Ethics are included in the topics from other disciplines. [RA21]<br>It can be said that the promotion policy of the museum is not diversified enough and doesn't seem to be a priority for the management of this institution, given that [...] [RA4]<br>First, they all seem to need a large number of data points for robust estimation. [RA6] |
| | *assum\** | Drawing the conclusions from previous literature, it is quite clear that the fiscal policy in EU is confronted with various difficulties and we may assume that fiscal policy is vulnerable and may have an exposure to liquidity and/or solvency risk. [RA28] |
| | *suggest* | All these responses suggest [RA18]<br>Given this context, the results suggest that Irish government run a more flexible fiscal policy and didn't aim in adjusting it to shocks on public debt. [R33] |
| author stance | *believe* | Thus, we tend to believe [RA18]<br>Hence, we believe that studying fiscal sustainability based on fiscal reaction function will provide useful insight regarding how governments' response to shocks on public debt. [RA33] |

*Table 7.5* Examples of stance lexical bundles in the discussion and conclusion sections of English-medium research articles by Romanian economics researchers

| Subcategory | Examples |
| --- | --- |
| Epistemic | the fact that the, from the fact that, be explained by the, can be seen to |
| Obligation/directive | should be able to |
| Ability | to be able to |

own field. The respondents to this study justifiably expect academic institutions to support their efforts by providing training and development opportunities. Indeed, the data presented in this study reveal that international publication seems to be regarded as a joint venture between researchers, reviewers and academic institutions.

We hope that the data reported in this study have shown the overwhelming desire of these semiperipheral researchers to be accepted and recognized internationally, as well as the development of their linguistic abilities. They constantly update their research and writing strategies and make efforts to remain well informed in their respective fields, sometimes spending, as the interview data show, *'several days on obtaining data that other researchers may get access to in minutes.'* (Interview 5)

Participation in the researcher development MA programme at the Bucharest University of Economic studies is one concrete step some respondents have taken, with to date over 100 members of academic staff having graduated from the programme. The classroom activities proposed within the programme aim to highlight the genre specificity of research articles and the choices writers can make in selecting the most appropriate language items to express their intended meanings. By drawing on the participants' considerable experience in their fields and exposure to academic texts, the tutors aim to help the participants construct their own understanding of the conventions of research writing, and by doing so, the tutors as 'literacy brokers' (Lillis and Curry 2006) develop professionally themselves.

The participants in this study tend to have a rather pragmatic attitude towards their own progress as members of the international academic community. The role of English as a gate to international participation seems to be accepted, and most respondents prefer to build on this reality rather than contest it for ideological reasons. Although they do voice their frustration at the inability to express complex thinking with limited language resources, the participants in this study tend to reflect on what they can do themselves in order to alleviate existing circumstances rather than to contest those circumstances and expect them to change. We would argue that such an attitude may turn out to be far-reaching in terms of its practical effects. In line with recent reflections on the nature of foreign and second language writing, the data presented in this study have shown that 'writing involves more than words', to include diverse social, semiotic and ecological resources (Canagarajah 2013, p. 440). The implications, therefore, involve consideration of how best to address the complex needs of researchers and of developing appropriate institutional frameworks that foster and support professional development.

# 8
# Looking Back from the Centre: Experiences of Italian Humanities Scholars Living and Writing Abroad

*Raffaella Negretti*

## 8.1  Introduction

It seems bizarre to characterize as semiperipheral the homeland of Dante, Michelangelo and Leonardo da Vinci. Throughout the centuries Italy has enriched the world's culture in all areas of thought and human knowledge, and the Italian language, culture and way of life now more than ever seem to exert an international fascination with a recognized – if rather stereotyped – identity worldwide. However, Italian culture has also been known for its complexity and contradictions, and as Pirandello in *L'Umorismo* well realized, it is through these paradoxes that the real nature of things is revealed. Realities, thoughts and lives tend to open themselves to a plurality of interpretations, and Italy is the place where opposites coexist. This may be said also for the situation of Italian academia, caught in a web of contradictions and multi-layered influences, and for the experiences of Italian academics – especially humanities scholars – whose lives are emblematic of the need to juggle contrasts and reconcile seemingly irreconcilable phenomena.

Many characteristics of the Italian university system suggest the type of paradoxes often encountered in the 'semiperipheral' countries in their struggle to adapt themselves to the practices of centre-oriented culture (Gizycki 1973, Bennett, Introduction to this volume). Many economic and bureaucratic aspects, in particular, could be considered almost peripheral (Canagarajah 2002). However, at the same time, Italian cultural practices resist categorization into a periphery/centre dichotomy, first of all because the notion that the centre is by definition Anglophone is already an ideological assumption, and secondly because Italian traditions of thought and expression have matured a strong identity and prestige over the course of many centuries.

In recent years, and especially since the start of the Bologna process, Italian universities have been increasingly pushed to embrace the academic practices and culture of the centre, in terms of both mobility and attitudes to research (Aittola et al. 2009), in an attempt to rejuvenate an obsolete organism slowly causing its own demise. The Italian academic system is a system in transition, both practically and culturally, and it is therefore interesting to investigate if these changes also entail relinquishing traditional discourses and practices in favour of a superficial and somewhat problematic integration of practices and discourses from the centre.

Although many articles have been written about the Italian brain drain, both in the general press and in academic journals, most of the research has focused on macro-level economic models explaining the migration patterns primarily of academics in the 'hard sciences' and medicine. This emphasis cannot explain much about ongoing cultural changes. A few studies have focused on the individual experiences of Italian academics, either in Italy (Aittola et al. 2009) or abroad (Morano Foadi 2006, Monteleone and Torrisi 2012), but none have investigated the experiences of humanities scholars, whose academic discourse is culturally and epistemologically rooted in non-Anglophone traditions (McNally 1969). In terms of discourse, this different rhetorical tradition is evidenced by contrastive studies of Italian/English academic writing (Giannoni 2008, Molino 2010, Vergaro 2011) and in patterns of change in Italian argumentation (Manuti et al. 2006). On a general level, the aim of this chapter is therefore to throw some light on the current situation in Italian academia, and the influences (Anglocentric?) that underlie possible changes in Italian cultural traditions of academic thought and rhetoric. More specifically, this chapter aims to shed light on potential changes in the discourse practices and experiences of Italian humanities scholars living and writing abroad. Do they face conflictual and contradictory experiences in writing in English and Italian? If so, how do they negotiate the need to bridge different writing and cultural practices? Through the personal accounts of Italian academics who live and work outside the country, the aim is to give voice to those who experience at first hand the need to mediate between the ideological centre, embodied by Anglo-derived academic discursive practices, and an ancient and fascinatingly complex cultural tradition.

## 8.2   Italy as semiperiphery?

Italian academia has several characteristics that place it into a typical semiperipheral position. Since the post-war period, many of these characteristics have led to a phenomenon described by the Italian press and by many scientific journals as a 'brain drain'. The phenomenon has been investigated primarily in the fields of science and technology, but many of the reasons outlined as the cause of this phenomenon apply to the Italian university system in general. First, Italian policies and resources fail to attract scholars from foreign countries and do not offer many opportunities to enable those who have moved abroad to return (Morano Foadi 2006). Although Wallerstein (1984) considered economic status as one of the characteristics of the semiperiphery, Italy is a curious case in this sense: despite recent signs of crisis, Italy has still one of the largest economies in Europe, and it is among the most industrialized countries in the world. Why, then, is Italy still affected by the brain drain, stagnant academic mobility and lack of international appeal so typical of semiperipheral countries (Nunes and Gonçalves 2001)? The answer is to be found in the economic and bureaucratic nature of the Italian *university*, which fits the description of the *periphery* advanced by Canagarajah (2002): limited material resources, a resistance to innovation, recruitment and career systems based on fiefdoms rather than meritocracy, and traditional knowledge practices different from those imported from the centre.

There is no doubt that the Italian university has been facing a decades-long decline, and that it is unable to offer meaningful opportunities for employment and growth to its graduates and researchers. In a famous study of the economic consequences of the emigration of talented youth, Becker et al. (2004) showed that, as early as the 1990s, emigration of Italian college graduates increased at staggering levels and that – contrary to other major European economies – this phenomenon was one of no return: brain drain rather than brain exchange. Focusing on the personal experiences of expatriate Italian scientists, Morano Foadi (2006) suggested that among the causes was a lack of material resources, not just in terms of sheer investment in research – 'the University of California alone invests more in research than the whole science market in Italy' (p. 214) – but also in the lack of work opportunities. The 'brain drain', or 'fuga di cervelli', in Italy poses dire economic consequences, and despite an increasing awareness of a phenomenon that is by no means moribund, the actual research on it 'is still scanty' (Piras 2013, p. 143). Yet anecdotal evidence of this massive 'escape of brains' abounds, with newspapers reporting stories of Italian academics finding fortune abroad. Indeed, it has become such a trope in Italian popular culture that countless comic strips ('the best brains are escaping' – 'the ones that are left are doing politics'), TV debates, books, fiction and even a successful movie have been released on the topic.

Unfortunately, Italian academics moving abroad are seldom willing or able to return home (Monteleone and Torrisi 2012). Re-entry is hindered by the lack of transparency, alleged nepotism and overall politicization of power within Italian universities (Abbott 2001, Battiston 2002), which do not offer a nurturing climate for young talents, especially women. A recent report by the Italian Ministry of Instruction, University and Research (MIUR 2009) underscored the considerable age of the Italian teaching body: only 0.4 per cent of the tenured faculty is under 29 years of age, with the bulk of the tenured professors – 78.8 per cent – over 60 years of age. The same report indicates that women make up only one-third of Italian teaching staff, and their presence decreases markedly along the career pathway: they do not even constitute a fifth of the full professors (18.8 per cent). It has been well documented how women, despite graduating in greater numbers and with higher grades than their male colleagues, face even greater challenges when it comes to pursuing an academic career, due to 'stereotypes, segregation practices and gender discriminations' (Frattini and Rossi 2012): the Italian university system seems thus to be a 'country for old men'.

Not only do young scholars face scarce career options, they must also being part of a system that is not ruled by the principles of meritocracy. Almost all the scientists interviewed by Morano Foadi (2006), for instance, referred to the existence of an unofficial 'law' which privileged not the better qualified, but those who had better connections and were willing to adhere to existing power structures. The grim reality of Italian research, where highly-skilled individuals are either jobless or forced into 'precariato' (temporary contracts, usually with conditions bordering exploitation), is extensively documented in the personal stories described in the number of newspaper and journalistic reports on the topic. In journalist Sergio Nava's book *Fuga di Talenti* (2009), describing the experiences of Italian expatriates, Cristina, a philosophy graduate from a prestigious private university in Milan, talks about the post-laurea limbo where 'you live in a condition of unpaid collaboration with your professor, waiting for him [sic] to fix you up'. This situation is not only harmful for the individual, but for the research projects as well, which suffer from the lack of continuity and constant change of hands.

The Bologna agreement,[1] with its focus on a knowledge-based economy (Fairclough and Wodak 2008), spurred the Italian government to introduce several changes aimed at modernizing the Italian academic system, though this was not always unproblematic. Several policies and practices were implemented top-down, to support mobility and internationalization in both teaching and research (Aittola et al. 2009); these include new laws promulgated by the Italian parliament in 2009, which explicitly linked career advancement and funding to 'internationally acknowledged parameters' and 'indicators reflecting quality of scientific research' (MIUR, see Gazzola 2012, pp. 139–140). This pull towards the centre has been manifested in an attempt to adopt the academic practices of countries typically viewed by the Italian public and scientists as achieving 'excellence': traditionally the United States and more recently also the UK, Germany and France. This change has been often accompanied by heavy criticism of the Italian academic system and a negative perception of Italy's reputation in academic and scientific domains (Morano Foadi 2006).

Since Bologna, Italy seems to be moving towards more centre-oriented practices, such as international publication, teaching and studying networks, and new mobility policies. However, at times, the espousal of centre practices at the institutional level has created conflictual dynamics in the nature of individuals' academic work. Although most of the academics interviewed by Aittola et al. (2009) demonstrated a positive attitude toward the need to publish internationally in English, many also stressed a sense of unease at the disappearance of the old traditions, especially in relation to culturally rooted epistemologies and ways of delivering knowledge: 'the traditional idea of free and autonomous university teaching jointly with free-of-charge studying is challenged by the reforms' (p. 307). The loss of traditional ways of interpreting, delivering and imparting knowledge in Italian universities is thus experienced with mixed feelings at the individual level, and aspects of Anglophonic academic culture such as competitiveness, internationalization and academic discourse seem to have created a struggle similar to that described by Belcher (2007) for off-network non-native-English-speaking (NNES) scholars attempting to publish in English, who are forced to reposition their work in a way that is consistent with Anglophone discourse and traditions.

The issues inherent in the adoption of evaluation practices incentivizing the use of English for scientific publication are summarized critically by Gazzola (2012), who pinpoints how the use of bibliometric indicators and journal impact factors (JIFs) to evaluate quality are de facto fostering a language bias, creating a somewhat inaccurate and uncritical perception of what 'internationalization' really means. As for the need to publish in English, the creation of programmes taught exclusively in English (PTEs) also seems to be a top-down process, which institutional and governmental agents have promoted in an effort towards 'internationalization', but which has led to policies and realities favouring Anglophone institutions. This raises questions of fairness in scientific communication: 'drawbacks are usually not sufficiently and critically characterized in Italy, and the advantages are sometimes assumed rather than proved' (Gazzola 2012, p. 150). This may explain why even in technical fields there is still a strong resistance towards the use of English for teaching and research: as late as 2013, faculty at a major Italian technical university petitioned against the requirement of providing English-only learning opportunities (Angelini 2013). These dilemmas are possibly perceived even more strongly by humanities and social science scholars, whose disciplinary discourses are embedded in strong cultural and philosophical traditions (De Swaan 2001). An attention to individual experiences can shed light on how traditional Italian ways of constructing and disseminating knowledge are changing.

## 8.3   Italian academic discourse

Few studies have investigated Italian scholarly discourse, especially in contrast to English. In relation to medical discourse, Giannoni (2008) suggests that the adoption of English has hybridized local written and spoken practices, especially with regards to opening/closing strategies and first-person markers. Differences in the use of personal authorial reference are also identified by Molino (2010), who compared the expression of authorial objectivity in English and Italian linguistics articles, stressing that a divergent use of impersonal and first-person verbs in argumentation may be a strong indicator of cultural identity and of different knowledge-construction practices in academic written discourse. The most significant differences seem tied to aspects of rhetoric rather than language: 'the use of English and Italian corpora seem not to differ so much in the choice of interpersonal strategy as in the type and frequency of retrospective metadiscourse acts being made, which has an impact on the overall incidence of use of authorial references' (p. 97). In another study of discourse, Vergaro (2011) points to the fact that Italian students of English also privilege impersonal discursive strategies as a rhetorical device to express authorial stance. At the same time, a study of Italian academic discourse in non-published communicative genres (Manuti et al. 2006) suggest that Italian 'academese' is gradually incorporating a 'meta-discursive rhetoric of credibility' driven by the influence of economic (and Anglo-based) models of the university as 'industry, firm, market of knowledge', pushed by the institutional efforts to reorganize the Italian university as more efficient and competitive (p. 122). It seems thus that the main issue for Italian academics is not the language itself, but rather the need to find different ways to rhetorically frame their ideas and achieve 'clarity'. Historically, these differences are rooted in philosophical divergences dating back to Renaissance humanism and 'the views of the Italian humanities scholars on the relationship between logic and rhetoric, views which differ markedly from those subsequently advanced in Northern Europe' (McNally 1969, p. 169).

Although rhetorical and discursive differences exist, there is no evidence suggesting that Italian academics are uncritically espousing discursive practices deriving from the Anglophonic scientific centre, nor that their publishing and career advancement opportunities at the international level may be hampered by being NNES authors. Despite explicit guidelines for research evaluation requiring a publication record in English (MIUR 2003), for scholars in the humanities publishing in English may still be a somewhat limited requirement, and often occurs as a parallel activity to disseminate already established work published in Italian fora: only 25 per cent of the publications submitted to the Committee for the Evaluation of Research in 2001–2003 by the humanities was in English (Gazzola 2012). Many Italian humanities scholars – art historians, literary scholars, philosophers, musicologists, semioticians (e.g. Umberto Eco) – produce internationally known work that is primarily published in Italian and that is uniquely imbued with Italian traditions of thought.

Yet again, Italy seems to embody a paradox, contradictorily merging the need to meet European and international academic practices with a strong humanist identity that defies linguistic imperialism. Possibly, as Vergaro (2011) points out, the notion of 'intercultural rhetoric' is better suited to capture the complex interaction of conventions, culture, language and genres in the construction of authorial identity by Italian academics. Rather than contrasting different rhetorical traditions, it is thus more significant to understand the social reality and the personal experiences of those who create the texts (Connor 2008). It is at the individual level that this paradox finds its life, and the following personal experiences may shed light on what it means, for Italian humanities scholars living abroad, to write and publish in English.

## 8.4 Methodology

The exploratory study presented here aims to illustrate some of the complexities described above through the experiences of three Italian humanities scholars currently living in Sweden (but with scholarly experience in English-speaking countries). The method adopted was in-depth qualitative interviews, varying in length from an hour to an hour and a half (Miller and Glassner 1997), following a semi-structured, active and almost conversational approach to interviewing (Holstein and Gubrium 1997) around a set of themes such as their personal (academic) history, their views on the Italian university and their experiences with publishing in English. Although this approach can only aim to illustrate a personal, mediated view of the social world, it has been widely acknowledged as valuable to 'provide access to the meanings people attribute to their experiences of the social world' (p. 113). The interview data was analysed using a thematic approach (Miles and Huberman 1994), which allowed common themes to be foregrounded across the three participants without sacrificing the description of their individual stories. To verify interpretative accuracy and reduce the potential bias of the researcher's perspective (Miller and Glassner 1997), the interpretative recount was submitted to each participant for approval and revision. Overall, the voices represented below[2] depict a variegated reality that challenges schematization.

## 8.5 Results

### 8.5.1 The literary/film scholar: Tarcisio

Tarcisio is a true humanist, deeply engaged in the dissemination of the Italian culture and language. An expert in Italian literature and cinema with a PhD in comparative literature, he teaches university courses as an adjunct lecturer in Sweden, and regularly publishes and gives talks in collaboration with the local Institute for Italian Culture. Like many other Italian academics,[3] Tarcisio left the country because of the lack of positions and funds, and obtained a temporary post abroad partly financed by the Italian Ministry of Culture. However, like many academics worldwide not groomed through the Anglo-American academic career system and thus with an extensive record of publications in English, Tarcisio's experience mismatches the requirements for a permanent post, which are also increasingly modelled after Anglo-American examples. His research, focused on the intersection between literature and cinema, has been summarized in a monograph (in Italian) and several other publications in Italian and international collections

Tarcisio's account of leaving Italy to pursue an academic career abroad highlights both advantages and challenges. He stresses how leaving Italy has made it easier to participate in international events, such as conferences and symposia, and has provided him with more opportunities for meeting scholars worldwide, to be part of a network. At the same time, the move has forced him to relinquish contacts in Italy, a situation he describes as 'just like "Risiko"[4]: you conquer some ground and lose some other piece of land'.

His view of the Italian university is that is 'suffocated' by restructuring problems tied to its effort to open up to the international scene. For instance, the idea of promoting 'centres of excellence' has again played in the hands of those who already have power and thus attract funding, suffocating emergent talents. Although he recognizes the value of Italian universities offering courses in English, he also points out that this is the opposite approach to that adopted by universities in the Anglophone world: rather than the students having to learn the language of instruction, it is the institution that adapts to meet the needs of the international students.

About the need to publish in English, Tarcisio points to the fact that at the international level his opportunities to obtain a permanent post have been limited by the fact that most of his academic work has been published in Italian, and thus has not 'counted': 'this work is second-rate for those who take the decisions when it comes to academic qualifications'. Although he recognizes the value of publishing in English, he sees the need to balance it with publication in other languages, because publication in English 'impoverishes the language' and is furthermore creating a culture that 'penalizes publications in other languages, which are considered less academically valuable'. Referring to the experiences of Italian colleagues close to him, he says that there are institutional (and financial) incentives to publish in English, an ideology of marketing in which research is valuable only if it is marketable at an international level in a PRI (Progetto di Ricerca Internazionale – International Research Project). Furthermore, he stresses 'a misalignment between the traditional humanistic education offered by Italian universities, and the actual requirements one needs to fulfil to continue along an academic career'. Like him, many thus seek employment abroad – the well-known phenomenon of the 'brain drain'. About these 'brains that escape', Tarcisio notes that it is mostly the scientific brains that seem to receive attention: 'the "other brains", such as those of humanities scholars, have limited opportunities in findings universities abroad with traditions of study in their specific areas of interest'.

Tarcisio also lucidly summarizes the conflicts inherent in writing English academic discourse (EAD) and the need to reformulate one's thought and ideas in a different way: 'what you write is a different thing. It is not just the language, it is the whole text that needs to be structured differently, to meet a different tradition'. Tarcisio mentions that, whereas in Italian we have a tradition of 'digressive richness', in the Anglophonic culture there is pressure for 'compactness', for 'bringing up and hammering in the main idea repeatedly and as clearly and transparently as possible'. This feature of EAD stems from a strong rhetorical tradition of persuasion, whereas 'in Italian the need to persuade the audience is not as strong, but rather Italian texts are aimed at offering a plurality of points of view, and open up vistas of interpretation'. This different approach that forces the writer to 'stay on track' is also – according to Tarcisio – a bit frightening because it creates the habit for mental rigidity and limits the writer's ability to flexibly combine and connect different pools of ideas and thoughts.

To offer an example of how discursive practices exemplify different epistemological grounds, he mentions an article he recently published in an international collection. It is already telling that the article, despite being about an Italian author, had to be written in English because Italian was not one of the permitted languages. Tarcisio mentions that when writing in Italian, he is not used to 'list' the critical references in the introduction to an essay: the object of the inquiry, the central idea, is explored and presented in a multifaceted way, through different paragraphs, and connections to critical key theories are made progressively as the idea is developed. A common criticism among the reviewers of the article was that it needed more explicitness and clarity about which and how literary criticism references were used. However, when Tarcisio requested the opinion of an Italian colleague on the revised version, she commented that his introduction was 'inelegant and a bit simplistic: by listing the critical references in this way he seemed to be trying too hard and almost sounded like a student'. This comment suggests that rhetorical differences not only represent different ways of constructing knowledge, but also convey different values in terms of how mature intellectual thought is manifested in a text and on how a writer's ethos is constructed. The evidence-based, clarity-oriented tradition of positivistic thought embodied in EAD rhetorical practices results in discursive features that in the Italian tradition may come across as simplistic, amateur and awkward. Tarcisio also suggests that these issues are stronger for those who write within the humanities, because those who publish in the 'hard sciences' face fewer problems as regards the epistemological imprint that the text needs to have.

### 8.5.2   The architect: Agnese

The experiences of Agnese and Michela present some affinities in regards to publishing in English: both are established scholars with several publications in major international journals.

Agnese is an established architect with an extensive academic record, who works both in Italy and abroad, and who still teaches for a technical university in Milan. After her degree in architecture in Italy, she moved first to Norway, Sweden and Finland, and then to the United States, where she acquired a master of science in environmental architecture at the prestigious MIT and learned the basis of the scientific discourse in English. However, her approach to architecture is imbued with humanist sensibility, and much of her work on the perception of human space is historically rooted in classical studies and phenomenological thought.

After years of scholarly work in English, Agnese considers it as her main language both in her teaching and in her publication. She mentions that her first attempts at publishing in English were more 'courageous', and she admits to having become more demanding in this respect over the years. About writing in English, Agnese stresses the need to write 'with the right formulation' to obtain quality, not just transposing ideas and expression from one language to the other. Twice she mentions how disturbing it is that a 'badly written' text opens itself for misinterpretation, and that problems of language and correctness 'distract' the reader from the content. Interestingly, as a result of her international experience, she also acknowledges the differences between Italian and English academic written discourse tied to different pedagogical cultures:

> in Italian, we often make connections to the history of a phenomenon and the etymology of a word, and try to tie it to philosophical or literary themes, to classical antiquity. They [Anglophones] are not so concerned with the origins of a language, which in Italy we acquire through many years of study of Latin and Greek, besides Italian, in our schools.

About the Italian university's attempt to internationalize, she is aware of many efforts to offer courses completely in English in order to attract students from abroad. However, she also stresses the poor proficiency of Italian students and teachers in regards to academic English, and the need to overcome prejudices and a 'timid' attitude, as this may still cramp the possibilities for Italian doctoral students, researchers and scholars to create international networks. She says that we Italians are too 'self-critical', and compared to Scandinavian students (who experience English every day, through television, films in original language and lectures in English, and therefore are more likely to 'dive' into it), Italian students are more 'ashamed' of their English. She also points to a generational gap: many of those who are now professors in Italian universities are not likely to know English, whereas the younger generations are much more proficient. The problem is that few of these younger, talented academics stay in Italy and become professors themselves. Yet, she also recognizes the recent drive on the part of Italian universities to adopt internationally 'marketable' models in which English covers a purely utilitarian role: 'the Italian university now wants to 'become more international by offering courses in English to support learning and stimulate proficiency in English to Italian students as well as to attract international students through specialized masters, and this has created the need for faculty who is fluent in English.'

### 8.5.3  The linguist: Michela

Michela is a successful computational linguist who obtained her PhD in the UK, and who has an impressive record of participation in internationally funded projects with an extensive publication record in English. Given her empiricist orientation, she has always published and operated primarily in English, and considers this use of language for scientific communication as unproblematic. Yet, like her colleagues, the beginning of Michela's academic career coincided with her departure from Italy: she says that her 'academic life really only began in 2002, after leaving Italy for her PhD'. Only then did Michela acquire visibility at the international level, with publications and opportunities to participate to international projects. Her country of reference is Britain, and she has no ties to any Italian university.

With regards to academic writing, Michela admits that

she cannot write about scientific subjects in Italian. I learned to write according to the [English] way of writing. If you write a paper in a way that does not correspond to the informational packaging that they[5] want, they will reject it. There is a well-established way of structuring a paper, and if you do not respect it your paper will be rejected.

As someone interested in textual analysis, she recognizes the fact that a text is an expression of what she call 'forma mentis': 'when I read an article in English written by an Italian, or a French academic, it is very evident that there is a different way of thinking behind. It goes beyond grammar and lexicon'. She also recognizes that EAD in her field is

> very structured and revolves around giving the readers exactly what they want. I know what I have to say and what my readers expect. This way of writing by focusing on what is new and evidencing it is very much an Anglo-Saxon tradition, and I see that in Romance countries there is a completely different way of formulating arguments.

She is also very aware of the issue of fairness in scientific communication (see Gazzola 2012) posed by the fact that only the publications in English seem to count, something also mentioned by Tarcisio. She says that 'when I make references to other work, I cannot include work written in Italian or French, because it has no value. We need to make an active effort to publish in other languages than just English'. At the same time, she points to new trends in her field where despite the fact that the most 'established research is published in the traditional genres, there are many fora that are increasingly open to alternative formulations and even in important conferences you can present experimental ideas, and you can play around with the argumentation'. About humanities scholars and Italian academics working in Italy, however, she also stresses that most professors do not use or speak in English and that for humanities scholars – such as those involved in the study of the history of Italian language – there may not be a need to publish in English.

## 8.6   Concluding remarks

The fact that discourse and language are symbolic vehicles to consolidate social realities and ideologies has been recognized by Bourdieu (1991), among others, and some of these dynamics seem to find embodiment in the experiences of Tarcisio, Michela and Agnese. Encounters between differing cultural norms are never neutral, and as critical discourse analysis has often underlined, discourse not only reflects reality, it also creates it: 'it constitutes situations, objects of knowledge, and the social identities and relationships between people and groups of people' (Fairclough and Wodak 1997, p. 258). Writing in English is therefore not simply a utilitarian choice; it creates a social and professional identity for the writer, opening or closing avenues to academic advancement and recognition. These conflictual dynamics are echoed in the words of Tarcisio, whose experience underscores the fact that publications in Italian are 'valued less' and have less 'market value' in the eyes of international gatekeepers (see also Curry and Lillis 2004). Also, the words of Tarcisio and Michela seem to confirm that the need to publish in English entails epistemological changes of thought and authorial persona (Belcher 2007, Bennett 2010b). Yet, if the espousal of centre rhetoric derived from EAD practices and a knowledge-based economy may be becoming more familiar to Italian humanities scholars, there is definitely not an uncritical acceptance of these models, quite the contrary. These academics seem to have quite a refined metacognitive awareness of the genre and how to adapt it to the specific conditions of the various publications they address (see Negretti 2012, Negretti and Kuteeva 2011). Tarcisio's words denote an awareness of the epistemological differences embodied in discourse, and his critique shows a deep understanding of the dilemmas posed by the need to encase ideas into English academic discourse, dominated by the need for explicitness and persuasiveness.

The cases of Michela and Agnese seem to confirm that epistemological misalignment may be more problematic in the humanities than in areas of research that are nearer to Anglophonic models for scientific writing. Agnese, the architect with an interest in philosophy, admitted to using a more digressive, more 'erudite' way of writing that is typical of Italian discursive ethos and aimed at establishing expertise through breadth of knowledge rather than specialist competence – a tie to 'classical antiquity' rooted in the vision of the Italian humanist thought: 'we are more anchored to history and the evolution of human experiences, from antiquity to now'. Michela, despite her complete adherence to EAD in her work, is also very aware of a different way of thinking deriving from different traditions, and says that 'it is important to be able to preserve and cultivate also one's national language. Maybe everyone should write in their own language and then we could translate to English later. I wish I could write about my research in Italian'. Both cases point to the paradox experienced by Italian humanities scholars, raised in a tradition but faced with the need to adopt another in order to have opportunities abroad.

These experiences also suggest the need to go beyond characterization of the spread of EAD as inherently positive or negative, and to focus instead on what is changing and how to bring about change in academic cultures. The fact that discursive practices typically adopted by certain (Anglo-centric) cultures are now adopted almost as a rhetorical lingua franca by academics of different backgrounds also entails that more scholars of different cultures move around and achieve academic recognition, and may likely introduce variation in the genre itself as cultures intermingle and penetrate each other (Matsuda and Atkinson 2008). As Michela points out, 'I don't agree that writing according to those [EAD] structures means also a standardization of thought. You can express many interesting new arguments even if you use those formulations'. An intercultural perspective on rhetoric, highlighting connections and change rather than differences, may be a fruitful avenue for investigation (Vergaro 2011).

Texts can also serve as catalysts of change within discourses and genres, as some authors (for example, Kohnen 2001, Lillis 1997) have already pointed out. As Italian academic brains continue to escape toward international shores, the Italian style of academic discourse, with its centuries-old tradition of humanist rhetoric stemming from a 'less scientific, more humane culture and pedagogy of classical civilization' (McNally 1969, p. 168), may paradoxically become a worldwide source of renovation, the 'principal means by which academic members create a [new] coherent social reality that frames the sense of what they do' (Manuti et al. 2006, p. 106). In the current climate, such mutual cross-fertilization could only be a good thing.

## Notes

1. The 'Bologna agreement' refers to the declaration signed in Bologna in 1999 by Ministers of Higher Education in many European countries. It is often said to have triggered a process of renovation operated through a series of directives and policies at the European and the national level, which encouraged a knowledge-based economy in Europe (Fairclough and Wodak 2008).
2. The interviews were all carried out in Italian and have been translated into English by the author (the translated report has been reviewed and approved by the interviewee). The participants' names are fictitious.
3. See the experiences reported in Nava (2009).
4. The Italian name for the famous board game 'Risk'®.
5. It was unclear who exactly the referents were, but from the content of the conversation it is safe to infer that 'they' refers to the editors, peer-reviewers, and fellow academics involved in the dissemination of international scientific publications (in English).

# Part III
# Publication Practices

# 9

# Turkish Academic Culture in Transition: Centre-Based State Policies and Semiperipheral Practices of Research, Publishing and Promotion

*Hacer Hande Uysal*

## 9.1 Introduction

For geopolitical, cultural and economic reasons, Turkish academia is an excellent example of the kind of semiperipheral culture that forms the subject of this book. While Turkey has always turned its face more towards Europe than Asia, due to its unique history and geopolitical location it is still caught in the conflicts between West and East, past and future, modernization and nationalism (Akarsu 2000, Kinzer 2001). Its academia is currently in transition, moving rapidly towards the centre in terms of state policy, while still preserving more peripheral characteristics at the institutional and personal levels. Therefore, this chapter focuses upon the tension that exists between the centre-oriented state policies, on the one hand, and institutional and personal practices of research, scholarly publishing and promotion on the other.

The chapter begins with a historical description of Turkish state policies on scientific research and publication, which makes publication in high-impact international journals a mandatory requirement for academic promotion. It then goes on to describe a field study conducted in two major Turkish universities (one Turkish-medium and one English-medium) to gauge the relationship between state policy, institutional implementation and scholars' actual publishing behaviour. This was done by means of a survey distributed to 115 scholars, supplemented with interviews with academics about the institutional and personal attitudes towards research and publishing, and their publishing and promotion experiences. The results reveal conflicts between the centre-oriented state policies and the traditional Turkish academic culture, which prioritizes personal or political connections and seniority over publication for the purpose of institutional promotion and power-related decision taking. This discrepancy was particularly evident in the Turkish-medium university, though considerable variations were also found in publishing behaviour and attitudes in both universities in accordance with discipline (social sciences vs. hard sciences), age and educational background (locally educated vs. Western-educated scholars).

## 9.2   Turkish state policies in scientific research and publishing

### 9.2.1   The peripheral phase: struggles for independence and industrialization (1923–1980)

The Turkish Republic was founded as a democratic nation-state in 1923 after the collapse of the Ottoman Empire. It inherited a severely damaged economy that had failed to industrialize, lost income sources with the changes in trade routes and become financially dependent on Western foreign powers (Hanioglu 2008, Kent 1996, Shaw and Shaw 1977); and World War I and the Independence War had put additional strains on the already financially bankrupt state (Coskun 2003). As a consequence, at its earlier phases, the Republic was in a terrible condition in terms of its economy, human resources, education and literacy rate (only 6 per cent), making Turkey 'the first peripheral area to become an independent nation state after a long history of capitalist penetration' (Keyder 2009, p. 3).

Therefore, in the 1930s priority was given to industrial development and building the basic infrastructure of the country, as well as to a series of radical social reforms in the areas of language and education to Westernize and modernize the country (Erichsen 1998, Ucuzsatar 2002). One important characteristic is that Turkey has always turned its face towards the West more than to the East. Under Ataturk's[1] leadership, it adopted the principles of Western civilization and started a 'Westward March' (Khosla 2001, p. 347) joining the United Nations in 1945, Council of Europe in 1949, NATO in 1952, OECD (Organization for Economic Cooperation and Development) in 1961 and OSCE (Organization for Security and Cooperation in Europe) in 1975, and applying for European Economic Community membership in 1959 (Erickson 2006, Eurydice 2010).

However, despite the country's desire to westernize, industrialize and integrate into the expanding world market, an important prerequisite was neglected, for although effective development in science, technology and innovation is a critical condition for industrialization, these were all delayed (Goker 2004). Technology was simply imported from the developed countries, which meant that there was no demand from industry for research (Kiper 2004). This, coupled with the Turkish academic culture, which was based on acquiring and transmitting existing knowledge instead of producing new knowledge, led to serious delays in understanding the importance of conducting and disseminating scientific research for economic and technological development (Cooper 1971 cited in Goker 2004).

Nonetheless, in the 1960s some governmental attempts were initiated in terms of research and scientific development through two institutions: the State Planning Organization (Devlet Planlama Teşkilatı-DPT), which was established in 1960 to target economic, social and cultural development (DPT 2006a, b), and the Turkish Scientific and Technological Research Council (TUBİTAK), set up in 1963 to promote and develop theoretical and applied research particularly in the natural sciences within the first five-year development programme (1963–1967) (TUBİTAK 2012). In 1964, a Scientific Policy Unit was also established within TUBITAK to take responsible for policy making in the field of scientific and technological research and advancements. This later became the Institute of Science and Technology (STHI) in 1983 (Al 2008).

### 9.2.2 Transition to a semiperipheral stage: awakening to the demands of the information age for scientific research and publication (1980–1990s)

As Turkey missed its chance to be a part of European industrialization, the 1980s was characterized by the country's struggles to simultaneously industrialize and meet the global pressures of the new information age. Influenced by the rapid pace of the scientific and technological advances shaping the world, Turkey launched some attempts at scientific research and technological improvement. For example, in 1983 the Institute for Science and Technology (STHI) published a report that established the country's long-term scientific and technological policies, specifying the most important areas of research and development, laying out plans and programmes and identifying the necessary human resources. Research responsibilities were also distributed to related institutions, and regulations and legal documents were prepared (Al 2008, Goker 2004). However, although this was a critical period for adapting to the needs of the new information age, the non-functional status of the STHI, and the political and social instabilities in the country, meant that this policy could not be implemented until 1993 (Erickson 2006, Goker 2004).

As for the universities, which were responsible for most of the research and publishing activity, an important development took place in the early eighties. With the Higher Education Law No. 2547 of 1981 and the complementary Higher Education Institutions Structure Law No. 2809 of 1983, all Turkish higher education institutions were centralized and restructured under the supervision of the Higher Education Council (HEC) and its subunit, the Inter-University Council (IUC). With this, the principles of the Anglo-American university system were adopted, highlighting the importance of research and publishing, and giving rise to a new understanding within the long-established teaching-oriented Turkish university culture (Ak and Gülmez 2006, Ardınç 2007). Now, international publications were given importance alongside national ones (Ardınç 2007).

### 9.2.3 Adoption of centre-oriented approaches to research and publication through macro-level state policies (1990s–present)

The economic situation started to improve in this period, as the Turkish economy moved from a closed-market system toward a free-market one (Erickson 2006). The country steadily developed, becoming the 16th largest economy in the world in 2012 and the 6th largest among EU countries, with an annual real growth of 5.2 per cent (IMF 2012). This continuous growth naturally brought pressures for technical and scientific competition. After a ten-year delay in the implementation of the science and technology policies, a more detailed policy document (the Turkish Science and Technology Report of 1993–2003) was published by TUBITAK in the second STHI meeting in 1993. The main aim of this new policy document was to catch up with the developed countries in terms of science and technology (Goker 2004). This report was noteworthy because, for the first time, matters regarding scientific publishing were also included in a policy document.

More specifically, the 1993–2003 report identified a number of problems with research and publishing (such as low research output, overworked and underpaid academics, limited library resources and poor access to scientific journals), and established a series of important goals, considered to represent the minimum global indicators of a country's scientific development. These included increasing the proportion of researchers from 7 to 15 per 10,000 people, expanding the research and development budget from 0.33 per cent to 1 per cent, and boosting Turkey's world ranking in international publications from 40th to 30th place (TUBITAK 1993).

Although the first two goals have not yet been achieved, there has been a surprising increase in the number of international publications over the years, well in excess of the desired objectives. State policies encouraging publication in prestigious international journals were probably the major factors behind this increase. For example, in 1993, TUBITAK started an economic incentive programme supporting only international publications (Arıoğlu and Girgin 2002), which was followed by initiatives from individual universities offering financial incentives and rewards for international publications. Moreover, Turkey's participation in the Bologna Reform Process, in 1999, forced it to integrate with global academia by bringing its higher education system into line with European standards (HEC 2010), resulting in the development of new standards for academic promotion, research and publishing. For the first time, centralized criteria for academic promotion were established by the Inter-University Council (IUC, 2000), making proficiency in a foreign language (generally English) and publications in ISI-indexed journals mandatory requirements for associate professorship in most fields. International publications were now attributed twice the value of national publications in these promotion criteria. Most universities also started to add extra criteria of their own, going beyond the basic HEC requirements for foreign language proficiency and international publications for academic appointments and promotions. Then in the 2005 meeting of STHI, it was decided that the country's science and technology performance would be monitored based on the number of scientific publications and citations (TÜBİTAK 2005).

In two consecutive years (2009 and 2010), the HEC continued to raise its standards for academic promotion, demanding more scholarly ISI-listed publications (IUC-HEC 2009). In 2010, TUBITAK excluded from its economic incentive programme Category C journals in the SCI index and Category D journals in the SSCI index (ULAKBIM 2010). As a result, academic performance started to be associated merely with the number of publications in the ISI database, and national publications were largely discouraged.

The new HEC publishing criteria for associate professorship and government attempts to support publications in the ISI database had an immediate influence on the publication behaviours of academics, manifested by a rapid increase in publications (46 per cent between 2002 and 2005) (Baskurt 2007). Turkey moved from 45th position in the world rankings in 1980 with only 439 publications (Ak and Gülmez 2006) to 18th in 2008 with 24,821 publications (TUBITAK-ULAKBIM

2011), exceeding the STHI's targets as stipulated in its policy reports of 1993–2003. This increase in Turkey's scientific output was eight times faster than the world average and the third fastest among large countries in the last 30 years (Archambault 2010, p. 11).

However, detailed analysis revealed that the increasing *quantity* of the articles published in this period was not positively correlated with their *quality*, as manifested by the decrease in citation statistics between 1993 and 1999 (Arıoğlu and Girgin 2003). Although Turkey was in a good place in world rankings in terms of publication numbers, when it comes to citation statistics and impact factors, it was 42nd out of 45 countries, with a total of 548,547 citations and an impact factor of 4.55 between 1981 and 2007 (Akıllı et al. 2009). In another study, Turkey was found to be the 29th of 30 European countries in terms of citation numbers (Al, in press).

Hence, the quality of Turkish publications was below the desired levels because the policies and activities of HEC and TUBITAK had prioritized quantity over quality. In consequence, this led to publishing mostly with instrumental reasons such as meeting the promotion criteria and meeting economic incentives, resulting in numerous publications with no direct benefits to the scientific world or to society, and the discontinuation of publishing activity once a person had been promoted (Ortaş 2009). Another reason for low-impact scores is 'the emphasis not on basic research but on the development of applied sciences, as much of the published material is in the form of case studies and technical reports, whose conclusions cannot be generalized' (Erichsen 1998, p. 11). In addition, it was suggested that research was constrained by the lack of laboratories and necessary equipment, thus resulting in small-scale studies (Yucel 2006). It should also be taken into account that 75 local journals were included in SCI or SSCI indexes in the meantime; and many publications, especially in the social sciences, were in these low-impact Turkish journals.

Hence, despite the centre-oriented nature of the government policies, Turkish scholars' publication tendencies clearly seem to demonstrate distinct local characteristics that are not in complete harmony with Western academic publishing culture and practices. These may indicate a gap between centre-based state policy and local institutional and individual academic practices, especially in the social sciences. This chapter goes on to describe a study undertaken in a micro-context in Turkey (two major Turkish universities) that aimed to better understand the relationships between government policies and local institutional realities and implementations.

## 9.3 Tensions between the centre-oriented policy-making and actual research, publishing and promotion practices: a case study in two Turkish universities

In order to explore more closely how academics are dealing with recent government policies concerning scientific research and publishing, and to what extent the macro-level state policies are actually put into practice, a small-scale study was conducted in two Turkish state universities (a micro-research context). Universities were chosen as research site because around 98 per cent of publications in the SCI index were reported to be produced by scholars in universities (HEC 2004, p. 106). The findings regarding the institutional practices of research, publishing and promotion at these universities are presented below.

### 9.3.1 The research context

The two universities, which constitute the research context, were selected because they are both among the most prestigious universities in the rankings, but have different academic orientations and perspectives. Gazi University (GAZI) – a Turkish-medium university – was established in 1926, with a nationalistic and teaching-oriented view aiming at educating mass numbers of students to be appointed mainly as government officers and teachers. It is one of the most crowded universities in Turkey with double-shift education (daytime and evening programmes). The Middle East Technical University (METU), on the other hand, was established in 1957 around a US university model offering 100 per cent English-medium education. It is elitist and research oriented, selecting only high achieving students. As for academic promotion and appointments, while GAZI adopts the basic HEC criteria, METU requires additional qualifications and higher standards of English proficiency and international publications from academics.

### 9.3.2 Methodology

The data were collected through two sources. First, a survey was distributed to 115 subjects (58 academics in METU and 57 academics in GAZI). It was administered on a one-to-one basis, allowing the inclusion of a diverse range of academics from different disciplines and of different ranks. A short questionnaire was distributed to the academics in various departments based on their availability and consent to participate in the study. The main aim of the questionnaire was to explore whether there has been a change in the publishing behaviours of academics since the year 2000, which was when centre-based state policies of publishing and research came into effect. More specifically, the questionnaire aimed to gauge whether academics have a stronger preference towards publishing in international journals and in English than they did prior to 2000. The survey included multiple-choice questions, and was given to the subjects in Turkish (see Appendix A).

Second, a face-to-face interview was conducted with eight people – four from each university and each with a different status (instructor, assistant professor, associate professor and full professor), and thus representing different age groups. The interviews included semi-structured questions and were conducted in Turkish with academics that have high levels of English proficiency, a decision made to control the language variable, which is considered an important factor affecting international publications. In addition, as there are fewer international publications in the social sciences in Turkey, the interviews were given in a social science department better to reveal any gaps or tensions between the state policies and local practices of research and publishing. The main aim of the interview was to understand the level of importance attached to publishing and research at the institutional level, to find out whether research and international publications, which have been strongly emphasized by state policy, are also supported by universities or departments and, finally, to learn whether or not practices of promotion and departmental decision-making are directly related to the research and publication activity of scholars in line with state policy.

### 9.3.3   Results

With regard to the demographics, 58 subjects were from METU and 57 subjects were from GAZI. Sixty-one (53 per cent) were from the hard sciences, while 54 (47 per cent) were from social sciences; 64 (56 per cent) were males and 51 (44 per cent) were females, and their ages ranged from 22 to over 65. Four (3 per cent) were instructors, 38 (33 per cent) were assistant professors, 35 (30 per cent) were associate professors and 38 (33 per cent) were full professors. Their self-assessed level of English was 'low and mediocre' in the case of 9 subjects (8 per cent) and 'good and very good' in the case of 106 (92 per cent). Fifty-four subjects (47 per cent) had received a higher-education degree from an English-speaking country.

As for the publication behaviour of the subjects before and after 2000 (when centre-based policies took effect in terms of research and, particularly, international publishing), it was found that subjects' international publication activity immediately increased after the state policies were implemented in both universities, but particularly so in METU, confirming that state policies of publishing influenced academics' publishing behaviour. The following table and figure display that finding (Table 9.1, Figure 9.1)

The increases in publications after 2000 also varied according to discipline. It was found that international publications increased in both disciplines, but this increase was higher in hard sciences than social sciences (Table 9.2, Figure 9 2).

In short, after the implementation in 2000 of state policies encouraging research and publications that resulted in the adoption of the centre-based philosophy of 'publish or perish', an immediate effect was observed at the micro level. Scholars from both universities and from both disciplines seem to have published more in international journals

*Table 9.1* International publications by 115 Turkish academics before and after 2000 (by university)

| | GAZI | | | METU | | | $\chi^2$ | SD | Sig. |
|---|---|---|---|---|---|---|---|---|---|
| Publication # | 0–2 | 3–8 | 9+ | 0–2 | 3–8 | 9+ | | | |
| International publications before 2000 | 74% | 18% | 9% | 66% | 14% | 21% | 3.296 | 2 | .192 |
| International publications after 2000 | 26% | 33% | 40% | 12% | 35% | 53% | 4.112 | 2 | .128 |

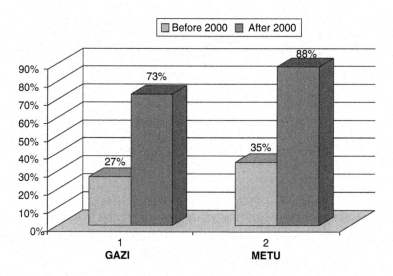

*Figure. 9.1* International publications by 115 Turkish academics before and after 2000 (by university)

*Table 9.2* International publications in the hard and social sciences by 115 Turkish academics before and after 2000

|  | Hard Science | | | Social Science | | | $\chi^2$ | SD | Sig. |
|---|---|---|---|---|---|---|---|---|---|
| Publication # | 0–2 | 3–8 | 9+ | 0–2 | 3–8 | 9+ | | | |
| International publications before 2000 | 57% | 20% | 23% | 83% | 11% | 6% | 9.979 | 2 | .007* |
| International publications after 2000 | 3% | 31% | 66% | 37% | 37% | 26% | 26.945 | 2 | .000* |

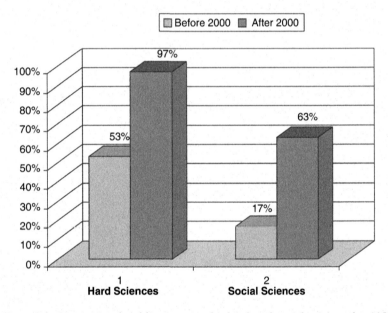

*Figure 9.2* International publications in the hard and social sciences by 115 Turkish academics before and after 2000

after 2000. However, it should also be noted that international publications were preferred more by scholars from METU and from those working in the hard sciences. In addition, scholars who had received part of their education in English-speaking countries tended to produce more international publications.

The interviews, however, provided more detailed information about the relationship between the centre-based state policy and institutional attitudes towards scientific research and publishing, on the one hand,

and the role of research and publishing in promotion and power-related decision-making practices on the other. For example, for the first two interview questions asked about the value of research and publishing in universities, and about any institutional support provided to encourage more research and publishing in participants' universities. The responses revealed that in both universities there is increasing support for research and publishing, in the form of research grants for scientific projects, travel grants for conference presentations and economic incentives for international publications in line with the state policy. However, it was also found that academics were only superficially rewarded for their publication and research endeavours, particularly at Gazi University, as academics with a higher research and publishing performance do not gain any immediate benefits and rights in academic decision-making or even in promotion mechanisms. This situation is naturally demotivating for academics, and it conflicts with the macro-level state policy, thereby reflecting peripheral characteristics. Participants from Gazi University expressed the situation as follows:

GAZI, Instructor:

> *When we publish in ISI-indexed journals, we are given a certain amount of money in a commendment ceremony, but we cannot feel any effect of doing more research or publications in our department. No one says, you have published in the best journals, now you can teach graduate courses or supervise more dissertations. Your word does not count more than anyone else who is not at all active in research or publishing. There is no concrete influence of publishing in this department, but I can say it can be a protective shield and people may personally respect you more. Still, it definitely is not a factor determining our academic identity.*

GAZI, Assistant Professor:

> *It looks like research and publications are valued, but with regard to getting promoted or being appointed to administrative positions, the person who has more publications has no more advantages. So, there is no difference between publishing a lot or a little in practice.*

GAZI, Associate Professor:

> *When I look at what I have experienced so far, I don't think research and publishing is valued. I am not a worldwide known researcher, but although I have more publications than my colleagues, I have always been somehow at disadvantage.*

GAZI, Full Professor:

> *Actually, it is somewhat valued; there is a reward ceremony for people publishing internationally, but one is not appreciated more just because one has more publications in practice. For example, no one takes the publications into account while appointing the head of department or members of certain administrative committees.*

It was evident from the participants' accounts that research and publishing activities are much more highly valued at METU than at GAZI, and that they contribute decisively to promotions and other decision-making mechanisms. Therefore, research and publishing is the number one priority for this institution, and accordingly, the academics are acclaimed and rewarded, both psychologically and physically, for research and publications. Consequently, they are more motivated towards doing more research and publishing especially in international journals in line with the state policy. The accounts of academics from METU on this issue can be seen below:

METU, Instructor:

> *Research is definitely given importance. It is a seriously valued issue which all the academic staff agrees on and tries hard to realize.*

METU, Assistant Professor:

> *It is valued a lot, and it should be valued because the spoken word is fleeting, but the written one endures. Research should be considered important, though in the education faculty at least, teaching should also be valued and good teaching should be encouraged and rewarded.*

METU, Associate Professor:

> *Everything in this university is based on research and publishing. When you meet the publishing criteria of the university, you are promoted. The most important criteria is always academic publications.*

METU, Full Professor:

> *It is the most important thing here. The whole promotion and reward system is based on research and publishing. For example, the faculties which have the highest number of publications and the top 20 per cent of*

*the academics in publishing are rewarded economically. When you publish in SSCI-indexed journals, you are given around 1000 TL (around $550) economic incentive; if the impact factor of this journal is over 1.5, you are given even a higher amount of incentive. An extra travel grant is also given to the person who makes two SCI/SSCI publications a year.*

When it comes to the physical conditions facilitating research and publishing, such as time for research, grants, library resources, equipment, support for academic writing and so on, the answers revealed that research and travel grants are available at both universities, but in lower amounts in GAZI. METU also has better working conditions for research-oriented academics, such as better library resources, a free interlibrary loan system, an academic writing centre for academic staff and graduate students, and fewer teaching hours compared to GAZI. For example, while an assistant professor teaches 12 hours a week in METU, an assistant professor teaches between 20–25 hours a week in Gazi. Therefore, conditions for doing research and publications seem to be more favourable in METU in harmony with the state policy. However, it should be noted that when compared to centre countries such as the US and UK, conditions in METU also fall short in terms of research support, resources, technical equipment and teaching hours, thus reflecting the university's semiperipheral status. The accounts of the participants can be seen as follows:

GAZI, Instructor:

> *The conditions are not suitable for instructors to do research. I cannot even apply to get a grant for an individual research project. I am teaching almost 30 hours a week, I am being kept busy all the time with non-academic burdens such as invigilating students in exams, student registrations, answering official letters coming to the department, updating the department web site and so on. For me, these all means, stop, don't do any research! Also the library is very poor in terms of resources and especially in terms of books.*

GAZI, Assistant Professor:

> *There is some support, but it is not sufficient. Travel grants don't cover all our expenses, we have to pay for at least half of the expenses by ourselves. The library is not sufficient for our field so we have to buy our own books or go to other universities' libraries. But the electronic database of the university is good. There is also no support for academic writing or editing, we try to do research and write articles with our own resources.*

GAZI, Associate Professor:

> It is much better than before, but when we were younger we did not have time even to breathe; I remember invigilating students in completely unrelated exams such as exams for chefs, even at the weekends, so it was impossible to do research. We can find time for research only after we get our associate professorship. As for the library, the electronic resources are good, but books are insufficient.

GAZI, Full Professor:

> You can get around 10,000 TL (around $ 5,600) from Individual Research Project grants, but if you need more than that, you will have problems. The economic support for research is limited. The library closes at 5 pm, and because not much extra economic support is given to research, the academic staff wants to teach more classes and earn more through teaching.

METU, Instructor:

> There are Individual Research Project grants supported by the university, but because of bureaucratic obstacles, you cannot buy the equipment you require on time. Conferences are only partially supported. In terms of resources, we need to buy most things by ourselves.

METU, Assistant Professor:

> Academics that want to do research are supported through Individual Research Project grants. I am not pleased with travel grants; they only partially cover your conference expenses and only once a year. I don't have much time, I am teaching four classes, I have an administrative job, supervising dissertations, so I have to steal time from my family and from my vacation time.

METU, Associate Professor:

> I have been in METU for 7 years, and so far whenever I requested a book or a journal article, my requests have never been refused. It may take time, and some resources arrive 6 months or up to a year later, but eventually everything I request comes. They give travel grants for one international conference and one national conference each year. We teach only two days a week and have three days for research because the promotion criteria are very high and challenging here.

METU, Full Professor:

> *There is an Individual Research Project grant, and there are ongoing seminars about how to do projects throughout the year, and there is an academic writing centre. In short, there are all kinds of support for those who want to do research.*

For the third question asking about the supportiveness and motivation for carrying out and publishing research at departmental level, the results paralleled the institutional practices. At Gazi University, the respondents reported little departmental support for research due to its teaching-oriented heritage and background, while in METU the situation seemed to be more encouraging. However, in both universities, a hierarchical order was reported in which lower-ranking academics, such as instructors and assistant professors, had more problems trying to do research.

GAZI, Instructor:

> *The older professors here don't have a research and publishing culture. They come from a background when they had become academics quickly when this institution was transformed from a teacher training college in 1982. I am not accusing anybody, but they were not able to guide us academically. Nobody taught us how to write articles, and even our dissertation supervisors did not give us support or feedback. Most of the time, professors don't even read dissertations. A very small group is doing research here, people don't collaborate, they don't have an academic culture or spirit. Therefore, it is not motivating.*

GAZI, Assistant Professor:

> *There is no such support in the department. The ones with higher status don't collaborate with people with lower status. So we cannot learn from others, there is no culture of apprenticeship, no collaboration among colleagues. No one is interested in whether we are doing research or not. The salaries are very low so I take about 30 hours of courses a week or do extra things with immediate economic return, and don't have the energy to write papers when I go home. I can only write papers during my summer vacation, but it is not enough to publish in international indexes.*

GAZI, Associate Professor:

> *In other universities, they encourage their staff to publish in journals, but this is not the case in our department.*

GAZI, Full Professor:

> *We publish a journal, give suggestions to research assistants to do research and publish to move towards a more research-oriented faculty. But this is not at sufficient levels yet. Our current faculty doesn't have an academic or research culture, because it was a teacher-training college in the past, and its job was to educate future teachers, but not to conduct research. Academic staff in those times did not even have PhDs, they were only responsible for teaching and transmitting their knowledge; they did not have to do research and produce knowledge themselves. This was the tradition until 1982 when HEC was founded and certain standards started to be employed. For example, all the academic staff were forced to get their PhDs. That is when most got retired because research and academic career were the least known things here. The young people at that time tried to adapt to the situation, had their PhDs and stayed. This once younger generation is now senior professors, but because they come from that teaching tradition, they are not research-oriented either. They are good teachers, but when it comes to research they do whatever they can.*

METU, Instructor:

> *It seems there is support at first, but there is a hierarchical order and I have to teach the most time-consuming classes. Although I also have a PhD and want to become an assistant professor, my attempts are constantly being obstructed.*

METU, Assistant Professor:

> *It is very demotivating, I am not content with the situation here. A group has the power and they make decisions without our consent. Even though I am one of the most senior staff, I feel things are not fair and transparent. I am stuck under never-ending responsibilities and I feel burned out.*

METU, Associate Professor:

> *I feel we are very lucky; for example, I hear that in other universities people are forced to work from 9 am to 5 pm. Here research is the priority so we are given 3 days off to do research and write papers. That is why the academic ranking of our department is higher than most other universities.*

METU, Full Professor:

> *I think it is more related to individual effort, but a professor with no administrative duties in METU always has time to do research and publish. The*

*teaching hours are flexible, you can work at your home or library, you don't have to be in your office all the time.*

The fourth question concerning personal promotion experiences aimed to gauge the role of research and publishing in promotion practices, thereby offering an important indicator of the local academic culture in the two universities. As promotion mechanisms and criteria prioritizing academic research and publication would have a positive effect on academics in terms of their research and publishing endeavours, they are important indicators of actual practice.

Although promotions to associate professorship are undertaken by HEC through a central evaluation mechanism involving both the assessment of publications and an oral exam, promotions at the levels of instructor, assistant professor and professor are administered internally by the universities themselves. In addition, after having been awarded the title of associate professor by HEC, academics still need to apply to their institutions for a position to be opened and to be officially appointed as associate professor. Therefore, institutions still have considerable power in promotion decisions regarding individual academics.

However, the participants' accounts reveal that institutional promotion practices, especially at Gazi University, seem to be lacking in objective institutional standards, and the administrative bodies, which have a great deal of authority, may interfere with promotions by delaying or even completely obstructing the process based on mostly non-academic factors. Furthermore, instead of academic performance, factors such as seniority and good social and political relationships with the administration are found to be more effective in promotion decisions than research and publishing, possibly causing a negative effect on academics in terms of motivation to conduct and publish research. This is clearly in conflict with the goals of state policy. This situation seems to be even more problematic at lower-ranking positions, such as promotions from an instructor to an assistant professor. The promotion stories of academics from both universities can be seen as below:

GAZI, Instructor:

*I got the instructor position quite easily ... due to good relationships between the dean and the department, but I had serious problems when I wanted to apply for assistant professorship one year after having my PhD. Although I had worked hard during this period and published several international publications, when I applied for the assistant professorship, I saw that the academic criteria of the university was not in effect any more due to changes in the university administration. This lack of academic criteria*

*and the clash between my personal political views with the new adminis-*
*tration caused many problems.... Although the position was opened twice,*
*I was warned by the upper administration not to apply to the position as*
*it was already reserved for a more senior person from another university.*
*But this person could not pass the language test so the position was in a*
*way wasted. The second time the position was opened, I was warned again*
*not to apply as it was reserved for another senior member who had only*
*two national publications, but had better social and political relationships*
*with the administration.... Although I had more, better quality publica-*
*tions than the other person, I could not even apply to the position due to*
*psychological pressure from above.*

GAZI, Assistant Professor:

*I got my doctorate degree in 1999, but because the relationships between*
*the head of the department and the president of the university was not*
*good, I could not become an assistant professor for seven years. However,*
*during this time, some other people got assistant professorship due to per-*
*sonal and political relationships with the administration. After seven years*
*of waiting, I rebelled and insisted on being given a position and upon my*
*insistence and determination, the head of the department took me to the*
*dean of the faculty and eventually despite the opposition of the university*
*president, I got the position.*

GAZI, Associate Professor

*When I got my PhD, a position for assistant professorship was opened,*
*but the department did not want me to apply as the position was opened*
*for a more senior person. I knew that this person was not academically*
*competent and most of his publications were heavily plagiarised, so I*
*decided to apply despite the oppositions. I faced a lot of delays for a year*
*and the decision could not be made for no apparent reason. I had to write*
*a lot of petitions asking the reason, and could not get any answer. At the*
*end, I learned that the position had been given to the other person. Then*
*I went to court ... and the court decided I should be the person to take the*
*position and I was appointed as assistant professor. Then I got the title*
*as associate professorship after I met the criteria from HEC, but I again*
*could not get my position from my own university for 3.5 years because*
*the administration that I had sued returned to power and delayed my*
*promotion.... Although all others got their positions in a very short time,*
*I was consciously discriminated against. I believe this was a totally*

*political thing as everybody knows I am not from the same political orientation as the administration.*

GAZI, Full Professor:

> *I got my PhD in 1989 and I got my assistant professorship easily as there was not much competition in those times. We had two assistant professors in the department and there were no others with a higher title. I applied to HEC for associate professorship, I failed the first time because 4 out of 5 people on my jury were from literature departments, but I got my title the second time. I could not get the position immediately from Gazi and I don't know what the criteria were that they were looking for. I was appointed two years later. It was the same for my professorship, there were not many academic criteria, but I could only get my professorship after three years of a delay without any reasons. The people who are closer and have connections with higher administrative bodies were appointed immediately.*

Although in METU a more objective and standardized procedure for promotion based on academic performance and more democratic decision-making mechanisms are expressed, the promotion stories of the participants revealed the presence of hidden institutional traditions, bureaucratic delays and even misuse of authority by department heads causing problems, especially at lower ranks as in GAZI. This too contravenes macro-level state policy and HEC regulations.

METU, Instructor:

> *I first started to teach as a part-time instructor in our department while I was working as a language instructor in the Department of Basic English. Then after working for 2 years, I was offered a full-time position as an instructor in the department. I did not have any publications at that time, but I was told I was going to be supported if I wanted to apply for assistant professorship. Later, however, I was told that my position had no promotion prospects and I would not be able to be promoted to a different position in a departmental meeting. I don't think that people should be divided as academic and teaching staff, we all have our PhDs, attending conferences, writing articles. This mentality is really disturbing, I am constantly obstructed, I can't supervise theses, I cannot teach graduate classes, there is a discrimination in the department so this lowers my motivation to do research and publish.*

METU, Assistant Professor:

> *I got my PhD in 1995 from a university in UK, I was a successful student, but I had to wait for five years to be appointed to the assistant*

*professorship here. I was told there were no vacancies, but two people from outside were given assistant professorship positions while I was waiting. Because I started to work here when I was really young, I was maybe too passive at that time out of respect to old professors, but this led them underestimate me. Promotions should not be given upon our character or attitude, there should be institutional standards and when someone meets the criteria he/she should be automatically promoted. The head of departments have too much authority, if they don't want you to be promoted, it is almost impossible for you to get the promotion.*

METU, Associate Professor:

*I got my PhD from a university in UK in 2003 and worked there until 2005. Then when I came here, after meeting the publication criteria, I immediately got my assistant professorship without any problems. I also got my associate professorship from HEC without any problems and after meeting the additional institutional publishing criteria, I got appointed.*

METU, Full Professor:

*I got my PhD from a university in the USA and applied to METU, but was first given an instructor position. I stayed as an instructor for two years, and after two years I got my assistant professorship by talking with the department head and insisting on my desire to be appointed. If you don't insist they won't give you the position despite your academic performance, they don't care about your promotion. After 2000, the institutional academic promotion criteria became more clear and publications in SSCI index became mandatory. Then after publishing many papers and studying hard for the oral exam, I got my associate professorship from HEC. I got appointed one year later, and after meeting the institutional criteria for professorship I got my position one year later due to some bureaucratic paperwork and delays.*

Overall, interview results revealed the complexities and differences in policy implementation between the two universities. While in METU, research and publications are supported and encouraged and have a high impact on promotion and power-related decision-making, in line with state intentions, in GAZI more peripheral characteristics such as personal and political connections, age and seniority are still in effect and are more influential in such decisions. However, even in METU, which works in accordance with the Western philosophy and follows centre-oriented academic traditions, the practices seem to be more of a semiperipheral nature due to economic and cultural factors.

## 9.4 Discussion and conclusions

The historical analysis of Turkish scientific research policies has revealed that, having been established from the ashes of Ottoman Empire which had fallen behind the West especially due to problems in education, science and technology, the new Turkish republic experienced similar delays in science and technology during its early years. Although radical political, economic and social reforms took place in this early stage to Westernize and modernize, most reforms and policy-making activities have taken place as top-down government initiatives that are not effectively implemented in practice and thus have little or no effect on the general public (Yucel 2006).

With the increasing pressures of globalization and the new demands of the information age, Turkey was later forced to realize that it had to leave behind its traditional closed mentality in economics, science, research and technology to be able to survive in the new world order and compete internationally. Therefore, state policies and planning have targeted the production of new knowledge and technology through research and development (Yucel 2006).

Furthermore, having been influenced by global developments and a centre-based academic philosophy, Turkish state policies have encouraged research and publishing in international journals as a means to integrate with Europe and the global scientific world. Accordingly, the Anglo-American academic ethos of 'publish or perish' was adopted through a shift of focus from teaching to research and from national publications to international publications in English. As a consequence of these state policies, which highlighted publications in the ISI database as an important indicator of one's academic success, scholars' publication activity increased considerably (Erichsen 1998). This has also been confirmed by the findings of the present study, which point to a significant expansion in international publications on the part of scholars in the two universities after the state policies were issued. It was revealed that international publications were preferred more by scholars in METU and by scholars working in hard sciences.

However, it should also be noted that despite the steep increase in the amount of research and number of publications indicated by both government statistics and the present study, the scientific quality of these publications was considered to be low, as reflected by the citation statistics. Reasons for the low citation statistics include state policies that continuously emphasize quantity over quality, research with non-generalizable results that do often not contribute to general theories, a preference for low-impact Turkish journals over ISI-indexed periodicals and a lack of physical conditions for research.

Therefore, Turkish academia clearly demonstrates local characteristics that are different from the centre-based academic culture. For example, unlike the Western academic culture in which academic communities are built bottom up by research and publishing (Canagarajah 2002), the situation in Turkey seems to be more of a top-down policy instituted by state policy. Therefore, the kind of motivation behind research and publishing is extrinsic or instrumental (resulting directly from the desire for promotion) rather than intrinsic (that is, generated by the desire for professional development or to contribute to knowledge building in discipline-specific communities). Consequently, scholars have preferred to publish as many papers as possible in a short time, mostly in ISI-indexed Turkish journals, just to meet the criteria rather than producing fewer, higher quality publications, which would receive more citations (Pazarlıoğlu and Özkoç 2009).

Turkey also seems to be caught in the process of a transition from a teaching-oriented academic community reflecting peripheral characteristics such as subjective institutional promotion standards, to a research-based academic or scientific community. While Western or centre-based academic culture is formed around scientific research and academic writing practices in which one's academic identity or status is determined by one's role in knowledge production (such as being a journal editor, referee, proponent of a theory, Canagarajah 2002), in Turkey the academic roles and status are determined by factors such as teaching, seniority and social or political connections with upper administrative bodies. These factors were found to be particularly influential in promotions and power-related decisions at Gazi University, which has more traditional characteristics and is also representative of more universities in Turkey. Therefore, it can be claimed that the Turkish micro-context tends to encourage the cultivation of personal, social or political connections in order to preserve better positions and status in academia rather than spending long hours working in isolation under hard conditions to be able to publish in high-ranking international journals.

Moreover, physical conditions seem further to discourage scholars from doing more research. For example, scholars have few hours to devote to research and publication activities because of their low salaries (they often seek extra jobs for additional income), heavy teaching loads and lack of sabbaticals, which means they can only find time for publishing in holiday times. The complex bureaucratic procedures necessary to apply for research funding, as well as insufficient library resources and laboratory conditions, further discourage academics from doing research and publishing (Erichsen 1998, Koksal and Razi 2011).

In conclusion, Turkey's geographical situation right between West and East and its economic status somewhere between the developed and underdeveloped world is accompanied by the kind of semiperipheral academic culture that forms the subject of this book. Turkish academia's semiperipheral structure is revealed by the tensions between macro-level state policies reflecting the adoption of centre-based academic tendencies that prioritize research and international publications, and the peripheral implementation of these policies at institutional level. These micro-level practices indicate some indifference or even a kind of resistance to centre-based policies that may hamper *high-quality* scientific productivity and innovation, which are important prerequisites for survival in today's global world.

## Appendix A

### Questionnaire

1. Please indicate your age group:
a) 22–35     b) 36–45     c) 46–55     d) 56–65     e) 66+

2. Please indicate your gender:
a) Male     b) Female

3. Please indicate your area of specialization (for example, language teaching, psychology, science education)

_____

4. Please indicate your current position
a) Instructor     b) Assistant professor     c) Associate professor
d) Full professor

5. Please indicate your current English language proficiency.
a) Elementary     b) Intermediate     c) Upper Intermediate
d) Advanced

6. Have you completed any of the following degrees in a university in an English speaking country? If yes, please circle the degree you completed.
a) Undergraduate     b) Masters     c) Doctorate

## Publishing practices in international versus national venues Before 2000

7. Did you publish any academic books, book chapters, journal articles.... **before 2000**?

   Yes_____        No_____ (If no, go to question 10)

8. How many **international** books, book chapters and journal articles did you publish before 2000?

   _____

## After 2000

10. Have you published any academic books, book chapters, journal articles.... since 2000?

    Yes_____        No_____ (If no, go to question 13)

11. How many **international** books, book chapters and journal articles have you published since 2000?

    _____

# Appendix B (Interview)

1. How much value do you think is attached to conducting and publishing research in your institution?
2. Are you supported/encouraged by your university to do research? Do they provide necessary conditions to facilitate your research and publication (for example, time, financial support, library resources, equipment, academic writing centre...)
3. Do you think the academic atmosphere in your department is motivating for you to conduct and publish research? Why/ Why not?
4. Can you describe the promotion process you went through while getting your current position?

# Notes

1. Mustafa Kemal Ataturk was the founder and the first president of the Turkish Republic.

# 10
# English-Medium Journals in Serbia: Editors' Perspectives

*Bojana Petrić*

## 10.1   Introduction

The dominant position of English in international scholarship and increasing pressures on scholars worldwide to publish in English are now well documented (for example, Belcher 2007, Buckingham 2014, Canagarajah 2002, Curry and Lillis 2004, Ferguson et al. 2011, Flowerdew 1999a, 1999b, 2000, Hamel 2007, Hanauer and Englander 2013, Lillis and Curry 2006, 2010, Uzuner 2008). One of the less-explored consequences of this trend is the growth of English-medium journals in non-Anglophone countries. While the extent of Anglicization of periodicals varies across countries and disciplinary areas, with the hard sciences more prone to Anglicization than the humanities, this trend seems to be pervasive and ongoing (see, for instance, Gibbs 1995, Lillis 2012, Lillis and Curry 2010, Pérez-Llantada et al. 2011, Swales 1997). As English-medium journals are on the rise, those in local languages seem to be disappearing from the scene, as scholars increasingly publish in English rather than in their local languages. For instance, between 1999 and 2006, the numbers of papers in Spanish-language journals published in Spain decreased by half (Pérez-Llantada et al. 2011); similarly, the proportion of medical publications in Italian in the PubMed database fell by 60 per cent between 1986 and 2005, showing 'the gradual peripheralization of Italian' as the language of medical science (Giannoni 2008, p. 105). Giannoni (2008) also cites data showing that the entire output of Italian researchers in some areas (mathematics, food quality, chemistry) is now published in English, either in international journals or in Italian English-medium journals. As Moreno (2013) half-jokingly stated in a recent conference presentation commenting on the situation in Spain, discourse analysts must act fast if they wish to collect academic papers in local languages while they still exist, especially in hard science and technological areas.

Despite this rapid global shift towards English in scholarly periodicals worldwide, few of the 'national' English-medium journals from countries outside the Anglophone centre achieve substantial international visibility, as measured by inclusion in international scientific databases. According to Gibbs (1995), journals from developing[1] countries make up only 2 per cent of all Science Citation Index journals. More recently, Lillis (2012) reported that 93 per cent of the English-medium psychology journals listed in the Social Science Citation Index are published in the Anglophone centre countries (that is, US and UK). This raises some pertinent questions about the nature of the majority of English-medium journals on the semiperiphery. Is their current status just a temporary stage in their transition from being national to becoming international? Or are they bound to remain of national significance only, despite their use of English and their availability online? What kinds of roles do these journals perform in their national contexts and in wider regional and international contexts? More broadly, how should we understand the terms 'national' and 'international' when describing the status of English-medium periodicals in semiperipheral geopolitical locations? These are some of the questions that motivated the present study of English-medium journals in Serbia, a non-Anglophone country on the semiperiphery of knowledge production, where a similar growth of English-medium journals can be observed. Specifically, the study aims to gain an insight into the nature of English-medium journals on the semiperiphery by investigating the motivations for these journals' adoption of English and their related goals. These issues will be explored by focusing on the perspectives of the journals' editors, who, in this context, are both shapers of their journals' policies and practices and scholars from the semiperiphery themselves.

The role of editors as gatekeepers and the factors impacting on their selection of articles for publication have long been the subject of research in sociology of science (see, for instance, Crane 1967), and have more recently come into the focus of scholars working in the field of writing for international publication. McKay (2003), reflecting on her role as editor of *TESOL Quarterly*, outlines three central roles editors play: in their *policy-making* role, editors ensure that policies developed by the editorial board are implemented; in their *decision-making* role, they decide on a number of important parameters of the journal (such as the composition of the editorial board and the selection of manuscript reviewers); finally, they also have a *political* role as they are accountable to the contributors, editorial board members and the body that funds the journal. McKay stresses that although editors do not act alone, they are not unbiased, but actively participate in shaping the nature of the journal, its policies and practices. Because of the importance of these roles, editors' views have been investigated in studies such as Gosden (1992) and Flowerdew (2001), who surveyed editors of prestigious journals in the Anglophone centre countries about their perceptions of and attitudes towards manuscripts submitted to their journals by speakers of English as an additional language. The editors in these studies identified both positive and problematic issues specific to non-centre scholars' submissions. They also showed a sympathetic and supportive attitude towards scholars writing in English as a foreign language and sometimes helped with editing their manuscripts if they felt the research was worthwhile. Thus, we see that editors can act as both gatekeepers and literacy brokers (Lillis and Curry 2006). This, however, is not a universal attitude, as shown by Lillis and Curry's (2010) reports of instances where manuscripts by non-centre scholars, written in L2 English, were treated in a discriminatory manner.

While these studies focused on the editors of centre journals, typically L1 speakers based at prestigious universities in the Anglophone world, the participants in the present study are editors from the semiperiphery, who are themselves speakers of English as an additional language, and whose roles, practices and attitudes are thus likely to be different. Indeed, the few accounts available in the literature (for example, Lillis' 2012 study of English-medium 'national' journals, and a series of articles and editorials by the editors of the *Croatian Medical Journal*, such as Marušić and Marušić 1999, 2001, 2012; Mišak et al. 2005) show that editors of English-medium journals in non-Anglophone countries may play an important role in supporting scholars from their national research communities. This study, however, does not focus on the role of editors; rather, it takes their special position as policy makers, decision makers and political actors (to use McKay's words) and their insights into the often unwritten decisions and attitudes surrounding editorial language policies as a starting point for an exploration of the nature of English-medium journals in non-Anglophone countries. This chapter therefore does not aim to provide a country profile. The participants have been selected due to their specific role in academic publishing in Serbia, and their views may not be representative of other (or even of the majority of) researchers in Serbia.

Like other contributors to this volume, I use the term 'semiperiphery' with reference to Wallerstein's (2004) world-systems analysis, which distinguishes between three economic-political zones, that is, the core, semiperiphery and periphery, with semiperiphery displaying features of both core and peripheral zones. The terms are used here to denote geopolitical areas of knowledge production characterized by differential levels of access to material and symbolic resources, and therefore differential levels of power to define and validate knowledge.

## 10.2   Context of the study

As one of the successor states of the former Yugoslavia, Serbia suffered a period of political instability and a severe economic decline during the 1990s wars and eventual disintegration of the former state, which had a considerable effect on the country's research infrastructure and community. Like Bulgaria, Croatia and Romania, Serbia has a 'semi-developed science system' (Radošević 2010, p. 183), characterized by poor support for scientific research. Serbian gross domestic expenditure on research and development (GERD) is less than 1 per cent of its GDP, and although it increased from 0.3 per cent in 2000 to 0.92 per cent in 2011 (Radošević 2010), it is still far below the EU average of 2.03 per cent. Among the many challenges facing Serbian science is the 'massive and continuous brain drain' (Dall 2007, p. 169), with Serbia ranked 141st for brain drain out of 144 countries analysed in the latest report on global competitiveness (Schwab 2012). It is not surprising, then, that the number of researchers (around 10,000, according to Kutlača 2007) remained almost constant during the first decade of the 21st century.

Nevertheless, despite the slow process of recovery of the once reasonably developed science system that existed in the former Yugoslavia, there is a trend towards greater internationalization of science in Serbia, understood as the greater participation of Serbian researchers in projects, conferences and publications beyond the national borders, inevitably accompanied by a growing need for and use of English. Participation in researchers' informal networks (see Curry and Lillis 2010) and in official projects such as UNESCO's Venice Process (launched in 2001), and the inclusion of Serbia in the European Union's 7th Framework Programme for Research and Development in 2007, have opened up opportunities for researchers in Serbia for greater international cooperation and better funding for research projects. This has led to a rise in the numbers of papers authored by researchers from Serbia in international peer-reviewed journals (for instance, between 2002 and 2008 their numbers rose by 172.1 per cent; for further information see Radošević 2010).

Internally, the Ministry of Science and Technological Development[2] has implemented policies that have also contributed to the increased need for English, such as the point system for evaluating scholars' research outputs. As is common elsewhere (see, for example, Burgess and Uysal, this volume; also Lillis and Curry 2010), this rewards scholars who publish in international, typically English-medium, journals on SCI and SSCI lists. Of particular relevance to this study are governmental measures relating to journal editing in Serbia, such as the *Act on Editing Journals*[3] (2009), which recommends that journals should use Serbian,[4] English or both languages as their medium; that all journal articles should be accompanied by abstracts in English; and that journals publishing articles in Serbian only should also include extensive English summaries. Journals are ranked annually by disciplinary[5] panels of experts, and are classified into one of the following five categories: (1) international journal published in Serbia; (2) national journal of international importance; (3) leading national journal; (4) journal of national importance; and (5) scholarly journal. The rankings have implications for funding and other benefits. Needless to say, journals in the first two categories must use English in order to be able to reach an international readership, although, technically, English is not a prerequisite for a journal to be included in the SCI list.

Given these external and internal factors, it is not surprising that an increasing number of journals in Serbia have started to use English as their medium. It is not uncommon to find the following in the guidelines for authors in journals publishing articles in both English and Serbian: 'The Editorial Board give absolute priority to submissions written in English' (from a social science journal) or 'Manuscripts submitted entirely in English have a priority in publication' (from a medical journal). This shows that the language of publication alone may increase its author's chances to get published in local journals.

In terms of the extent of Anglicization, journals in Serbia can be grouped into the following four categories: (1) Serbian-medium journals, where all content (excluding abstracts) is in Serbian only; (2) mixed-language journals, where some articles are in English while others are in Serbian (but no article appears in both languages); (3) bilingual journals, where all content is published in both English and Serbian; and (4) English-medium journals, where all content (excluding abstracts) is in English only. Of these categories, only the latter is steadily increasing, driven both by newly founded English-medium journals and by growing numbers of formerly bilingual, mixed-language or Serbian-only journals switching to English as their only medium. Specifically, between 2006 and 2009 the proportion of English-medium journals rose from less than a quarter (23.9 per cent) to almost a third (31.9 per cent) of all journals published in Serbia.[6] In contrast, in the same period the proportions of Serbian only and mixed-language journals fell from 31.8 per cent to 26.8 per cent, and from 47.3 per cent to 41.3 per cent, respectively.

As elsewhere (see, for instance, Giannoni 2008), this trend is marked by considerable disciplinary variation, with the highest proportion of English-medium journals in the hard sciences and mathematics, and the lowest in the social sciences and humanities. With reference to Becher and Trowler's (2001) taxonomy of disciplines, which combines the distinction between hard and soft disciplines on the one hand and pure and applied on the other, in 2009, 84 per cent of all journals in hard-pure (for example, chemistry, mathematics) and hard-applied disciplines (for example, engineering) were English-medium, in contrast to 23 per cent of soft-applied (for example, education studies) and 9 per cent of soft-pure (that is, humanities) journals. The figures also reflect the fact that the most active parts of the Serbian science system are in hard-pure and hard-applied disciplines, particularly clinical medicine, chemistry, engineering/technology, and physics (Radošević 2010).

However, despite this shift towards using English as the main medium of publication, only 16 per cent of these journals were classified as 'international' by the local research authorities at the beginning of the 2010s. It is therefore particularly interesting to explore the goals and functions of the majority of English-medium journals in Serbia that are not ranked as international.

## 10.3   Methodology

### 10.3.1   Identifying and selecting English-medium journals published in Serbia

In the first stage of the research, bibliometric data were used to identify and select English-medium journals published in Serbia whose editors could then be invited to participate in the study. The main criteria for journal selection were that the journal was English-medium, bilingual or mixed-language, and that it was edited and published in Serbia. A list of all locally published English-medium and mixed-language journals was compiled from the data available in the Serbian Citation Index database and the *Journal Bibliometric Report*,[7] totalling 81 regularly published journals. After eliminating journals whose editors' contact details were not available online, 35 editors of English-medium journals were contacted by email and invited to participate in the study. The selection was made following the principle of maximum variation sampling (Miles and Huberman 1994), so as to include as diverse a range of journals as possible in terms of disciplinary areas (using Becher and Trowler's 2001 classification), the size of the university centre with which the journal is affiliated, the journal's lifespan and – of particular importance to this study – length of use of the English medium.

Of the 35 editors contacted, 19 (67 per cent) initially agreed; however, four dropped out at a later stage due to other commitments, so the final number of informants was 15. The intended diversity of journals in the sample was achieved along a number of dimensions: in terms of their lifespan (with journal launch dates ranging from 1955 to 2007), the length of time in which English had been used as their medium (some were English-medium from the beginning while others recently switched to English) and the balance of articles by local vs. non-local authors. The journals were based in five different geographical locations, including both major universities and smaller research centres. In terms of disciplinary areas represented, the majority of the journals were from hard-applied disciplines (8), followed by soft-applied (4) and hard-pure (2), with none from the soft-pure (that is, humanities), which is in line with the proportions of English-medium journals in these areas, as explained above. In terms of journal rankings, the sample included journals from all categories, with the majority occupying categories three (leading national journal) and four (journal of national importance) according to the 2010 report.[8]

### 10.3.2 Data collection and analysis

To elicit the editors' perspectives on the issues of interest to the study, a set of open-ended questions was developed, which was used as a basis for face-to-face interviews (with five informants) and for email correspondence (with ten informants who were not available for face-to-face interviews). The schedule consisted of general and journal-specific questions, with the former covering issues such as the journal's aims and motivations for using English; their intended readership; the editor's perception of the nature of their journal; their attitudes towards the role of English and Serbian in academic publishing in their discipline; and the difficulties of editing an English-medium journal in a non-Anglophone country and the strategies editors use to overcome them. The journal-specific questions, which were developed after examining each journal in detail, concerned the journal's history, ranking, proportions of articles authored by local vs. other scholars, language-related guidelines and support for authors (if any), use of English in the editor's discipline and other relevant issues (for example, reasons motivating the change in the journal's title). Both the interviews and the email correspondence were in Serbian, the language shared by the researcher and the interviewees (for an English translation of a sample schedule, see Appendix).

Although in both cases a similar range of topics was covered, the difference in the format resulted in differences in the amount and quality of data obtained. The interviews were semi-structured (Patton 2002), which enabled me to probe into the issues under discussion in more depth and allowed the participants to introduce topics they found relevant, resulting in richer and more varied data. Additionally, visiting the informants' offices and institutions to conduct the interviews provided further information about the context in which they work and their work routines. Nevertheless, the data obtained via email were also useful, as the editors answered the questions with precision and in varying degrees of detail, in some cases providing further information, which showed their interest in this topic.[9] A further indication of their willingness to participate can be seen in the fact that there were no instances of unanswered questions, even though all questions were open-ended, thus requiring time and effort.

Interviews were transcribed and coded together with emailed data for the following major themes: goals and motivations for using English; editors' views on the nature of their journal (national/international); attitudes towards publishing in English and Serbian; and difficulties of journal editing in a non-Anglophone country and strategies to overcome these difficulties. This chapter reports on the first two topics only due to space limitations.

### 10.3.3　Research ethics

As this study concerns a relatively small academic community, special care was taken to protect the identity of the participants, particularly since the editors are quite prominent figures in their disciplinary communities. Although all gave consent for the information to be used for research purposes, I was aware of the sensitive nature of it, especially when it involved other individuals and bodies. Lillis (2012) faced a similar difficulty when reporting data from a study of four journals in the same discipline in four different countries, and maintained the anonymity of the editors by unlinking interview excerpts from descriptions of the journals' profiles. Following this, I will unlink the individuals' accounts from the universities, locations and disciplinary areas of the journals they edit. Editors will be referred to by codes (for example, E1, E2), with no further personal information provided. In cases where the journal's discipline is specified, the code will not be provided as this may reveal the informant's identity. If the disciplinary area is extremely specific, a more general disciplinary label will be used. This will both minimize the risk of data loss and maintain the participants' anonymity.

## 10.4 Findings and discussion

Using mostly interview data, supported by bibliometric information where relevant, two major themes will be discussed: editors' perceptions of the goals and motivations for their journals' adoption of English as their medium, and their views on the nature of their journal.

### 10.4.1 Why English?

A survey of points during the journals' lifespans when they switched to English shows that all journals launched after 1990 (a total of 11, with six launched in the 1990s and five in the 2000s) have used English from the beginning, with only one starting as a bilingual Serbian-English publication. Of the four journals established prior to 1990, two used to be Serbian-only but switched to English in the 2000s, one has been English-only from the beginning, and one initially accepted articles in English in addition to French, German, Russian and Serbian, but in the 1980s adopted English as its only medium. Journals starting off as English-medium tended to choose English titles from the beginning, while those switching to English later adopted an English title either by translating the original title from Serbian or by introducing a new title in English, Latin or Greek.

Most editors cited multiple motivations for using English as the language medium of their journals. The use of English is intended to achieve certain goals, some of which are related to the international sphere, while others are aimed at the local context.

#### 10.4.1.1 *Reaching beyond the national context*

For most editors, the main goal of publishing the journal in English is to 'foster international scholarly exchange', a phrase repeatedly used by many participants. However, the editors differed in terms of which aspect of exchange they emphasized as the most desirable. For some, the primary goal is to promote the work of Serbian scholars beyond the national borders; for others it is primarily exchange in the opposite direction – that is, enabling knowledge flows from the international circles towards the Serbian research community; still others aim for bi-directional exchange.

Most editors strongly believe that English-medium journals are an excellent vehicle for presenting research by Serbian scholars to an international audience, especially if they are also open-access and available online, even if they are not included in SCI/SSCI lists. Editors whose journals recently switched to English describe the positive outcomes in terms of 'expanding the readership' of their journals and creating 'greater opportunities for being cited' (E10) for Serbian researchers. Some editors keep track of the geographical locations of their journals' readership using Google Analytics tools, which allow them to check the number of viewings and downloads of the journal's content by country. E9, for instance, shared data showing that, in the month before our correspondence, only 7 per cent of his online-only journal's readers were from Serbia, with the majority based in the US and various European countries. He also noted an interesting pattern among the journal users: in the preceding three months, papers by foreign authors published in his journal were viewed almost twice as often as papers by local authors; however, papers by local authors were 25 per cent more likely to be downloaded, suggesting that while papers by Serbian authors were less likely to be browsed, those that did attract readers' initial attention had a higher likelihood of actually being downloaded and possibly read. According to the editor's data, then, the presence of foreign authors in the journal increased the likelihood of papers by local researchers getting noticed. Editors also provided examples of the work of Serbian authors published in their journals cited by foreign authors publishing in English-medium journals in other countries, using information provided by the national library. Some editors, such as E8, received requests for permissions to include papers by Serbian scholars published in her journal in international collected volumes. These examples show that the journals' goals related to the promotion of Serbian scholarship are, in many cases, being fulfilled, although most editors expressed hopes for further developments in this direction.

While greater exposure of Serbian scholars' work to a wider international readership is seen as an important function of English-medium journals by most editors, some explained their journal's use of English specifically in terms of making articles by international scholars accessible to the local readership. This function of English-medium journals is particularly important in a country whose institutions have subscriptions to a limited number of publications (as also noted by Lillis and Curry 2010, for other contexts); as E14 describes it, 'most of our researchers do not always have access to the latest publications'.

However, even where access is not an issue, as E1 points out, local English-medium journals play a role in bringing to the attention of the local community work which uses theoretical frameworks or research methodologies with no or little presence in the local research tradition, which is particularly relevant in some social science disciplines. As E1 states, one of the goals of his journal is 'to free [his discipline] from the remnants of socialist-era dictates' by encouraging the use of more diverse and up-to-date research frameworks.

Another motivation for using English is to create a top-quality journal and promote it internationally; as E4 explains, 'to enable the journal to be visible outside the local context, to be cited in relevant journals and to find its place in the world scientific literature'. While English is seen as a prerequisite for this goal, editors are aware that 'it is not sufficient to publish in English to become a well-known and well-respected journal' (E4), and that 'the quality of published articles is more important than the language [in which they are published]' (E11). E14 also points to the importance of the journal being indexed in prestigious databases, which 'in theory don't require the use of English but in practice English is necessary'. Most editors see the inclusion in the SCI/SSCI list as the yardstick of recognition of the journal's quality; therefore, reference to Thompson Reuters' criteria and procedures was frequently made. Although a few editors challenged the objectivity of the impact factor and other bibliometric measures of journal quality, the majority view this procedure as fair and objective, which is in some cases seen as a contrast to the local authority's evaluation system.

Finally, creating a unique journal was a goal mentioned by the editors of three journals covering inter/transdisciplinary areas, where English is necessary as the communities of scholars in these areas are small and geographically dispersed. One of these editors explains that his journal is currently the only one in the world to cover the particular combination of disciplines in his research area; hence, it is not surprising that papers in this journal are authored by researchers from across the globe. By finding a niche area at the intersection of several disciplines that are brought together in a novel way, these journals are illustrative of the semiperiphery's greater freedom for experimentation and openness to 'fringe' topics, something that mainstream centre journals cannot always afford (see Introduction to this volume).

### 10.4.1.2 Goals in the local context

The use of English was also motivated by goals related to the local context, at both national and institutional levels, revealing some important functions of these journals in the local environment. The cases below show that local factors may be a crucial driver of the journals' use of English.

While many editors referred to the Ministry's journal evaluation system (some welcoming while others criticizing its criteria and procedures), in one case, it was identified as the main factor behind the journal's move towards English, aimed at improving the journal's ranking in the Ministry's evaluation table. The editor of this journal was ambivalent about the shift towards English, although he was instrumental in setting up the necessary procedures. On the one hand, he welcomed the move and described some of the positive outcomes of switching to English, such as the increased regional exchange and the fact that the journal was under consideration for inclusion in the SCI list. On the other hand, he resented the assumption (which he perceived was behind the Ministry's evaluation criteria) that publications in the local language are by definition inferior to those in English. Commenting on the previous issues of his journal, launched in the 1950s, he pointed to the arbitrary nature of such evaluation: 'Is this not science because it's not in English?' adding that 'if it weren't, it wouldn't be considered by Thompson [for inclusion in the SCI list]'. This example shows the complexity of attitudes surrounding language policies but also the powerful effect of local 'push' factors, in this case the evaluation regime awarding governmental funding to top journals.

English-medium journals may also be used as a vehicle for fulfilling the institutional goals of the journals' funding body. One of the editors explains that his journal was launched as a result of a departmental decision with the aim of raising the department's profile in the national context and creating a space for its staff to develop a track record of international publications necessary for promotion. Publishing an international journal was also intended to support the department's application for accreditation of its newly established doctoral programme. Although the journal also aimed to foster international exchange, the primary motivation behind its language policies was to achieve institutional goals in the local context.

Finally, local readers' and authors' perceived needs also featured as a factor in deciding on the language policy of the journal. The editor of the only bilingual journal in the sample explained that both languages were needed because the journal's intended readership included both researchers and practitioners. The Serbian version was seen as necessary to reach the practitioners, most of whom were not proficient enough to read an English-only publication; however, this was only a temporary measure in order to 'educate the practitioners' and prepare them for reading professional literature in English, as the journal planned to switch to the English-only version in a year's time in order to avoid high translation costs. The editor stressed that ultimately the practitioners in the field 'must understand that English is essential for professional development'. Several other editors also mentioned that one of their journals' aims was to raise standards of journal publishing in Serbia through measures such as rigorous peer review procedures involving reviewers from other countries, which was perceived as a break with the practices of some poor-quality local L1 journals (see Salager-Meyer 2008). At the same time, many of the editors described their efforts to help local authors publish in English, with some editing manuscripts themselves if they felt there was potential for a good contribution. Support for local authors was also offered on some of the journals' websites, through features such as a 'model' research paper and detailed guidelines for authors. Some editors point to the educational role of 'local, easily accessible journals, to encourage junior scholars to read and write better' (E8). These measures, reminiscent of the extensive support for local scholars offered by the *Croatian Medical Journal* (Marušić and Marušić 1999, 2001, 2012 and this volume; Mišak et al. 2005), and also identified by Lillis (2012), show that English-medium journals on the semiperiphery have an educational role as well, helping local authors develop skills needed for publishing in English. However, the support-ive role these journals perform may be perceived as conflicting with the goal to achieve and/or maintain high standards, with some editors see-ing support as a temporary measure only, and others – primarily those concerned with creating a high-quality journal – rejecting the notion that journals need to help local authors altogether.

As can be seen, the journals' use of the medium of English is moti-vated by a complex combination of locally and globally oriented goals, which are not mutually exclusive but are not necessarily congruent either. Rather, they simultaneously operate at different levels: while English is primarily used as a tool for reaching beyond the national boundaries, it is also intended to serve local purposes. Drawing on Blommaert's (2005) take on world system analysis, the multiple func-tions of English in academic publishing on the semiperiphery can be seen as a result of the position these journals occupy vis-à-vis the cen-tring institutions to which they orient, that is, the Anglophone centre on the one hand, and the national research authority on the other, and the overlapping yet distinct value attribution regimes of the two. The goals of these journals, as described by their editors, show that many are oriented towards the Anglophone centre and its institutions such as Thompson Reuters, which Lillis (2012) describes as the effect of a centripetal force. At the same time, we have seen that some of these journals aim to function, as Lillis (2012) describes it, 'as a centrifugal force by opening up intellectual spaces that are often not available in either English-medium centre journals or longstanding journals in local languages' (p. 716). Still others have important roles in a more narrowly defined local context, where English is primarily used due to its ability to index 'international'; hence 'top-quality' (Lillis and Curry 2010), needed for institutional purposes. In all these cases, English is perceived as a necessary or helpful tool for reaching the journal's goals. Editors differ in their perspectives about whether these forces are 'pull' or 'push' factors. Some editors foreground the pressures to adopt English as their publication medium, with journals forced to switch to English in order to avoid marginalization even within the national context. Such push factors are typically evident in the case of journals with a long tradition of publishing in the local language, which have recently had to switch to English. In some cases, both pressures and opportunities surface as motifs in the editors' accounts. Overall, however, pull factors seem to feature more strongly, with the majority of editors perceiving the use of English as a vehicle for opening up new opportunities and fulfilling goals both locally and beyond.

In sum, the findings suggests that English-medium journals on the semiperiphery are located at the intersection of conflicting centripetal and centrifugal forces, a position fraught with possible tensions. This is particularly evident in the accounts of editors of journals in applied fields, which cater for both researchers and practitioners. At the other end of the spectrum, however, are editors of journals in hard-pure sciences, where publishing in English has long become standard practice; as one of the editors states, 'simply, nothing is written in Serbian any longer' in her field. In these cases, the language medium is not a matter of choice, and the use of English is so normalized that even my question of 'why English?' seemed superfluous.

## 10.4.2   The nature of English-medium journals on the semiperiphery

Bibliometric data show that the journals in the sample vary widely in terms of the national affiliations and geographical locations of their published authors. While some publish mainly papers by local authors, others publish almost exclusively papers by non-local authors (although the latter are fewer in number). In between are journals with varying proportions of articles by local and non-local authors. However, while 'local' can be easily defined as researchers affiliated with institutions in Serbia, 'non-local' is a rather heterogeneous category, including authors from ex-Yugoslav countries (who not long ago were part of the same local context), other neighbouring countries and other semiperipheral countries, as well as the countries of the Anglophone centre. To add to the complexity, some of the authors located in centre countries are originally from Serbia, therefore formerly (and perhaps still to some extent) 'local' authors. Clearly, bibliometric data alone are not a reliable indicator of the scope and nature of English-medium journals in non-Anglophone contexts.

The editors' perceptions show a seemingly more homogenous perspective, as all but three editors chose 'international' as the best descriptor of the nature of their journal, quoting evidence such as the fact that the journal's authors, readers and editorial boards include academics from a range of countries and, in some cases, that the journal is included in international databases. Of the three remaining editors, one opted for 'regionally international' (E11) as his journal serves primarily as a vehicle of knowledge exchange in the Balkan region; another editor described his journal as '50 per cent national, 30 per cent regional and 20 per cent international' (E12), while the third considers his journal 'transnational', which he also views as one of the features of science (E9). None of the editors qualified their journal as 'national', and those whose journals were ranked as 'leading national' by the Ministry tended to disagree with this classification, pointing to problems in the criteria and procedures, such as perceived bias against journals affiliated with institutions located outside of the capital and against marginalized research areas within core disciplines.

However, further analysis revealed some ambiguity behind the editors' use of the term 'international'. First, being international is implied to be a process, and therefore also a matter of degree. For instance, some of the editors who qualified their journal as international described the future goals for the journal as 'greater internationalization' (E6), achieving 'a higher proportion of papers by foreign scholars' (E12), or 'becoming more international' (E8). In other words, 'international' tends to be perceived as a gradable, dynamic and measurable quality. Secondly, while a few editors spoke of 'international' as involving exchange specifically with 'the countries of the Anglo-Saxon area' (E10), that is, the countries of the Western core, this was not a uniform, nor even the majority view. For many, what is important is that the journal is not restricted to the local research community, and is instead open to knowledge flows to and from areas beyond the national borders.

Several editors emphasized the regional context as the most relevant for their journal; however, even 'regional' was defined in diverse ways, with some focusing on the ex-Yugoslav area, others on the Balkans, still others on Central European or Eastern European countries. The regional aspect was perceived as particularly important in disciplines dealing with topics related to the shared cultural and historical space or common geographical and climatic features. The editor of an agricultural journal gives an example of his own research paper on a local breed of pig, which was rejected by a US journal due to, as the reviewers phrased it, the topic's lack of interest for the journal's readership; yet the topic was important to the regional research community. The knowledge flows, however, can be established with other, geographically remote, semiperipheral regions as well, based on a shared interest. For instance, one of the editors in economics gives bibliometric evidence of increased knowledge exchange with South American research communities on topics of relevance to similar economies. This is similar to the *Croatian Medical Journal*'s strategy of publishing articles from developing countries on topics of joint interest, aiming 'to serve as a bridge between mainstream science and the scientific periphery' (Mišak et al. 2005, p. 123). Thus, English-medium journals on the semiperiphery have an important role to play in showcasing research of interest in the regional and semiperipheral context, which may be rejected as 'parochial' (see Flowerdew 2001) by centre journals.

While it may be tempting to replace the problematic national/international binary by a more fine-grained continuum (national-regional-international), these all remain contested terms in the context of academic publishing, as shown above and in previous literature. Lillis and Curry (2010), for instance, refer to 'international' as a 'sliding signifier' which is 'often used as a proxy for "English medium"' (p. 6) and, drawing on bibliometric studies, suggest the term 'internationality' instead, while Lillis (2012) tellingly uses inverted commas when referring to English-medium 'national' journals, questioning this status. Hamel (2007) also points to the blurring boundaries between the national and international spheres of academic publishing. Clearly, 'national' and 'international' cannot adequately describe the scope and the nature of English-medium journals in non-Anglophone countries.

The complexity surrounding the issues of location, scope and nature of these journals is aptly illustrated by a segment from the interview with E1, who received an offer from a prestigious international publisher to take over his journal, which at the time of the study was being monitored by Thompson Reuters for inclusion in the SSCI list. The editor did not accept the offer, explaining 'I want the journal to be from Serbia'. Yet one of the important goals of the journal for him is, as he calls it, 'de-ghettoization' of Serbian scholars in his discipline, and he emphatically states that research and publishing 'should not be local'. The seeming contradiction in this politics of location can be explained with reference to the notion of translocality (for a recent critical review, see Greiner and Sakdapolrak 2013), a perspective used to explain phenomena of interconnectedness not restricted to national boundaries. The translocality framework offers concepts that can be fruitfully applied to the study of English-medium journals on the semi-periphery, such as local-to-local flows and relations (for instance, the South American economists publishing in a Serbian journal, as shown above); the importance of locality (shown in E1's firm decision to keep the journal locally based); and connectedness, networks and transfer (unanimously perceived as important goals of these journals by all editors in this study).

Considering English-medium journals on the semiperiphery as a *translocal* phenomenon thus helps accommodate both their rootedness in the local (institutional and national) context and their ability to open up spaces for knowledge flows connecting the local context both with other localities and with higher-than-local levels. While such spaces are in some cases created as a result of internal and external pressures, they may also play an emancipating role in the local community, offering local scholars a more supportive environment than English-medium journals in the centre and an opportunity to publish in 'locally international' journals as a stepping stone to publishing in more high-stakes journals. We can also see that while the 'international' dimension is seen as an important overarching goal of these journals and the yardstick against which to measure their quality and development, the local is of equal significance: on the one hand, it is a source of affordances and constraints that shape the journals' practices (such as the local research authorities' regulations); on the other, it provides a motivation and an arena for the journals' goal-oriented activities (such as increasing the standards of publishing in the local research community). Their translocal nature, that is, the fact that they are not restricted to the local context, which is enabled by the use of English, contributes, in turn, to the fulfilment of their goals in the local context. In other words, the more successful they are in developing local-to-local and local-to-higher-than-local knowledge flows, the more valuable they will be perceived to be in the local context.

## 10.5   Conclusion

This study has explored the growing phenomenon of English-medium journals on the semiperiphery by investigating the perceptions of editors of English-medium journals in Serbia. This phenomenon is relatively recent and marks a new development in small research communities. While scholars from 'small' language backgrounds have always had to write in a foreign language in order to reach a wider international audience, what is new is that increasingly the option to publish in the local language is disappearing due to decreasing numbers of periodicals in the local language and the growing pressures on scholars to publish in English. Instead, the choice is increasingly between publishing in local or centre-affiliated English-medium journals.

The findings of this study lead to several interrelated conclusions. First, English-medium journals in Serbia, and quite possibly in other non-Anglophone countries, constitute a diverse category, with different histories, goals, and practices related to the use of English. This variation is due to a range of factors, including disciplinary differences, institutional affiliations and personal editorial styles. While this study has identified general patterns, future research should investigate specific categories of journals in more depth and explore the factors that impact on their policies and practices.

Second, it is shown that these journals use English in order to achieve a variety of goals at different levels, from local institutional goals to the goals at the international level. As the journals operate in a polycentric environment, and are oriented towards centring institutions at both local and higher-than-local levels, tensions may occur as a result of conflicting goals and priorities. Importantly, however, English-medium publishing is seen as a necessary although not sufficient condition for achieving these goals. Journals in hard-pure disciplines are a special case in this regard, as the editors in these disciplines do not perceive English as adding to the value of the journal; its use in these disciplines is normalized to such an extent that publishing in the local language is seen as impractical.

Third, I have argued that English-medium journals on the semiperiphery should be considered as a *translocal* phenomenon due to the knowledge flows they enable between different local contexts as well as with higher-than-local levels. The translocal perspective also accommodates the firm ties these journals have to their localities and the affordances and constraints on their practices arising from the local context.

Importantly, this perspective allows a way out of the local/global and national/international binaries and places emphasis on activity at levels in between, showing that English-medium journals on the semiperiphery serve important functions in a continuum of contexts.

Of the many issues raised by the findings of this study that are worth pursuing further, I will select two as particularly pertinent. One concerns the use of English in these journals and the question of whether it should be seen as a sign of oppression and inequality or empowerment through appropriation of a language resource for one's own purposes. It is useful to quote Blommaert (2005) here: 'What happens to resources such as English, their value and identity-articulating potential in one place is not necessarily predictable from what happens to them elsewhere' (p. 211). Hence, to answer this question, further research is needed, focusing on the attitudes and practices of English-medium journals' readers and authors, to understand what the use of English does to them (echoing Blommaert's question about what language does to people) and what they are able to do with and in it.

The second question raised by this and similar studies is how to understand the role that English-medium journals on the semiperiphery play in global academic publishing. As we know from the world system analysis literature (Wallerstein 2004), it is typically the centre that has direct communication channels to various semiperipheral and peripheral zones for economic and other flows, while connections among different semiperipheries are less common, as semiperipheries tend to orient to the centre. This study has shown that some English-medium journals are able to and have an interest in forging links and exchanging knowledge with other semiperipheries in addition to with the centre. Are English-medium journals such as these opening up a space for new routes of knowledge flows? If so, what processes of knowledge validation and circulation are involved? Or is this a temporary phenomenon bound to disappear as a result of increasing pressures to publish in centre journals only? More broadly, should a parallel be drawn to how the semiperiphery is seen in economic terms as a factor that stabilizes the world system (Wallerstein 2004) and should we similarly regard English-medium journals on the semiperiphery as a balancing factor in global academic publishing? Or does this phenomenon play a different, yet undefined, role? Future research is needed to answer these and other questions arising from the dynamic landscape of academic publishing in the 21st century.

# Appendix

## Sample interview schedule

[Journal title] has been recently launched, and from the start it has used English as its medium. Can you tell me about the reasons for this decision?

What conditions were necessary for this to be made possible?

To what extent have the goals that motivated the decision to publish in English been achieved?

Can you tell me something about the readership of the journal? To what extent does the readership consist of scholars/users from Serbia, the ex-Yugoslav/Southeast European region, or a broader range of countries?

Some have expressed concerns about journals in English being inaccessible to scholars in Serbia who don't speak English well enough. What is your opinion about this?

According to the Ministry's report on the ranking of journals for last year, [title of journal] is ranked [x]. Can you comment on this, please? Are you satisfied with this ranking? What are the implications of this ranking for the journal (for example, for funding, for the journal's appeal as a potential outlet to other academics)?

Regardless of the ranking, how do you see the journal, as national, regional, international, transnational or something else?

According to the latest bibliometric report, [title of journal] has published [%] of articles by international authors. Are you satisfied with the proportions of articles authored by local and foreign authors? How has the journal managed to attract the attention of international academics in the short span of time since its launch?

In your opinion, what are the benefits of publishing articles by foreign authors in the journal you edit?

Are there any indications that the works by Serbian authors published in the journal have attracted the attention of international readers since they are published in English and are available online?

From your experience, are Serbian researchers facing more difficulties when preparing manuscripts in English? If so, what particular difficulties? Do you know of authors not submitting manuscripts to English-medium journals because of their lack of English knowledge or English writing skills?

How does the journal address this issue? Does the journal offer support? Do you see this as a role of the journal or some other body or the authors themselves?

What difficulties do you face as an editor of an English-medium journal in a non-Anglophone country? (prompts: communicating with authors from a range of countries, selection of reviewers, members of the editorial board, text editing and proof-reading). How do you deal with these difficulties?

How would you characterize the nature of the journal, given its readership and users: as a national, international, regional, transnational or something else? How do you see the journal in 5 or 10 years' time in that respect?

What is your opinion of the fact that a growing number of journals is switching to use English as its main medium of publication?

What is the future of scholarship in Serbian and other 'small' languages?

Is there anything else you would like to comment on in relation to the themes we have discussed?

## Notes

1. Gibbs' (1995) use of the term 'developing' is based on indices of economic development. While 'developing' is likely to overlap with 'semiperipheral' in most cases, it should be borne in mind that the two terms are not identical. For instance, Giannoni (2008) uses 'peripheral' when referring to knowledge production and academic publishing in Italy; however, based on economic criteria, Italy belongs to developed, rather than developing countries.
2. Due to the recent restructuring of the government, the Ministry is now called Ministry of Education, Science and Technological Development.
3. Available at http://www.mpn.gov.rs
4. I use 'Serbian' for convenience, although the language is Serbo-Croatian (see, for instance, Kordić 2010).
5. The number of disciplinary areas has risen from 17 in 2009 to 22 in 2013. A journal can be assessed within more than one area, as is the case with interdisciplinary journals.
6. Data about journals published in Serbia used in this study were compiled from the Serbian citation index database (www.scindex.ceon.rs), which indexes locally published academic journals, and the annually published *Journal Bibliometric Report*, which provides various scientometric analyses of Serbian journals. Both are provided by the Center for Evaluation in Education and Science (CEES), a non-governmental, non-for-profit organization promoting 'open, data-driven, and permanent evaluation of academic entities of Serbia' (www.ceon.rs).
7. See note 6.
8. See note 2.
9. It should be acknowledged that this is a self-selected group, as the informants were among those who responded to my email.

# 11
# The Croatian Medical Journal: Success and Consequences

*Matko Marušić and Ana Marušić*

## 11.1   Introduction

In the European context, Croatia fits the definition of a semiperipheral country very well. It is located between the centre and periphery both geographically and economically, developing at a slower rate than the centre (but faster than the periphery), with fewer material resources, and characterized by a tradition of corruption, including in the academic community. Relative to the centre, research productivity is low and resistance to innovation high; there is also inefficiency, a lack of organization, limited access to equipment and resources, and an inability to attract or fix top-ranking researchers (Marušić and Marušić 1999). Most scientific production is restricted to the university environment, and university departments are run as 'minifiefdoms' (Canagarajah 2002, p. 195) rather than meritocracies; hence, it is generally considered to be more important to cultivate influential connections than an impressive curriculum. As for Croatian science journals, these have been mostly 'domestic' in language, scope and management, and publications are either not peer-reviewed or the process is conducted in a less than rigorous manner (Marušić and Marušić 1999).

After emerging from the communist regime that had governed it since World War II, Croatia suffered military aggression between 1991 and 1995, which left 16,000 dead, half a million displaced and much of its industry devastated (Lang and Marušić 1993). Since 1991 it has been a free country, recovering and learning to live as a democratic society. Despite all odds and disappointments (M. Marušić 2010a, 2010b), it joined the European Union in 2013.

The *Croatian Medical Journal* (*CMJ*) was launched in 1991 and has accompanied the birth of the country as an independent state, experiencing all the phases of its growth and development since then (M. Marušić 2010b). It achieved inclusion in MEDLINE in 1998 and in Current Contents/Web of Science in 1999 (Marušić et al. 2002), and was awarded an impact factor of 1,796 in 2011 (the highest in the history of all Croatian scientific journals). However, with the growth of journal's importance and international prestige, the pressures on its editorial freedom also increased. In 2003, the medical school hosting it (Zagreb) began its bid for editorial control, initiating a conflict that lasted until June 2011, when the entire editorial board resigned. Nevertheless, the *CMJ* has been successful in establishing standards for editorial work in Croatia, and its experiences are potentially motivating and instructive for other countries on the semiperiphery.

## 11.2  The niche

From the outset, the journal aimed to offer a window through which the world would be able to see Croatian medical science, and a door through which Croatian science could achieve the best international standards (M. Marušić 2011). It also hoped to contribute to the modernization of medicine, academia and society through its international orientation, openness and strict application of rigorous editorial and publishing standards (Marušić and Marušić 1999). However, its attempts to solicit good-quality works from the local scientific community proved much harder than expected, because domestic scientists preferred to send their best works to internationally renowned journals, while reputable foreign scientists did just the opposite, contributing articles that would not be published in more prestigious journals (M. Marušić 2010b). Hence, the *CMJ* was left with a clearly defined niche, which did contain relevant and interesting works, though in general produced by rather inexperienced authors (Marušić and Marušić 2001, 2011, M. Marušić 2010b).

The journal learned a great deal from the 1991–1995 war (Marušić and Marušić 2002, Sambunjak and Ivaniš 2006). Despite resistance from some members of the editorial board, it took to soliciting and publishing reports of war medicine experiences, from surgical innovations to the documentation of war crimes and the organization of field hospitals. This led the editors to develop activities that combined editorial work with medical work in war:

- War medicine: *CMJ* editors actively approached physicians who volunteered on the battlefronts to solicit their war medicine reports and helped them write and publish their experiences. Some 360 articles were published in the *CMJ* and other medical journals via this process (Marušić and Marušić 1996).

- Peace promotion initiatives: the *CMJ* stimulated debate about peace among health care professionals and students (Glunčić et al. 2001), and contributed to the promotion of human rights and the development of a peace-building 'Colledex' (collaboration, education, experience) project (Marušić and Marušić 2001). After the war, it published a series of essays on 'Medicine and Peace', which later came out in book form.
- Humanitarian work: in 1991, the *CMJ* became the official journal of the World Association of Croatian Physicians (WACP), a voluntary association engaged in humanitarian work (Baća et al. 1999). In 1993, its editorial office operated as the centre for the coordination of a huge humanitarian action in Bosnia and Herzegovina (A. Marušić et al. 1994), and the journal participated in actions to provide psychosocial support to refugees (Arcel et al. 1995) and deliver humanitarian aid to all warring sides in Bosnia and Herzegovina (A. Marušić et al. 1994).
- 'Challenge of Goodness': this was a series of articles published in the *CMJ* by the renowned humanitarian and human rights activist, Slobodan Lang. The basic idea was that humankind should identify the good deeds performed in war as meticulously as the war crimes, and that the experience of goodness should be used in future conflicts (Lang 1998).

Hence, it became clear that this journal could make an effective contribution to society and help ease the suffering of the people.

## 11.3   The versatility of editorial work

The experience of providing editorial assistance to war-engaged physicians not only taught the editors ways of helping inexperienced authors who have valuable data to transmit, but also revealed the great need for such work (Marušić and Marušić 2001). It was clear that these doctors were competent and committed professionals, but were unaware of the importance of publishing and unskilled in writing scientific reports. Hence, after the war, this wartime editorial strategy broadened to include peace-time themes, which reflected the attempts of a semi-peripheral society to improve its quality of life.

## 11.3.1 Editorial work in the journal

The strategy of soliciting specific reports from authors meant that the journal could work with its authors in peacetime in much the same way as it had in war. This work had many facets:

- Active acquisition of manuscripts: the editors continued to solicit manuscripts that were pertinent to the journal's niche, which was defined as 'medicine and health in a transitional post-war southeastern European country and its neighbours'.
- Open access: visibility was chosen above profit, as the journal's readership was unable or unwilling to pay for access to it. For this reason, offers to join the commercial electronic packages of prestigious journals were declined (Kljaković-Gašpić et al. 2007).
- Author-helpful policy: manuscripts that were poorly written or organized yet had relevant themes and/or interesting core data were not rejected outright but repeatedly corrected ('pre-review') until ready for international peer review (Marušić and Marušić 2001, M. Marušić et al. 2004). Indeed, the *CMJ's* author-helpful policy became its international trademark (Marušić and Marušić 2012). It soon became clear that the problem was not just about the authors' command of English, but went much deeper. In fact, four layers of editing were distinguished (Mišak et al. 2005) concerning problems with: (i) study design; (ii) textual organization; (iii) scientific reporting style (terminology, tables and figures); and finally (the easiest to deal with) (iv) language (clarity, grammar, style).
- Legal regulation: the roles of all the stakeholders in the journal were defined in an 'Agreement on the *Croatian Medical Journal*', which served as the official core document. This focused on the administrative details of transforming the need for a balance between editorial freedom and responsibility to the practice of editorial work (M. Marušić et al. 2003). The document was praised and recommended to other journals, large and small (Huth 2004).
- Journal research: the journal was viewed as a research model under the editors' control, and various aspects of its work were investigated in a formal scientific manner: manuscript inflow, origin and destiny (M. Marušić et al. 2004), the review process (Kljaković-Gašpić et al. 2003, A. Marušić et al. 2002), authorship (Bates et al. 2004, Ilakovac et al. 2007, Ivaniš et al. 2008, 2011, A. Marušić et al. 2006), impact factor (Golubić et al. 2008, Kovačić et al. 2008), the journal's image and role in the eyes of its readers (Sambunjak et al. 2009). This activity significantly improved the journal's work.

- Essays: these were introduced to add colour to the dry scientific content with an aim to extend the readership, and covered subjects such as patients' experiences ('Patient Voice') and essays about corruption and other problems in the Croatian health care system by an expert investigative reporter ('Rights and Wrongs').
- The *CMJ* Book Collection: collections of approximately twenty essays on the same topic were transformed into books; these were treated as non-commercial products and were used mostly for educational purposes and journal promotion (Huić 2008).
- Croatian International Publications: this was a section in the journal devoted to abstracts of the best publications by domestic authors in international journals. The academic community liked the column, which increased the journal's visibility (Huić 2008).
- Themed issues: two or three issues a year (out of 6) were devoted to a single research theme, often associated with scientific conferences. Most of the *CMJ*'s cited articles came from the themed issues.
- Student *CMJ*: students were encouraged to publish their research in the journal, and were helped at all phases of their work. This attracted more authors, so that, from 2002 to 2006, each first issue in the year contained students' work or articles that had themes related to students' issues (Huić 2008).
- Artwork: when space allowed, poetry by doctors or about medical themes, and reproductions of doctors' paintings were included (Huić 2008).
- Editors' associations: the editors of the *CMJ* became members of the European Association of Science Editors (EASE), World Association of Medical Journal Editors (WAME) and Council of Science Editors (CSE), attending their respective meetings. This not only brought new collaborators, but also led to book chapters on important editorial issues in small journals (A. Marušić 2008, A. Marušić and Haug 2006, Nylenna et al. 2003). One of the *CMJ*'s editors served as president of WAME and CSE, and as the member of International Council of Medical Journal Editors (*ICMJE*).
- Collaboration with domestic journals: the *CMJ* assisted a number of editors with advice, software and documents. One editor contributed to the national policy of public funding of journals, which increased the quality of scholarly publishing, primarily by introducing quality standards. Croatia now has an official standard of editorial work, and an ethics flowchart from the Committee on Publication Ethics (COPE). During the four years of *CMJ*'s leadership on improving national policy on scientific publishing, the number of Croatian

journals listed in indexing databases (such as Scopus and those of Thomson Reuters) approximately tripled (Sambunjak et al. 2008).

• Collaboration with international journals: collaboration with esteemed journals such as *The Lancet* produced research comparing some aspects of their editorial work (A. Marušić et al. 2002).

• Journal design and technology: with the advances in publishing technology, the *CMJ* became an open-access journal, which won an international award for design and a domestic award for its website.

### 11.3.2   Education

The educational efforts made by the *CMJ* during the war continued after it, becoming an intrinsic part of the journal's editorial policy (A. Marušić, ed. 2005, Marušić and Marušić 2001). They included:

• Individual work with authors: the focus here was 'preventive', that is, systematic teaching of the skills needed to present research data.

• Undergraduate course: the *CMJ* helped persuade all four Croatian medical schools to introduce a mandatory course on the principles of research in medicine. This began in 1996, making the Croatian medical education system one of the first in Europe with compulsory teaching in research methods (Marušić and Marušić 2003).

• Postgraduate course(s): at the University of Split, *CMJ* editors stimulated the creation of study into 'Evidence-based Clinical Medicine' in which a systematic study/meta-analysis would be recognized as a doctoral thesis. To speed up the completion of PhD works, the teaching strategy focuses on planning research and data analysis and presentation.

• Continuous education: the *CMJ*'s 2-day intensive course (20 hours) 'Planning and writing in medical research' (Sambunjak and Ivaniš 2005) has attracted 438 participants over nine years.

• Research training in medical schools: starting in 2009, training in research and critical thinking became part of the medical curriculum at the University of Split (A. Marušić et al. 2013) through courses on medical statistics, medical informatics and clinical research methods.

• Educational programmes in neighbouring Bosnia and Herzegovina: *CMJ* editors helped modernize the medical school curricula (Šimunović et al. 2006), develop the first university-level nursing curriculum and improve the work of several scientific journals, all within the context of the promotion of peace and reconciliation (Sambunjak and Šimunović 2007).

- Research in medical education: in accordance with the 'enlightened routine' concept (Marušić and Marušić 2012), the science training projects in medical school became subjects for research, with the systematic exploration of topics such as medical students' attitudes towards research (Burazeri et al. 2005, Hren et al. 2004, M. Marušić et al. 2010, Vujaklija et al. 2010), the effects of mentoring in medicine (Sambunjak and Marušić 2011), and students' moral reasoning (Hren et al. 2006, 2011).
- The International Campaign for the Revitalization of Academic Medicine (ICRAM): in 2004 *CMJ* joined ICRAM, actively contributing to the analysis of the problems in academic medicine (Tugwell 2004), and soliciting a number of contributions as regards the state of academic medicine in different countries. These works were subsequently published as a book (A. Marušić, ed. 2005).

### 11.3.3  The practice and promotion of research integrity

Social responsibility in scientific research requires editors and journals to detect and prevent publishing misconduct (A. Marušić et al. 2007). With respect to the mentality of the environment in which *CMJ* had chosen to work, this strategy soon proved crucial for the scientific and cultural role envisioned for the journal. As happened with other activities, this facet of work soon branched out to include practice, education and research.

- Responsible conduct in research: in the setting of a post-war, post-communist transition society, it was felt that the introduction of a culture of research integrity would be an effective way to reform the scientific community (Petrovečki and Scheetz 2001). This involved the creation of the post of Research Integrity Editor in the *CMJ* (Katavić 2006), and the teaching of responsible conduct in research on undergraduate and postgraduate programmes (Marušić and Marušić 2012). This in turn contributed to the formalization of the work of the national Committee for Ethics in Science and High Education (Puljak 2007).
- The National Committee for Ethics in Science and High Education: The *CMJ* worked with the major public research funding body in Croatia (the Ministry of Science, Education and Sports) to establish a national Committee for Ethics in Science and High Education (CESHE) (Puljak 2007). One of the *CMJ* senior editors was elected president of CESHE.
- Promoting research integrity: The *CMJ* was the first journal in the region to introduce mandatory checking of all submissions for text similarity using CrossCheck. Two members of the editorial team engaged successfully in plagiarism research (Baždarić et al. 2012).

- Retractions: editors are responsible for the integrity and quality of the public record and are obliged to correct the mistakes that concern the publication record in their journal. *CMJ* was one of the rare journals in the region that retracted its articles.

- Research in authorship: In the relatively small academic community of Croatia, it was easy to recognize underserved authorship, including guest and gift authorship (M. Marušić et al. 2004). Research into causes of authorship misuse led to a number of studies describing the psychometric characteristics of authorship contribution declarations (Bates et al. 2004, Ilakovac et al. 2007, Ivaniš et al. 2008, 2011, M. Marušić et al. 2006), and the finding that decisions on authorship are often in the moral rather than conventional domain of social decision-making (Hren et al. 2007, 2013).

- Research into medical student ethics: a number of studies on student moral reasoning (Hren et al. 2006, 2011), cheating (Hrabak et al. 2004) and attitudes to science (Hren et al. 2004, Vujaklija et al. 2010) were conducted during the course of the research method training, with active student cooperation.

- Education and research on culture of research integrity: the CESHE has had an important role in changing public perception about research misconduct and has resolved several cases that were mishandled by institutions (Chalmers 2006, Markovitch 2008a, 2008b). Croatia was praised for this reform and its standards were called 'unusual in much of Europe' (Bosch 2008).

Unfortunately, these efforts to promote responsible publishing and social responsibility in research, albeit well intended (M. Marušić 2009) and patriotic (Marušić and Marušić 1996), met with resistance and hostility from the more traditional circles within the academic community, and ultimately led to the termination of the mandate of Editorial Board in 2011 (Tatalović 2011), as described in more detail below.

### 11.3.4 Improving medical practice

In medicine, the transfer of knowledge is inseparable from the development of skills, the reliance on scientific evidence and the exploration of population-related issues. Consequently, these efforts to improve science communication in Croatian medicine spread to medical practice.

- Quality of care: the *CMJ* introduced a series of essays on quality of health care, subsequently published in book form. In 2010, at the

Split Medical School, the basics of quality of care were incorporated into the teaching of the principles of evidence-based medicine. One of the *CMJ* editors joined the National Agency for Quality and Accreditation in Health Care (Mittermayer et al. 2010).

- Evidence-based medicine: *Post hoc* assistance to the authors in addressing the problems of study design required explaining and teaching basics of research methods, firstly the types of clinical studies; this led to the need to learn the principles of evidence-based medicine (EBM), statistics, ethics, clinical trial ethics and patient rights (A. Marušić et al. 2013).

- Cochrane Collaboration: With the support of the Cochrane Collaboration, the *CMJ* editors formally established the Croatian Branch of the Italian Cochrane Centre (Puljak and Rako 2009), and the senior deputy editor became its director. The centre has organized a number of seminars, including an online course in Croatian, and coordinated a number of systematic reviews by Croatian authors. This work is empowered by the policy of some Croatian medical schools to accept systematic reviews and meta-analyses that follow the Cochrane Collaboration methodology as eligible for PhD research.

- Clinical trial registration initiative: the *CMJ* participated in the clinical trial registration initiative (De Angelis et al. 2004), which subsequently influenced the national health policy.

- Croatian register of clinical trials: as part of the European Union accession process, Croatia was required to establish public access to information about approved clinical trials. One of the *CMJ* editors obtained a research grant from the Ministry of Science, Education and Sports to carry out a pilot register, using information about trials in Croatia available from the *ClinicalTrials.org* public registry (www. regpok.hr). In 2011 approval was granted by the Ministry of Health and Social Care to develop the official national register. At present, the *CMJ* editors are working on implementing the WHO criteria for primary registers at the International Clinical Trials Registry Platform (ICTRP), so that Croatia can join the countries with trial registries available to the public in the Croatian language.

- Good clinical practice: in order to introduce and promote the concept of good clinical practice (GCP) in clinical research, the *CMJ* editors joined the European Forum for Good Clinical Practice (EFGCP), and prepared the Report on the Procedure for the Ethical Review of Protocols for Clinical Research for Croatia as a European Union candidate country on behalf of the EFGCP Ethics Working Party (Huić et al. 2011).

## 11.4 Editorial freedom

The *CMJ* is perhaps no different from many other journals in its ambition to influence academia, and, in doing so, achieve visibility and respect (Marušić and Marušić 2012). However, the result is probably unique in the history of science journals. The journal's insistence on international standards and its high rejection rate were not welcomed by some powerful figures in the traditional academic community, who first attempted to override the editors by tampering with the document that set the standards of quality and integrity of the journal work (Hoey 2008). When this did not work because of the pressures from the international community (Callaham et al. 2008, A. Marušić 2008, Sibbald and Flegel 2008), the editorial team were harassed and threatened (M. Marušić 2008, 2010a, M. Marušić and Marušić 2007, Marušić and Marušić 2008a, 2008b).

At the outset, the Croatian medical community had seemed genuinely proud of the *CMJ*'s success, particularly of its inclusion in the Current Contents (CC) database. However, it soon emerged that many saw this as an opportunity to achieve publication in a CC-listed journal without having to comply with the rigorous standards imposed elsewhere (academic advancement in Croatia depends upon a minimal number of publications, of which roughly half should be in journals listed in Current Contents). Thus, the journal received numerous requests from colleagues and other potential contributors to relax its editorial standards and apply fast-track publication (M. Marušić 2010b). The editors did not give in to this pressure (of the thousands of works submitted, there is not a single case of bias as regards the decision of whether or not to publish), which brought it into conflict with the established academic community.

The controversy began with a number of informal objections against the board's decisions. Due to the large number of submissions, it had been deemed necessary to introduce an editorial rejection system in order to lessen the load for the reviewers. However, authors would insist that their works be sent to review, claiming that the editors were not experts in their field (M. Marušić 2010b). Then, at the end of 2002, the journal's rejection of a paper written by a powerful colleague led to a series of personal threats and attacks, followed by a number of disciplinary procedures against editors-in-chief by the Zagreb medical school (Marušić and Marušić 2007, 2008a, 2008b), which were overturned by relevant bodies (Škaričić 2009, Committee for Ethics in Science and High Education 2009). The struggle continued until June 2011, when the editorial board (35 out of its 37 members) resigned (A. Marušić 2011).

The journal's social engagement has been governed by its belief in the indispensability of ethics for all parties involved (for authors as regards basic research integrity, conflicts of interest, and so on; for editors, who are effectively safeguarding the integrity of the public record; and for clinicians in the context of war medicine, ethics of clinical research, good clinical practice, and so on), and this has underpinned its promotion of social responsibility in research. However, its struggle against the limitations of the semiperiphery brought it into conflict with other forces operating in Croatian academia, ultimately resulting in the resignation of the editorial board as described (Tatalović 2011).

## 11.5   Conclusion

The *CMJ*'s experience demonstrates that the role of a scientific journal is, or may be, much wider than that of mere 'gatekeeping' in the field of high-quality science reporting. As authors want to publish in the journal, they have to fulfil the journal's requirements, giving the editors a powerful educational role that impinges on several different domains: the social (medicine in war, peace promotion through medicine, open access policy), the judicial (research integrity issues), the clinical (EBM, quality and integrity of clinical trials) and even the political (confronting corruption and pressures, dealing with political and administrative structures, and so on).

However, as we have seen, the journal's very semiperiphality may also result in unsustainable tensions, as the dynamics and values of centre publishing enter into conflict with traditional attitudes and practices. Negotiating such a conflict is one of the greatest challenges facing such publications.

# 12
# The Academic Weblog as a Semiperipheral Genre

*Małgorzata Sokół*

## 12.1 Introduction

The development of the Internet as a collaborative networking technology has been intensified by the expansion of Web 2.0 tools. The term Web 2.0 refers to web services and applications such as weblogs (or blogs), social networking sites, video-sharing sites, wikis and so on, that is, tools that facilitate interactive information sharing, user-centred design and more dynamic user participation and collaboration (see for example, O'Reilly 2005). The widespread adoption of Web 2.0 tools by members of academia has reinforced changes in the way science is done today. It has transformed the ways in which scientific knowledge is produced and disseminated, and has altered patterns of how scholars communicate and conduct research – of how they are socialized into the academic community and gain professional status and recognition. As I have argued elsewhere (Sokół 2012), the intensity of these technology-driven changes may be indicative of a deeper transformation at the institutional level, where well-established scholarly norms and discursive practices are being challenged. This raises important questions pertinent to the discussion of the academic 'centre' and 'periphery'.

In the chapter, I extend the geographically based distinction between 'centre' and 'periphery' as introduced by Canagarajah (2002) in order to explore academic discursive practices in the communicative context of Web 2.0. More specifically, my aim is to discuss the role of the emergent genre of the academic weblog in scholarly exchange, and of its overall importance for contemporary academia. Following the discussion of the semiperiphery undertaken in the present volume, I will tentatively propose that the academic weblog can be considered a semiperipheral genre. The academic weblog is an academic genre in the making, whose enactment and development results from the evolving needs and expectations of academics who increasingly participate in online environments. With its potential to dissolve hierarchical systems (see for example, Campagna et al. 2012, Walker 2006), and such affordances of the medium as interaction and connection, immediacy, instant access and relatively low cost (see the discussion of the public affairs blogs in Miller and Shepherd 2009), the academic weblog may be regarded as an informal response to the 'publish or perish' policy, while at the same time offering evidence of a major shift in the traditional publishing practices of academia. The academic weblog is viewed as a hybrid genre, less rigorously constructed, fluid and permeable, characterized by a high level of personalization, and with an unclear status as far as recognition among peers is concerned – features which, among others, would indicate the semiperipherality of the genre.

The discussion of the semiperipheral status of academic weblogs as an emergent genre of scholarly exchange is supported by the quantitative-qualitative analysis of the corpus of posts from Polish academic weblogs (for the list of weblogs under investigation, see Appendix A), completed with an email questionnaire with the blogs' authors (for the questionnaire, see Appendix B). The theoretical-methodological basis of the investigation is the socio-pragmatic approach to the analyses of web-based discourse (see, for example, Grieve et al. 2010, Herring et al. 2004, 2005), which prioritizes communicative purpose as the main genre-defining criterion. Recognizing that this traditional, goal-oriented view of genre is challenged by the development of web-based textual forms (see, for example, Askehave and Ellerup Nielsen 2005, Campagna et al. 2012), I focus on the communicative purpose of the genre as it relates to form and offers a way of studying the community's motivations and expectations. As Yus (2007b, p. 22) emphasizes,

> ...there is a socially recognized purpose of genres that also affects their identification and interpretation, that is, genres are normally regarded as types of communicative actions habitually enacted to realize particular communicative and collaborative purposes. They are identified according to their socially recognized purpose and by their common characteristics of form. The purpose of a genre would not be an individual's private motive for communicating, but a purpose socially constructed and recognized by the relevant organizational community and invoked in typical situations.

The overall aim of my preliminary study is to find out whether the academic weblog has conventionalized and stabilized as a form of scholarly communication among Polish academics. Thus, apart from the focus on the function, the investigation also involves an analysis of the visual-structural properties of the academic weblogs. For this purpose, I adapt Yus's (2007a) approach to the analysis of the verbal-visual layout of the weblog genre. In general, the study proves that the academic weblog is a fairly stabilized genre, in terms of its function(s) and structure. The structural properties of academic weblogs are largely determined by the blogging software, but also result from the functionalities of the medium that meet the needs of the blogs' authors as well as those of the audience. As regards the dominant functions of the academic weblog, the genre mainly serves to share knowledge and information, and to educate.

## 12.2 From computer networking to science 2.0

Although academic weblogs are a relatively recent phenomenon of web-based scholarly exchange, their growing popularity confirms the attractions of Web 2.0 networking technologies for members of academia, and the inherently social nature of scholarship. As early as in the 1990s, Harrison and Stephen noticed that 'the major innovation in the development of computer networking is the ability to *share* [authors' emphasis] on a widespread and nearly instantaneous basis both information and ideas in a variety of symbolic forms (text, number, images, sound, colour, and so on)' (Harrison and Stephen 1996, p. 5). In addition, the increased interaction within academia enabled by the earlier forms of web technologies served to change the nature of scholarly networks. They emerged as structures that are strongly connected, though spatially dispersed and loosely delimited, revealing at the same time the ongoing 'glocalization', that is, the consolidation of local interconnections and enhancement of their global expansion (see Koku et al. 2001). Web 2.0 tools have intensified the sharing potential of computer networking, leading to the further restructuring of formal and informal scholarly networks, both globally and locally.

The emergent patterns of doing science today are referred to as Science 2.0 (for example, Waldrop 2008), and essentially involve increased collaboration among scholars and the sharing of digitally stored data, information and knowledge – Science 2.0 is claimed to be more collegial and more productive. Science 2.0 relates to an Open Science movement, Open Access scientific publishing and Open Data practices, which are realized in numerous collaborative initiatives (for examples, see Nikam and Rajendra 2009, Rowley-Jolivet 2012, Waldrop

2008). As Rowley-Jolivet emphasizes, this transformed science is new from a technological point of view, but it represents the Mertonian scientific norms of

> communalism, or the common ownership of scientific discoveries; universalism, according to which claims to truth are evaluated in terms of universal or impersonal criteria; disinterestedness, according to which scientists are rewarded for acting in ways that outwardly appear to be selfless; and organized scepticism – all ideas are subjected to rigorous, structured community scrutiny.
>
> (Rowley-Jolivet 2012, p. 127)

The potential for collective thought and group knowledge that is offered by contemporary media technologies is also appreciated by two great media theorists, Pierre Lévy and Henry Jenkins, whose theories help us to understand the contemporary transformations taking place in scholarly communication. A crucial term in Lévy's conception of the new media architecture is *collective intelligence*, which is understood as 'a form of *universally distributed intelligence* [emphasis in the original], constantly enhanced, coordinated in real time, and resulting in the effective mobilization of skills', the basis of which is 'the mutual recognition and enrichment of individuals rather than the cult of fetishized or hypostatized communities' (Lévy 1999, p. 13). The organization of the new knowledge space contributes to an intellectual and social transformation: social bonds are renewed through our relation to knowledge and collective intelligence. At the same time, a demand is put on scholars to acquire competencies and skills that would allow them to navigate smoothly through this new knowledge space. Lévy also points to another important implication of the distributed collective intelligence that is relevant for the discussion of the academic 'centre' and 'periphery', namely the deterritorialization of science and dissolution of boundaries between disciplines.

Jenkins follows on Lévy's concept of collective intelligence to advance his own theory of convergence culture, which explains the relationship between collective intelligence, media convergence and participatory culture[1] (Jenkins 2006). The culture of convergence means that scholarly communication has to operate within the new paradigm in which the new media do not compete but rather coexist with the old media in the process of knowledge dissemination (see also Kulczycki 2012, p. 1). This implies that the traditional means of knowledge distribution are transformed by the new opportunities and scholars need to learn how to make use of both the traditional and new resources, sometimes not being aware of the new possibilities. In addition, as Kulczycki notes (2012, pp. 2–3), media convergence means that amateurs are included in the content creation process, which, in the context of academic blogging, means that amateurs, as well as experts, are invited to be active contributors to knowledge exchange. Given the purposes of the present chapter, further issues that Science 2.0 brings include the reconceptualization of academic literacies and, potentially, the transformation of the established model of academic socialization, and, on the discourse plane, issues related to academic genre adoption and enactment. For instance, how effective are Web 2.0 media in helping novices learn academic writing practices and norms? Is active participation in Web 2.0 media and the development of relevant media literacies necessary for (expert) membership in an academic community? Finally, can 'owning' academic, web-based genres (in the Swalesean sense, Swales 1990) be a sufficient measure of membership in an academic community?

The Web 2.0 technologies and Open Access movement are transforming scholarly communication, and they offer numerous opportunities for academia: instant and rapid communication of science, research visibility and transparency, elimination of price barriers in accessing Open Access publications. However, Science 2.0 is received by some with mistrust and suspicion, as it challenges the established norms of scholarly exchange. The potential risks of the transformed science include, among other things, the violation of copyright, plagiarism, exploitation of credit for work, theft of intellectual property, reduction of citations of publications from paid journals (Nikam and Rajendra 2009), lack of reliability and a waste of time for activities which do not contribute directly to academic career advancement (Kulczycki 2012). An important issue is also the evolving patterns of peer review. As Harrison and Stephen note, 'scholars obviously engage in many activities in addition to communication (like analysing, observing, conducting experiments, and synthesizing), but the products of those activities are not regarded as knowledge until they enter into the stream of disciplinary discourse through which knowledge is created, justified, disseminated, and archived' (1996, p. 5). Therefore, pertinent questions that concern peer review are whether Science 2.0 needs a reviewing system, and whether Science 2.0 itself can provide a reviewing system to the 'traditional' printed journals:

[s]cience communication in the convergence culture faces many internal and external challenges. On the one hand, it must justify

and legitimize its place in the scientific process; on the other hand, it has to develop rules for merging with the 'old media', that is, the reviewing system, as well as, publishing in journals and books. (Kulczycki 2012, p. 21)

Academia will, rather sooner than later, have to address the numerous challenges that have been brought by Science 2.0, especially as the use of Web 2.0 media by academics is on the increase, as are the number of Science 2.0 initiatives,[2] and much of the relevant discussion is already taking place in Web 2.0 environments.

## 12.3 The academic weblog and the challenges for genre theory

With the unceasing popularity of blogging practices in general, the blogosphere is also developing into an important space for scholarly communication. The weblog (popularly referred to as blog) has become an attractive Web 2.0 tool for members of academia, as it offers the potential to dissolve institutions and organizations, and, as a result, reverses conventional power relations. It ensures sharing, freedom of expression and creativity, and it represents a relatively transparent and unedited view of thinking-in-progress (Halavais 2006, Kjellberg 2010, Mortensen and Walker 2002, Schiltz et al. 2007, Walker 2006). It gives the sense of being connected, where audience awareness is crucial (Kjellberg 2010, Walker 2006) and it enables users to customize content according to users' individual needs and purposes (Harrison and Barthel 2009). Thanks to its inherent technological characteristics, the weblog provides such affordances as interaction and connection, immediacy, instant access and relatively low cost (Miller and Shepherd 2009). Particularly hyperlinking, which is the foundation of web existence and organizes the structure of the blogosphere, enables a novel means of accessing, cross-referencing and verifying information (O'Reilly 2005).

Academic weblogs are thought to have many antecedents, but most often they are compared to personal home pages. However, what makes weblogs distinct from rather static home pages is that blogs are more about self-disclosure, whereas homepages serve more as vehicles for self-presentation (see the overview in Yus 2007a). In addition, weblogs are frequently modified and include dated entries, which are listed in a reverse chronological sequence (Herring et al. 2004). As regards their structure, weblogs are also marked by diversity and hybridity, but a large degree of conventionalization has been brought by the development of blogging software. On the one hand, blogging software facilitates a blogging activity: running a blog does not require advanced technical skills, knowledge of HTML[3] or web-design programmes (see Harrison and Barthel 2009, O'Reilly 2005). On the other hand, the use of blogging templates contributes to the standardization of the form and to the emergence of *internalized weblog schema*, that is, sets of prototypical verbal and visual properties of the weblog layout that are stored in users' minds, and which generally indicate what properties are expected to be found in the prototypical weblog genre (Yus 2007a). In this way, blogging templates are responsible for the stabilization of the weblog as a genre, but still, they do not determine the blog content, leaving much room for innovation and heterogeneity (see Myers 2010).

Much of the researchers' interest in academic weblogs (often from scholars who are bloggers themselves, for example, Halavais 2006, Kjellberg 2009, 2010, Kulczycki 2012, Mortensen and Walker 2002, Myers 2010, Walker 2006) centres on the functions of blogging practices. Academic weblogs are considered tools for the dissemination of content, expression of opinions, conducting research, writing, interaction and construction of relationships (see, for example, Kjellberg 2010). They are also used as publication tools, but as Kjellberg (2009) notes, researchers are aware that publishing in a blog is an intermediate stage before employing usual channels of communication. In addition, academic weblogs function as platforms for self-expression and self-promotion under the generally accepted 'traditional' norms of scholarly exchange (Sokół 2012). Given this diversity of uses, there are different names used to refer to blogs run by academics and for academic purposes: apart from academic blogs, other names include *science, research* or *scholarly blogs*. In this chapter, I am concerned with blogs that are run by single academics and I adhere to the term *academic weblog* or *academic blog*.

Blog researchers have also attempted to classify academic weblogs and to explore their relation to other academic and non-academic genres, in both the offline and online worlds (see for example, Halavais 2006, Kjellberg 2009, Mortensen and Walker 2002, Walker 2006). First, the diary-like nature of academic blogs is emphasized: academic weblogs are considered a hybrid between journal, academic publishing, storage space for links and site for academic discussion (Kjellberg 2009, Mortensen and Walker 2002). Walker (2006, p. 130) focuses on the research blog and argues that its different kinds form clusters. She distinguishes three types of research blogs: (1) blogs that are platforms for political debate; (2) research logs, which are records of research conducted and discussions of ideas that might be pursued in relation to somebody's research (a subtype of this kind of blog can, for example, be a dissertation log); and (3) pseudonymous blogs about academic life.

In his discussion of the generic integrity of the academic weblog, Halavais (2006) uses the metaphors of the third place or the visible college to refer to this emergent genre of scholarly exchange. Halavais relates academic blogging to three archetypal scholarly communication settings: the notebook, the coffee house and the editorial page (2006, pp. 119–120). Firstly, he argues that the academic blog replaces the notebook as a way of externalizing thought and serves to present work-in-progress. Secondly, just like the coffee house of 18th century London, the academic blog provides a setting for the free exchange of ideas among those who may come from a variety of backgrounds but who share particular interests (see the reference to the idea of the coffee house in the names of some academic weblogs in Polish: 'Polemiki i rozmówki w "Cafe Aleph"' http://blog.marciszewski.eu/ [Debates and chats in 'Cafe Aleph'[4], or 'presscafe.eu'). Finally, the academic blog allows scholars to fulfil their obligation to educate the public and engage in public issues, just like the editorial page.

The academic weblog emerges then as a diverse and evolving form of informal scholarly exchange, which poses challenges for genre theory. For one thing, constant and rapid change, malleability and multiplicity are inherent in blogs, like other web-based and offline genres (see Campagna et al. 2012, Giltrow and Stein 2009, Miller and Shepherd 2009): genre evolution over time is empowered by 'the variation inherent to any socially typified construction and provoked by differing complexes of social, psychological, economic, and technological change' (Miller and Shepherd 2009, p. 265). For another, the affordances of web-based communication and the developing expectations of the medium's users have enhanced genre change, meaning that web-based genres are even more functionally defined than 'traditional' genres (see Giltrow and Stein 2009, Miller and Shepherd 2009). In the web-mediated context, homogenous genres tend to turn into heterogeneous genre hybrids, which need to be studied in terms of their hypertextual character and the multimodal options they offer (Campagna et al. 2012).

Other issues that have been brought by the evolving nature of web-mediated genres and which are relevant for the discussion of scholarly communication relate to the transformed authoring practices in the web. As Campagna et al. (2012, p. 12) argue, following Friedman (2005), 'the new collaborative platforms are characterized by the increasing pervasive tendency among web users to *upload* rather than simply *download* [author's emphasis] information from the Internet, that is to express opinions, exchange ideas, produce materials and globalize the content directly on the Web'. This more active role of the user in combination with the dissolved hierarchies and institutions has led to the emergence of less constrained communicative practices. Some of the implications of these changes, pointed out by Campagna et al. (2012, pp. 12–13), are that web authoring involves multiple identities, and that the role of 'expert-in-the-field' is now challenged by the voices of several 'experts-in-the-field'.

## 12.4  Searching for genre stability: analysis and discussion

In my discussion of the semiperipheral status of academic weblogs as an emergent genre of scholarly exchange, I focus on the Polish blogosphere. In general, I aim to find out how academic blogging practices relate to the 'centre' and 'periphery', both on the social and discourse levels. In addition, my purpose is to estimate the degree of stabilization of the academic weblog genre. Given the complex and evolving nature of academic weblogs (see Section 12.3), in my preliminary attempt to identify the integrity of this genre, I conduct a quantitative-qualitative analysis of the functional and structural properties of the blogs under investigation. The linguistic analysis is complemented by an email questionnaire to the blogs' authors on the uses of blogs (see Appendix B for the questionnaire).

The research material used in the study consists of 520 posts that were retrieved from the websites of 26 academic blogs run in Polish (the total number of words in the corpus is 320,966). The blogs used in the investigation were found either through the Polish portal 'Agregator Polskich Blogów Naukowych Bloginaukowe.org' [The aggregator of Polish scientific blogs] available at http://bloginaukowe2.blogspot. com/, or through the links found on the blogs listed by this aggregator. All the blog authors whose blogs were involved in the study gave their consent to the investigation.[5] The general corpus was divided into two sub-corpora of 260 posts each, depending on whether the blog's author represents a humanities (sub-corpus A; the total of 139 334 words, with the average of 535.9 words per post) or non-humanities discipline (sub-corpus B; the total of 181 632 words, with the average of 698.6 words per post; for the list of weblogs under investigation, see Appendix A). The decision about how to classify a given blog in the sub-corpora was not simple, as some of the analysed blogs are interdisciplinary, some aim to discuss general scientific issues, and some mix scientific and non-scientific content. Sub-corpus A represents such disciplines as communication, psychology, pedagogy, sociology, history, digital philology and medieval studies, literary studies, media studies, philosophy and education, whereas sub-corpus B contains biology and biotechnology, physics and astronomy, climatology, medicine, neurobiology, statistics and information technology. While I recognize discipline-bound variation of academic discourse, rather than focusing on the characteristics of weblogs related to particular disciplines, in my study I aim to identify the tendencies in academic blogging as such, and search for the general properties of the academic weblog genre.

The theoretical-methodological basis of the investigation is the socio-pragmatic approach to the analyses of web-based discourse (see, for example, Grieve et al. 2010, Herring et al. 2004, Herring et al. 2005), in which genre is defined as a means of social action, and which prioritizes a communicative purpose as the main genre-defining criterion (see Miller 1984, Swales 1990). While I recognize that this traditional, goal-oriented view of genre is challenged by the development of web-based textual forms (see for example, Askehave and Ellerup Nielsen 2005, Campagna et al. 2012), I concentrate on the communicative purpose as it shapes a given genre: its schematic structure, choice of content, and style (Swales 1990, p. 58). In addition, the focus on a communicative purpose (or purposes) offers the way to study the community's motivations and expectations behind genre use, which, in turn, give important insights into how web-based genres are adopted and developed. For the investigation of the visual-structural properties of the academic weblogs in focus, I adapt Yus's (2007a) approach to the analysis of the verbal-visual layout of the weblog genre. Taken from the perspective of relevance theory, Yus's analysis proves useful for my present purposes as it focuses on the role of users' expectations in genre adoption, evolution and identification, and enables to assess the degree of genre stabilization.

### 12.4.1    The uses of academic weblogs

The investigation into the uses of academic weblogs and motivations behind blogging practices was based on the study of the communicative purpose(s) of the blog posts in the sub-corpora. The communicative purposes of the blog posts were determined through content analysis of these posts (for the results, see Tables 12.1 and 12.2), and the results of the analysis were confronted with the blog authors' views on the function of academic blogs that were revealed in the email questionnaire (Appendix B). Identification of the dominant communicative purposes allowed me to assign functional labels to the particular posts in the sub-corpora.

*Table 12.1*  The functions of academic weblog posts determined on the basis of the communicative purposes identified in sub-corpus A (blogs run by humanities scholars)

| Academic weblog functions | No. of raw occurrences | Occurrence (%) |
|---|---|---|
| Article | 58 | 17.06 |
| Announcement | 21 | 6.18 |
| Comment on higher and school education abroad | 0 | 0.00 |
| Comment on higher and school education in Poland | 19 | 5.59 |
| Comment on local life | 0 | 0.00 |
| Comment on public life in Poland | 9 | 2.65 |
| Conversation | 0 | 0.00 |
| Initiation of a discussion | 1 | 0.29 |
| Instruction | 20 | 5.88 |
| Interview | 5 | 1.47 |
| Invitation | 20 | 5.88 |
| Meta-post* | 3 | 0.88 |
| Note | 39 | 11.47 |
| Obituary | 0 | 0.00 |
| Reblogged post** | 19 | 5.59 |
| Report | 42 | 12.35 |
| Review | 31 | 9.12 |
| Self-disclosure | 5 | 1.47 |
| Self-promotion | 34 | 10.00 |
| Self-reference | 14 | 4.12 |

*Note*: * A post that directly relates to the blogging activity itself or discusses aspects of running a blog, for example, marking anniversaries of how long a given blog is run.
** A post that is redirected from another blog. I included this category into the investigation as the presence of reblogged posts marks the bloggers' activity in the medium, and points to their interests. In addition, reblogged posts contribute to the integration of the blogosphere.

The study into the functions of academic weblogs confirms the multi-functionality of the posts: more than one dominant communicative purpose was identified in numerous posts. In addition, the number of the functions that were singled out reflects the diversity of the users' needs behind the academic blogging practices, on the part of both the blogs' authors and, potentially, their audience.

The most frequent posts in both sub-corpora are articles, but in case of the blogs run by non-humanities scholars, articles vastly outnumber other posts by comprising more than half of all the occurrences (see 17.06 per cent for Sub-corpus A in relation to 58.08 per cent for Sub-corpus B). The high proportion of articles proves that the main use of the

*Table 12.2* The functions of academic weblog posts determined on the basis of the communicative purposes identified in sub-corpus B (blogs run by non-humanities scholars)

| Academic weblog functions | No. of raw occurrences | Occurrence (%) |
|---|---|---|
| Article | 169 | 58.08 |
| Announcement | 4 | 1.37 |
| Comment on higher and school education abroad | 1 | 0.34 |
| Comment on higher and school education in Poland | 9 | 3.09 |
| Comment on local life | 5 | 1.72 |
| Comment on public life in Poland | 6 | 2.06 |
| Conversation | 5 | 1.72 |
| Initiation of a discussion | 3 | 1.03 |
| Instruction | 9 | 3.09 |
| Interview | 0 | 0.00 |
| Invitation | 1 | 0.34 |
| Meta-post | 3 | 1.03 |
| Note | 37 | 12.71 |
| Obituary | 3 | 1.03 |
| Reblogged post | 0 | 0.00 |
| Report | 11 | 3.78 |
| Review | 1 | 0.34 |
| Self-disclosure | 7 | 2.41 |
| Self-promotion | 5 | 1.72 |
| Self-reference | 12 | 4.12 |

academic weblog is discussion of scientific issues and popularization of science. The articles in the sub-corpora under study are extended essays that are constructed according to the 'traditional', well-established rules of scholarly exchange, with care for reliability and adherence to the norms of academic interaction. They resemble research papers, though their style tends to be more conversational and straightforward, in order to be accessible also to the non-scientific audience.

Another frequent category in both sub-corpora is the note (respectively 11.47 per cent and 12.71 per cent), by which I refer to an informal, interactive post that realizes an informational purpose. With their informational content relevant to the blog authors' scientific and non-scientific interests, goals and needs, notes contribute to the pool of public goods from which all users can profit. Notes often include personalized content and thus additionally realize the functions of self-promotion and self-disclosure. The use of both articles and notes enhances the bloggers' position of an expert member of academia, who is aware of the audience and is willing to share knowledge, inform and educate.

As regards the proportion of other post categories, the investigation reveals major differences between the two sub-corpora. In case of the blogs run by non-humanities authors, the remaining post categories are considerably less frequent than articles and notes, with the proportion of particular categories no higher than 5 per cent. The frequency of some categories in Sub-corpus A is more considerable: apart from articles and notes, other substantial categories are reports (12.35 per cent), self-promotional posts (10.00 per cent) and reviews (9.12 per cent). Reports (which give an account of an academic event or book publishing) and reviews (usually of books) realize two important aims related to scholarly communication: information exchange and evaluation. The noticeable proportion of self-promotional posts indicates that academic weblogs have the potential to serve as platforms for publishing bloggers' research and informing about their scientific achievements (see also Sokół 2012), and generally these posts prove bloggers' commitment to scholarship. Another group of less frequent categories, though the proportions exceed 5 per cent, includes announcements (6.18 per cent), instructions and invitations (both amounting to 5.88 per cent each), and comments on higher and school education in Poland (5.59 per cent). These posts relate to the functions of information exchange (announcements and invitations) and tutoring and guiding (instructions). They also give evidence for the bloggers' sense of engagement in academic and public life (comments on higher and school education in Poland).

The function-oriented study of the blog posts is to a large extent confirmed by the results of the email questionnaire with the blogs' authors on the uses of academic weblogs. The questionnaire was returned by 28 Polish academic bloggers. The function that scored highest in the questionnaire was the popularization of science (20 bloggers). The importance of this function is supported by such motivations provided by the bloggers as the presentation of niche scientific issues, stigmatization of pseudo-science, answering questions related to one's discipline or reaching wide audiences (including students of universities and secondary schools, and amateurs; academic blogging is thought by the bloggers to have much in common with scientific journalism).

Other functions frequently pointed to by the bloggers include self-expression (15 bloggers); self-promotion (14 bloggers); reporting and documentation of current events (11 bloggers); cooperation with an academic community (9 bloggers); blog as a tool supporting the didactic process (8 bloggers); and publishing of research results (7 bloggers). The group of the least frequently indicated functions includes conducting/initiation of academic debates (5 bloggers); blog as a research tool (4 bloggers); and conducting/initiation of debates concerning public life, current news and so on (3 bloggers). As regards the additional functions specified by the bloggers, it seems that running an academic weblog supports one's research by teaching organization and self-control, and contributes to the honing of academic writing skills.

The results of the email questionnaire reveal that the academic bloggers under study are aware of the possibilities and limitations of blogging, and, following their experience, they also know which aims are not effectively achieved through a blog: for instance, research is better published in journals and books. The answers also prove that the bloggers act out different social roles in their blogs, and although the roles

*Table 12.3*  The visual-structural properties of the blogs from sub-corpus A (run by humanities scholars)

| Visual-structural properties of academic weblogs | No. of raw occurrences | Occurrence (%) |
|---|---|---|
| 1 main column text | 10 | 76.92 |
| More than one main text column | 3 | 23.08 |
| 1 sidebar | 8 | 61.54 |
| 2 sidebars | 2 | 15.38 |
| 1 rectangle at the top | 11 | 84.62 |
| White background colour | 13 | 100.00 |
| Other than white background colour | 0 | 0.00 |
| Explicit reference to the blogger | 7 | 53.85 |
| Link to a page with information on the blogger | 10 | 76.92 |
| Weblog title | 12 | 92.31 |
| Headlines | 13 | 100.00 |
| Date of posts | 12 | 92.31 |
| Location of the post by category or permalink* | 12 | 92.31 |
| No of comments displayed | 12 | 92.31 |
| Text only in posts | 0 | 0.00 |
| Text and images in posts | 13 | 100.00 |
| Links inside posts to other web pages of blogs | 13 | 100.00 |
| Links to other blogs or bloggers | 10 | 76.92 |
| Links to sites of possible interest | 11 | 84.62 |
| Archive | 8 | 61.54 |
| Search form | 10 | 76.92 |

* A permalink is an internet hyperlink that is intended to be permanent (online version of the *Collins English Dictionary*).

*Table 12.4* The visual-structural properties of the blogs from sub-corpus B (run by non-humanities scholars)

| Visual-structural properties of academic weblogs | No. of raw occurrences | Occurrence (%) |
| --- | --- | --- |
| 1 main column text | 12 | 92.31 |
| More than one main text column | 1 | 7.69 |
| 1 sidebar | 12 | 92.31 |
| 2 sidebars | 0 | 0.00 |
| 1 rectangle at the top | 12 | 92.31 |
| White background colour | 9 | 69.23 |
| Other than white background colour | 4 | 30.77 |
| Explicit reference to the blogger | 4 | 30.77 |
| Link to a page with information on the blogger | 10 | 76.92 |
| Weblog title | 13 | 100.00 |
| Headlines | 13 | 100.00 |
| Date of posts | 13 | 100.00 |
| Location of the post by category or permalink | 13 | 100.00 |
| No of comments displayed | 12 | 92.31 |
| Text only in posts | 1 | 7.69 |
| Text and images in posts | 12 | 92.31 |
| Links inside posts to other web pages of blogs | 1 | 7.69 |
| Links to other blogs or bloggers | 11 | 84.62 |
| Links to sites of possible interest | 13 | 100.00 |
| Archive | 7 | 53.85 |
| Search form | 12 | 92.31 |

are clearly marked in particular posts, the academic weblog as a genre mixes the private and the public, the individual and the communal.

### 12.4.2 The visual-structural properties of academic weblogs

The degree of stabilization of the academic weblog genre was analysed through the study of the visual-structural layout of the homepages of the blogs according to the properties adapted from Yus's approach (2007b). The results of the analysis for the respective sub-corpora are presented in Tables 12.3 and 12.4.

The structural analysis of the posts from both sub-corpora demonstrates that the academic weblog has a relatively conventionalized structure, which mainly results from the use of the blogging software. The academic weblog proves to be an *emergent* genre, to use the terminology used by Herring et al. (2005), which means that its structure is inherent in the medium (see also Miller and Shepherd 2009) and takes advantage of connection and immediacy of the medium enabled by hyperlinking. The reliance on the blogging software may also result from the bloggers' concern with the blogs' content more than with their visual-structural layout (see Yus 2007b). However, in some cases the study also indicates a creative use of the medium's visual and hypertextual properties, which gives evidence for how generic conventions can be used to mark the blogger's originality and innovation.

The standardized layout of the academic weblog as appears from the quantitative-qualitative analysis of the blogs includes, in the majority of cases, one main column text with one sidebar, with a rectangle at the top that contains the blog's title, explicit reference to the blogger and/or the link to a page with information on the blogger. The posts are displayed on the white background colour, and usually mix verbal and visual expression. They are categorized by headlines, the date of posting, the post category or permalink, which together with the inter-links between the blog's web pages, the archiving facility and the search form facilitate navigation through the blog's content. In addition, links to other blogs or bloggers strengthen the networking within the academic blogosphere, although frequently only within related disciplines; whereas links to sites of possible interest complete, extend and/or validate the blog's content.

## 12.5   Conclusions

As Miller and Shepherd (2009, p. 265) argue, '[g]enres originate not only from changes in situation, context, and culture but also from other genres, in an evolutionary process, and occasionally from the conscious effort of individuals to fill a previously unmet need'. It seems that academic weblogs have the capacity to fill the need for unrestrained scholarly communication and networking outside the 'traditional' channels, however with the adherence to the well-established norms of scholarly interaction transferred from the offline world, as well as from the earlier forms of academic web-based genres (for example, the discussion forum).

The academic weblog proves to be a relatively stabilized genre in terms of both structure and function, whose major aims are to share knowledge and information, and to educate. The academic weblog is a self-oriented genre, though with a clear orientation towards interaction with the scientific and non-scientific audience: the investigation shows that high value is given to the interpersonal dimension of discourse. The semiperipheral status of the academic weblog can be justified by its conflicting characteristics, where individuality mixes with communality, public and institutional aspects coexist alongside private ones, and personalized content occurs next to the factual and objective data. For one thing, the bloggers reveal care for reliability and a strong sense of intellectual property. For another, the boundaries between disciplines and domains appear to be more fluid, and the blogosphere has no settled patterns of peer review. Some degree of feedback, though, is obtained through the blogs' comment sections and other channels of communication.

The discussion of how the academic weblog is situated between the 'centre' and 'periphery' concerns also the status of the academic weblog in relation to other genres owned by an academic community. The academic weblog is not a central academic genre, whose adoption and use is essential for membership in an academic community. Still, it has the potential to fit into the transforming Polish reality to mediate a much-required change.

## Appendix A

**List of the academic weblogs involved in the investigation**

SUB-CORPUS A (blogs run by humanities academics)
warsztat badacza Emanuel Kulczycki http://ekulczycki.pl/
XJENTIFIKA http://xjentifika.wordpress.com/
pedagog http://sliwerski-pedagog.blogspot.com/
popblog http://www.piotrsiuda.pl/
marcin wilkowski http://wilkowski.org/
Filologia cyfrowa :: Mediewistyka 2.0 http://filologiacyfrowa.
    wordpress.com/
Komiks w bibliotece http://abrewiacje.wordpress.com/
HerstoriA http://herstoria.blox.pl/html
humanistyczny notatnik naukowy http://humanistycznynotatnik
    naukowy.com/
KOCHAM HISTORIĘ http://kochamhistorie.blox.pl/html
Człowiek i Technologie http://czlowiekitechnologie.com/tag/blog-
    naukowy/
blog.2edu.pl Obudź w sobie eduNinje http://blog.2edu.pl/
presscafe.eu blog o edukacji medialnej http://presscafe.eu/
SUB-CORPUS B (blogs run by non-humanities academics)
profesorskie gadanie http://czachorowski.blox.pl/html
Żywa Planeta http://zywaplaneta.pl/
http://zajaczkowski.org/
wduch http://wduch.wordpress.com/
borczyk~Il nome della Rosa http://bborczyk.wordpress.com/

Mroczna Sztuka Ogłupiania http://czajniczek-pana-russella.blogspot.com/
Doskonale szare http://doskonaleszare.blox.pl/html
Nie od razu naukę zbudowano http://kierul.wordpress.com/
„Pan inżynier' dziś bada http://marekopel.wordpress.com/
MathMed – blog lekarza medycyny http://mathmed.blox.pl/html
piękno neurobiologii Blog Jerzego Vetulaniego http://vetulani.
   wordpress.com/
http://smarterpoland.pl/
Sporothrix http://sporothrix.wordpress.com/
Other blogs involved (through taking part in the questionnaire):
Nowa Alchemia http://nowaalchemia.blogspot.com/
GMObiektywnie blog Wojciecha Zalewskiego gmo.blog.polityka.pl
blog.endokrynologia.net o medycynie i ochronie zdrowia http://blog.
   endokrynologia.net/
Czas na Historię czyli o historii trochę inaczej http://czasnahistorie.
   blogspot.com/ (the blogged stopped functioning in December 2013).

## Appendix B: An email questionnaire

May I ask you to indicate the purposes for which you run your blog?
Here is the list of potential possibilities. Please, mark the relevant
answers in your reply to this email:

– conducting/initiation of academic debates
– conducting/initiation of debates concerning public life, current news
   and so on
– cooperation with an academic community (for example, establishment of contacts)
– popularization of science
– publishing of research results
– blog as a research tool
– blog as a tool supporting the didactic process
– self-promotion
– self-expression
– reporting and documentation of current events
– other (please, specify them)…

## Notes

1. According to Jenkins' glossary, '[m]edia convergence refers to a situation in
   which multiple media systems coexist and where media content flows fluidly
   across them' (Jenkins 2006, p. 322); participatory culture is 'culture in which

fans and other consumers are invited to actively participate in the creation and circulation of new content' (Jenkins 2006, p. 331).

2. Apart from the proliferation of academic blogging, the Science 2.0 initiatives in Poland include, for instance, such Open Science undertakings as the portals 'Otwarta nauka' [Open Science] http://otwartanauka.pl/, Centrum Otwartej Nauki [The Centre for Open Science] http://ceon.pl/, or EBIB, which is a portal for librarians and a bulletin whose general aim is to educate on issues related to new technologies, information and librarianship.

3. HTML stands for HyperText Markup Language used to build web pages.

4. All translations from Polish throughout the chapter are mine.

5. I express thanks to all the blog authors involved in the investigation for their cooperation and participation in the questionnaire.

# Conclusion: Combating the Centripetal Pull in Academic Writing

*Karen Bennett*

What is remarkable about all the accounts that make up this book is the consistency of the experiences they describe. Despite emanating from very different parts of the European landmass and from cultures with very varied political and economic histories, most of them voice, to some extent or another, the experience of being torn by contradictory impulses. Indeed this is so marked a theme in this book that conflict would appear to be a defining characteristic of the semiperipheral condition. In general terms, it may perhaps be expressed as the dilemma between the urge to 'modernize' and become part of the hegemonic centre on the one hand, and a sense of loyalty to a traditional culture on the other. More specifically, it is manifested in these accounts by scholars' relationships with other members of the (local and international) academic community, in the decisions they take with regard to the publication of their work, the discourses they use and the values they espouse.

On the level of the system as a whole, the conflict could best be described in terms of centripetal and centrifugal forces (see Lillis and Curry 2010), the former encouraging assimilation with centre values and practices, the latter operating in the opposite direction, either in frank reaction or as a vestige of an earlier less centralized academic economy. The centripetal force might be conceived as analogous to the pull exerted by large cities in developing countries – an appropriate metaphor, given Becher's (1989/2001) famous distinction between urban and rural disciplines, quoted by several of the authors in this volume. This urban centre (which thus represents not only the wealthy northern countries of the economic system, but also, in epistemological terms, the 'scientific' disciplines, which claim to be universal in their reach and neutral in their discourse, and which are transmitted primarily through English) is perceived by those in its hinterland as a site of wealth, glamour and prestige. Hence, the occupants of the traditional rural economy increasingly view themselves as backward, poor and uncosmopolitan, and there will be a tendency for depopulation as younger talents head for the bright lights.

The problem with such centralization, however, is that the over-concentration on a single pole creates imbalances that have negative repercussions on the system as a whole. In the academic economy as in the real one, the centre is dependent on its hinterland for sustenance; just as farming is needed to feed all those hungry mouths in the megalopolis, so the wealth-creating applied sciences need to be counterbalanced by an intellectual culture that gives attention to the ethical, aesthetic and symbolic needs of the population. It is the awareness of this that has given rise to the centrifugal forces at work in the system, sometimes imposed from above like the European Union's LEADER programmes, at other times emerging from grassroots initiatives. In all cases, the aim is simultaneously to channel knowledge from the centre to the less privileged regions on the semiperiphery, and to stimulate those regions to develop their own resources instead of automatically looking to the centre for guidance and inspiration.

Before attempting to assess the success of these initiatives, let us look in more detail at some of the centripetal and centrifugal forces that are at play on the semiperiphery of academic culture, according to the various authors that have contributed to this volume.

## C.1 Centripetal forces

With the exception of the very tangible 'brain drain' mentioned by Negretti (Chapter 8) and Burgess (Chapter 5), perhaps the most compelling and widespread of the various centripetal forces described over the course of this book is the growing pressure upon semiperipheral researchers to publish in high-profile centre journals instead of in their traditional local or regional outlets. Indeed, many of the authors report that point systems are now being used in their countries to assess researchers' output, with 'International' or Anglophone publications inevitably worth more than national or non-English ones; and although the 'publish or perish' ethos is still less marked here than in centre institutions, career advancement and research funding are becoming increasingly dependent upon success in this domain.

While individual researchers usually experience this pressure as emanating from their own institutions, the true source of the thrust is likely to lie further upstream with the Ministry or a national funding body. Its purpose is primarily to combat insularity and encourage participation in forums outside the home country. Yet, as Lillis and Curry (2010, p. 56) point out, the words 'international' and 'English' used in this context are sliding signifiers, often employed loosely to mean 'high status' or 'high academic quality', irrespective of the mechanisms that are actually involved. One of the consequences of this imprecision may be that real research quality is actually sacrificed in the race to accumulate 'international' publications, as indeed Uysal (Chapter 9) explicitly asserts with relation to the Turkish context.

The drive for 'internationalization' is also having a detrimental effect upon national journals, as several of these chapters report (for example, Petrić, Chapter 10; Burgess, Chapter 5). Many are simply disappearing from the scene, reducing the available outlets for the kind of linguistically embedded knowledge that is produced in many humanities and social science disciplines. Others are switching to English or becoming bilingual in an attempt to boost status and sales. This in turn brings a shift in focus with regard to the material accepted for publication, as specialized scholarship dealing with aspects of particular cultural communities starts to be shunned in favour of research that is perceived as more generalizable or of a wider interest. Indeed, it is suggested (explicitly by Burgess in Chapter 5, implicitly by others) that the more status a journal accrues, the more it will begin to behave like a centre publication, rejecting studies perceived to be 'parochial' (Flowerdew 2001) unless they are susceptible to repackaging for central consumption (for example, through the mechanisms of 'exoticization' or 'relocation' described by Lillis and Curry 2010, pp. 145–147).

What is more, in fields that have traditionally been dominated by mother-tongue scholarship (such as Portuguese history, as described by Bennett in Chapter 1), the imperative to publish in English may actually be causing the state of the art to recede. An international readership rarely has the level of background knowledge or interest that home-grown experts can bring to bear on the subject; hence, the broadening of the debate to include interlocutors from beyond the national or linguistic boundaries may have a 'dumbing down' effect upon the discipline as a whole.

Anglophone dominance is also taking its toll on the academic discourses of other languages. Many are changing to become more like English, as a number of these contributors report (Dontcheva-Navratilova, Chapter 2; Vladimirou, Chapter 3; Bardi and Muresan, Chapter 7; Burgess, Chapter 5), while in at least one case (Portuguese,

Chapter 1) there is the suggestion that the traditional discourse may be heading for extinction, given its incompatibility with the values underpinning EAD. There are epistemological implications too, of course, for these discourses encode a theory of knowledge in their very structure; hence, their replacement by English or by a discourse that is calqued on English is effectively a form of 'epistemicide' (Bennett 2007b, Sousa Santos 1996, 2001).

One of the implications of these pressures is that researchers on the semiperiphery, writing in a language that is not their own, are often obliged to resort to the services of literacy brokers (Lillis and Curry 2006, 2010) in order to ensure that their work complies with the linguistic and rhetorical norms presiding in centre publications. As this is expensive and time-consuming, it constitutes an obstacle against these scholars' full participation in the international discourse community, thereby reinforcing the hierarchies that are already in place in the system. What is more, literacy brokering operates as a centripetal force in its own right in that it feeds the various language industries (EAP teaching, publishing, translation and editing services) that promote and perpetuate English academic discourse as the hegemonic vehicle of knowledge in the modern world (see Bennett 2014). That is to say, the more EAD is codified in manuals and course books, taught in universities and studied by linguists, the more authority it accrues, with the result that alternative discourses (such as the traditional humanities discourses described in some of these chapters) will gradually come to be perceived as defective, even by those that were brought up to use them.

Finally, the use of reward systems by semiperipheral institutions means that publication in centre journals is often perceived as an end in its own right (see, for example, Bardi and Muresan, Chapter 7; Uysal, Chapter 9; also Lillis and Curry 2010, p. 171). That is to say, where once publication served as the means of disseminating knowledge generated from a variety of perspectives and for a variety of motives, researchers are now increasingly tailoring their studies from the outset to suit the requirements of the dominant journals. This naturally has the effect of reducing epistemological diversity, particularly for scholars operating in the humanities, who are used to publishing in the less constraining formats of books and book chapters (see Burgess, Chapter 5).

In short, there are a number of centripetal forces operating on the semiperiphery which are encouraging researchers in these countries to assimilate their values and practices to those of the dominant centre. What is more, this cannot be analysed unproblematically as a top-down phenomenon; for though policies and practices are clearly being implemented at state or EU level, there also seems to be a general grassroots conviction that such changes are synonymous with 'modernization' and 'progress'. By systematically choosing centre practices and values over local ones, and perpetuating the hierarchy in their metadiscourse, many semiperipheral researchers are unwittingly colluding in the destruction of their traditional academic cultures. If unresisted, this will result in a loss of cultural specificity at all stages in the knowledge-making process, producing a situation of epistemological homogenization.

## C.2   Centrifugal forces

One of the most surprising aspects to emerge from this book as a whole is probably the extent to which the centripetal forces do *not* completely dominate the semiperiphery. Chapter after chapter report the existence of perceptions and actions that militate against this trend: the multilingual publishing strategies of humanities scholars in some countries (Barros, Chapter 6; Negretti, Chapter 8); the convictions of Spanish and Portuguese historians that better scholarship is found in local journals than in international ones (Burgess, Chapter 5; Bennett, Chapter 1); the careful negotiation of identity by Czech and Greek linguists in order to ensure that they are able to participate on the global stage without sacrificing their local interests (Dontcheva-Navratilova, Chapter 2; Vladimirou, Chapter 3); and even the mismatch between official policy and actual practice reported by Uysal in Turkey (Chapter 9). All of these suggest a keen awareness amongst semiperipheral scholars of the epistemological implications of internationalization and an interest in resisting takeover by the dominant culture.

On the level of pedagogy, solutions are put forward that suggest a growing concern at the demise of local academic cultures and a desire to protect them against colonization. Dontcheva-Navratilova (Chapter 2) and Bennett (Chapter 1) both advocate a contrastive approach to the teaching of second language writing that would give visibility to the native academic discourse and highlight its epistemological differences from English (as opposed to the monolingual approach, which silences alternative discourses, implicitly rendering them defective or second-rate). Gonerko-Frej (Chapter 4), for her part, laments the loss of creativity involved in conventional EAP writing classes and espouses the ELF model proposed by Mauranen et al. (2010, also Mauranen 2012, 2013). Based on the premise that English as a Lingua Franca (ELF) is no longer the property of native speakers, this model offers a formidable challenge to Anglo-Saxon dominance by allowing English the flexibility to become the tool of other identities and ideologies.

Centrifugal forces are also very evident in the domain of publishing. Petrić's study (Chapter 10) shows that not all English-medium journals on the semiperiphery are aspiring to centre status or, indeed, are particularly centre-oriented. On the contrary, many appear to have markedly local or regional goals, which include: promoting the work of their scholars beyond national and linguistic borders; enabling knowledge flows to enter the country in a relatively inexpensive format (thereby helping combat network exclusion in contexts where there are few resources for costly subscriptions to centre publications), serving as a node in a regional distribution network, and providing educational and editing services to enable authors on the semi- or even outer periphery to participate in international forums (the *Croatian Medical Journal*, described in more detail by Marušić and Marušić in Chapter 11 is a case in point). Some of these journals also take advantage of the greater epistemological freedom available on the semiperiphery to establish very specialized niches at the intersection of disciplines, thereby 'opening up intellectual spaces that are often not available in either English-medium centre journals or longstanding journals in local languages' (Lillis 2012, p. 716).

Finally, the academic weblogs described by Sokół in the last chapter are particularly subversive of centre values, as they undermine many of its fundamental principles with respect to discourse, genre, authorship and intellectual property. Indeed, the new technologies may ultimately prove to be the greatest centrifugal force operating upon the system, as they are inherently resistant to centralized control. Open-access publishing in particular may have the potential to break the stranglehold of the dominant journals, destroying the price wall that keeps many semiperipheral scholars off-network and setting more flexible standards for research publication. Whether this will also be able to reverse dominant trends on matters such as discourse, methodology and epistemology remains to be seen.

\*\*\*

This work started as an attempt to explore academic production in a series of countries on the semiperiphery of the academic system. The semiperiphery was initially defined in geographic and economic terms to group together countries located around the southern and eastern edges of the European landmass, countries that are financially disadvantaged in relation to the wealthier north and therefore do not have the resources – or in some cases, the will – to cultivate the most prestigious knowledge-making practices.

However, it soon became clear that there were other dynamics at work in the creation of these polarities. Language and epistemology, in particular, have also emerged as fundamental markers of centrality or peripherality, generating a picture of a system whose centre is characterized not only by its location and economic clout, but also by an Anglophone monolingualism and strong empiricist orientation. Hence, the subalterns in this system are not only the countries that formed the main focus of this book, they are also, to some extent, the non-Anglophones in the north (such as the French, who have traditionally constituted a focus of linguistic resistance) and practitioners of humanistic disciplines everywhere, whose epistemological credibility is gradually being eroded by the encroachment of quantitative and evidence-based methods.

It is thus becoming imperative to decentralize the system in order to break this iron bond between knowledge, language and capital. While we cannot really hope to return to the ideal of disinterestedness that once motivated the quest for wisdom, a step in the right direction might be to loosen some of the straps that currently hold this configuration in place, giving a voice to the figures on the margins that are currently being silenced because they are speaking in the wrong language or discourse, or because they haven't the funds to participate. In this process, as in so many others, the semiperiphery is likely to prove crucial. For its role is not only to provide a buffer zone between rich and poor; it is also, as we have seen, a between-space of contradictory impulses where resistance foments and new paths are traced. Any new paradigm that arises to challenge the one that is currently dominating the centre of the system is likely to have at least some of its roots here.

# Bibliography

Abbott, A. (2001) 'Forza Scienza!'. *Nature*, 412(6844). 264–265.

Ädel, A. and Erman, B. (2012) 'Recurrent Word Combinations in Academic Writing by Native and Non-native Speakers of English: A Lexical Bundles Approach'. *English for Specific Purposes*, 31. 81–92.

Aittola, E., Kiviniemi, U., Honkimäki, R.M., Huusko, M. and Ursin, J. (2009) 'The Bologna Process and Internationalization – Consequences for Italian Academic Life'. *Higher Education in Europe*, 34(3–4). 303–312.

Ak, M.Z. and Gülmez, A. (2006) 'The Analysis of International Publication Performance of Turkey'. *Akademik Incelemeler [Academic Investigations]*, 1(1). 25–43.

Akarsu, F. (2000) 'Transition and education: A case study of the process of change in Turkey'. In K. Mazurek, M. Winzer, and C. Majorek (eds) *Education in a Global Society: A Comparative Perspective*. NJ: Princeton Hall, pp. 315–329.

Akıllı, E., Büyükçınar, Ö., Latif, V., Yetgin, S., Gürses, E.A., Saraç, C. and Demirel, İ.H. (2009) *Türkiye Bilimsel Yayın Göstergeleri II 1981–2007 Türkiye Ülkeler Gruplar [The publication indicators of Turkey (II) 1981–2007, Turkey, Countries, Groups*, Ankara: TUBITAK.

Al, U. (2008) 'Turkish scientific publishing policy: A bibliometric approach based on citation indexes'. Unpublished Ph.D. dissertation. Hacettepe University, Ankara.

Al, U. (2012) 'Publication and Citation Performances of European Union Countries and Turkey'. *Bilig*, 62. 1–20.

Ammon, U. (ed.) (2001a) *The Dominance of English as a Language of Science: Effects on Other Languages and Language Communities*, Berlin: Mouton de Gruyter.

Ammon, U. (2001b) 'English as a future language of teaching at German Universities? a question of difficult consequences posed by the decline of German as a language of science'. In U. Ammon (ed.) *The Dominance of English as a Language of Science: Effects on Other Languages and Language Communities*. Berlin and New York: Mouton de Gruyter, pp. 343–362.

Ammon, U. (2008a) 'German as a Language of Science and Scholarship: Once a World Language, Now one of Many "niche Languages" '. http://www.goethe.de/ges/spa/pan/spw/en3889454.htm. Accessed 13 September 2013.

Ammon, U. (2008b) 'How Could International Scientific Communication be Made Fairer and More Efficient?' *The Scientist*, 1 April. http://www.the-scientist.com. Accessed 18 March 2014.

Ammon, U. and McConnell, G. (eds) (2002) *English as an Academic Language in Europe. A Survey of its Use in Teaching*, Frankfurt: Peter Lang.

Anderman, G. and Rogers, M. (eds) (2005) *In and Out of English: For Better, For Worse?* Clavedon, Buffalo and Toronto: Multilingual Matters.

Angelini, F. (2013) 'Politecnico: Stop ai corsi di Inglese'. *La Provincia: quotidiano di Como online*: http://www.laprovinciadicomo.it/. Accessed 27 May 2013.

Anthony, L. (2012) AntConc. [computer software]. Tokyo, Japan: Waseda University. http://www.antlab.sci.waseda.ac.jp.

Arcel, L., Folnegović-Šmalc, V., Kozarić-Kovačić, D. and Marušić, A. (eds) (1995) *Psycho-social Help to War Victims: Women Refugees and their Families from Bosnia and Herzegovina and Croatia*, Copenhagen: IRCT.

Archambault, E. (2010) 'Science Metrix, 30 Years in Science Secular Movements in Knowledge Creation'. www.science-metrix.com/30years-paperd.pdf.

Archontakis, F. (2008) *Health and Medical Research in Spain*, Documented Briefing series. Cambridge: The Rand Corporation.

Ardınç, F.N. (2007) 'Türkçe yayın ve akademik yükseltme kriterleri' [Turkish publications and academic promotion criteria]. *Sağlık Bilimlerinde Süreli Yayıncılık*, Tubitak-Ulakbim: Ankara. 35–38.

Arıoğlu, E. and Girgin, C. (2002) '1974–2001 döneminde ülkemizde bilimsel yayın performansının kısa değerlendirilmesi' [The evaluation of scientific publication performance of Turkey between 1974–2001]. *Science and Utopia Journal*, 95. 62–66.

Arıoğlu, E. and Girgin, C. (2003) 'Ülkemizin yayın sıralamasına eleştirel bir bakış' [A critical look at the publication rankings of Turkey]. *Science and Utopia Journal*, 105. 38–41.

Askehave, I. and Ellerup Nielsen, A. (2005) 'Digital Genres: A Challenge to Traditional Genre Theory'. *Information Technology and People*, 18(2). 120–141.

Atkinson, D. (1999) *Scientific Discourse in Sociohistorical Context: The Philosophical Transactions of the Royal Society of London, 1675–1975*. New Jersey and London: Lawrence Erlbaum Associates.

Baća, I., Bokan, I., Barko, V., Marušić, M. and Novak, D. (eds) (1999) *Chronicle of World Association of Croatian Physicians 1991–1997*, Zagreb: Croatian Medical Journal.

Baker, C. (1992) *Attitudes and Language*, Clevedon: Multilingual Matters.

Bardi, M. and Muresan, L. (2012) 'Student Perceptions of Programme Quality – a Tool for Improvement'. *Quality Assurance Review for Higher Education*, 4(1). 14–22.

Barros, R.Q. de (2009) 'English as an academic lingua franca: Introducing an exploratory study of its use and image in the Faculty of Letters of the University of Lisbon, Portugal'. Paper presented at the *International Conference on English Language and Literature Studies: Image, Identity, Reality* – ELLSIIR. Belgrade University, 4–6 December.

Baskurt, O. (2007) 'Akademik atama ve yükseltmelerde yayın etkinliğinin önemi ve kriterlerin standardizasyonu' [The importance of publication activities in academic promotions and standardization of criteria]. *Saglık Bilimlerinde Yayıncılık*. Tubitak-Ulakbim: Ankara. 85–88.

Bates, T., Anić, A., Marušić, M. and Marušić A. (2004) 'Authorship Criteria and Disclosure of Contributions: Comparison of 3 General Medical Journals with Different Author Contribution Forms'. *Journal of the American Medical Association*, 292. 86–88.

Battiston, R. (2002) 'A Lament for Italy's Brain Drain' (Book Review). *Nature*, 415(6872). 582–583.

Baždarić, K., Bilić-Zulle, L., Brumini, G. and Petrovečki, M. (2012) 'Prevalence of Plagiarism in Recent Submissions to the Croatian Medical Journal'. *Science and Engineering Ethics*, 18. 223–239.

Becher, T. (1989) *Academic Tribes and Territories: Intellectual Enquiry and the Cultures of the Disciplines*, Milton Keynes: The Society for Research into Higher Education and the Open University.

Becher, T. and Trowler, P. (2001) *Academic Tribes and Territories: Intellectual Inquiry and the Culture of Disciplines*, Buckingham/Philadelphia: The Society for Research into Higher Education and Open Education and Open University Press.

Becker, S., Ichino, A. and Peri, G. (2004) 'How Large is the "brain drain" from Italy?'. *Giornale degli Economisti e Annali di Economia, Nuova Serie*, 63 (Anno 117) (1). 1–32.

Belcher, D. (2007) 'Seeking Acceptance in an English-Only Research World'. *Journal of Second Language Writing*, 16. 1–22.

Bennett, K. (2007a) 'Galileo's Revenge: Ways of Construing Knowledge and Translation Strategies in the Era of Globalization'. *Social Semiotics*, 17(2). 171–193.

Bennett, K. (2007b) 'Epistemicide! The Tale of a Predatory Discourse'. *The Translator*, 13(2). 151–169.

Bennett, K. (2009) 'English Academic Style Manuals: A Survey'. *Journal of English for Academic Purposes*, 8(1). 43–54.

Bennett, K. (2010a) 'Academic writing Practices in Portugal: Survey of Humanities and Social Science Researchers'. *Diacrítica – Série Ciências da Linguagem*, 24(1). 193–209.

Bennett, K. (2010b) 'Academic Discourse in Portugal: A Whole Different Ballgame?'. *Journal of English for Academic Purposes*, 9(1). 21–32.

Bennett, K. (2011a) *Academic Writing in Portugal I: Discourses in Conflict*, Coimbra: Coimbra University Press.

Bennett, K. (2011b) 'The Scientific Revolution and its Repercussions on the Translation of Technical Discourse'. *The Translator*, 17(2). 189–210.

Bennett, K. (2012a) 'Footprints in the Text: Assessing the Impact of Translation Upon Portuguese Historiographic Discourse'. *Anglo-Saxónica*, 3(3). 265–290.

Bennett, K. (2012b) *English Academic Discourse: Hegemonic Status and Implications for Translation (with particular reference to Portuguese)*, Saarbrucken: Lambert Academic Publishing.

Bennett, K. (2014) 'Discourses of Knowledge: Cultural Disjunctions and their Implications for the Language Industries'. *Ibérica*, 27. 35–50.

Bennett, K. (forthcoming) 'The "butler" syndrome: academic culture on the semiperiphery', *Revista Canaria de Estudios Ingleses*, 69.

Biber, D. and Barbieri, F. (2007) 'Lexical Bundles in University Spoken and Written Registers'. *English for Specific Purposes*, 26. 263–286.

Biber, D. and Gray, B. (2011) 'The historical shift of scientific academic prose in English towards less explicit styles of expression: Writing without verbs'. In V. Bhatia, P. Sánchez, and P. Perez-Paredes (eds) *Researching Specialised Languages*. Amsterdam/Philadelphia: John Benjamins, pp. 11–24.

Biber, D., Johansson, S., Leech, G., Conrad, S. and Finegan, E. (1999) *Longman Grammar of Spoken and Written English*, London: Longman.

Bishop, D. (2012) 'How to Bury Your Academic Writing'. http://deevybee. blogspot.co.uk/2012/08/how-to-bury-your-academic-writing.html. Accessed 16 January 2014.

Blackwell, J. and Martin, J. (2011) *A Scientific Approach to Scientific Writing*, New York: Springer.

Blommaert, J. (2005) *Discourse. A Critical Introduction*, Cambridge: Cambridge University Press.

Blommaert, J. (2007) 'Sociolinguistic Scales'. *Intercultural Pragmatics*, 4(1). 1–19.

Blommaert, J. (2010) *The Sociolinguistics of Globalization*, Cambridge: Cambridge University Press.

Blommaert, J., Collins, J. and Slembrouck, S. (2005) 'Spaces of Multilingualism'. *Language and Communication*, 25. 197–216.

Bocanegra-Valle, A. (2014) ' "English is my Default Academic Language": Voices from LSP Scholars Publishing in a Multilingual Journal'. *Journal of English for Academic Purposes*, 13. 65–77.

Boletín Oficial del Estado, 279, 21 November 2013 Sec. III. P. 92880 http://www.boe.es/boe/dias/2013/11/21/pdfs/BOE-A-2013-12234.pdf. Accessed 16 January 2014.

Bosch, X. (2008) 'Integrity: Croatia's Standards Unusual in Much of Europe'. *Nature*, 454, 574.

Bourdieu, P. (1991) *Language and Symbolic Power*, Cambridge, MA: Harvard University Press.

Bradburn, N.M., Sudman, S. and Wansink, B. (2004) *Asking Questions: The Definitive Guide to Questionnaire Design. For Market Research, Political Polls, and Social and Health Questionnaires*, San Francisco: John Wiley and Sons.

Buckingham, L. (2008) 'Development of English Academic Writing Competence by Turkish Scholars'. *International Journal of Doctoral Studies*, 3. 1–18.

Buckingham, L. (2014) 'Building a Career in English: Users of English as an Additional Language in Academic in the Arabian Gulf'. *TESOL Quarterly*, 48(1). 6–33.

Burazeri, G., Čivljak, M., Ilakovac, V., Janković, S., Majica-Kovačević, T., Nedera, O. et al. (2005) 'Survey of Attitudes and Knowledge About Science in Medical Students in Southeast Europe'. *British Medical Journal*, 331. 195–196.

Burgess, S. (1997) *Discourse Variation across Cultures: A Genre-Analytic Study of Writing on Linguistics*. Unpublished Ph.D. Thesis. University of Reading, U.K.

Burgess, S. (2002) 'Packed Houses and Intimate Gatherings: Audience and Rhetorical Structure'. In Flowerdew (ed.) *Academic Discourse*, Harlow: Longman, pp. 196–215.

Burgess, S. and Fagan, A. (2002) '(Kid) Gloves on or off?: Academic Conflict in Research Articles Across the Disciplines'. *Revista Canaria de Estudios Ingleses*, 44. 79–96.

Burgess, S. and Fagan, A. (2006) 'From the Periphery: The Canarian Researcher Publishing in the International Context'. In J.I. Oliva, M. McMahon and M. Brito (eds) *On the Matter of Words in Honour of Lourdes Divasson Cilveti*. La Laguna: Servicio de Publicaciones, pp. 45–57.

Burgess, S., Gea-Valor, M-L., Moreno, A.I. and Rey-Rocha, J. (2014) 'Affordances and Constraints on Research Publication: A Comparative Study of the Language Choices of Spanish Historians and Psychologists'. *Journal of English for Academic Purposes*, 14. 72–83.

Burgess, S., Martín-Martín, P., Moreno, A., Rey-Rocha, J, López, I. & Sachdev, I. (2013) 'Spanish Medical science and History scholars writing to publish in English-medium journals: attitudes, motivation, strategies and difficulties'. Paper presented at the 31st Conference of the Spanish Association for Applied Linguistics (AESLA), La Laguna, 17–20 April.

Burke, P. (1990) *The French Historical Revolution: The Annales School, 1929–89*, Cambridge: Polity Press.

Burke, P. (ed.) (1991) *New Perspectives on Historical Writing*, Cambridge: Polity Press.

Byram, M. (1989) *Cultural Studies in the Foreign Language Classroom*, Clevedon: Multilingual Matters.

Byram, M. and Fleming, M. (eds.) (1998) *Language Learning in Intercultural Perspective*, Cambridge: Cambridge University Press.

Byram, M. and Morgan, C. (1994) *Teaching-and-Learning Language-and-Culture*, Clevedon: Multilingual Matters.

Callaham, M., Sahni, P., Winker, M., Overbeke, J., Habibzadeh, F. and Ferris, L. (2008) 'World Association of Medical Editors: Support for the Croatian Medical Journal's Editorial Independence'. *Croatian Medical Journal*, 49. 100.

Campagna, S., Garzone, G., Ilie, C. and Rowley-Jolivet, E. (2012) 'Introduction'. In S. Campagna, G. Garzone, C. Ilie and E. Rowley-Jolivet (eds) *Evolving Genres in Web-Mediated Communication*. Bern: Peter Lang, pp. 9–24.

Canagarajah, A.S. (1996) 'Non-Discursive Requirements in Academic Publishing, Material Resources of Periphery Scholars, and the Politics of Knowledge Production'. *Written Communication*, 13. 435–472.

Canagarajah, A.S. (1999) *Resisting Linguistic Imperialism in English Teaching*, Oxford: Oxford University Press.

Canagarajah, A.S. (2002) *A Geopolitics of Academic Writing*, Pittsburgh: University of Pittsburgh Press.

Canagarajah, S.A. (2013) 'The End of Second Language Writing?'. *Journal of Second Language Writing*, 22. 440–441.

Casanave, C.P. (2008) 'The Stigmatizing Effect of Goffman's Stigma Label: A Response to John Flowerdew'. *Journal of English for Academic Purposes*, 7(4). 264–267.

Castanheira, J.P. (2012) 'As livrarias estão cheias de lixo sobre Salazar', *Expresso*, 25 September: http://expresso.sapo.pt/as-livrarias=-estao-cheias-de-lixo-sobre-salazar-f745113#ixzz2tCkGM7at. Accessed 13 February 2014.

Chalmers, I. (2006) 'Role of Systematic Reviews in Detecting Plagiarism: Case of Asim Kurjak'. *British Medical Journal*, 333. 594–596.

Chamonikolasová, J. (2005) 'Comparing the structures of academic texts written in English and Czech'. In M. Huttová (ed.) *Slovak Studies in English 1*. Bratislava: Univerzita Komenského, pp. 77–84.

Charles, M. (2006) 'The Construction of Stance in Reporting Clauses: A Cross-Disciplinary Study of Thesis'. *Applied Linguistics*, 27. 492–518.

Chen, Y.-H. and Baker, P. (2010) 'Lexical Bundles in L1 and L2 Academic Writing'. *Language Learning and Technology*, 14(2). 30–49.

Chovanec, J. (2012) 'Written Academic Discourse in English: From Local Traditions to Global Outreach'. *Brno Studies in English*, 38(2). 5–16.

Clyne, M. (1987) 'Cultural Differences in the Organisation of Academic Texts'. *Journal of Pragmatics*, 11. 211–247.

Čmejrková, S. (1996) 'Academic writing in Czech and in English'. In E. Ventola and A. Mauranen (eds) *Academic Writing*. Amsterdam and Philadelphia: John Benjamins, pp. 137–152.

Čmejrková, S. and Daneš, F. (1997) 'Academic writing and cultural identity: The case of Czech academic writing'. In A. Duzsak (ed.) *Culture and Styles of Academic Discourse*. Berlin: Mouton de Gruyter, pp. 40–62.

Čmejrková, S, Daneš, F. and Sěvtlá, J. (1999) *Jak napsat odborný text* [How to write and academic text.] Praha: Leda.

Coffin, C. and Mayor, B. (2004) 'Texturing writer and reader reference in novice academic writing text and texture'. In D. Banks (ed.) *Systemic Functional Viewpoints on the Nature and Structure of Text*. Paris/Budapest/Torino: L' Harmattan, pp. 239–264.

Coleman, J.A. (2006) 'English-Medium Teaching in European Higher Education'. *Language Teaching*, 39. 1–14.

Connell, R.W. and Wood, J. (2002) 'Globalization and Scientific Labour: Patterns in a Life-History Study of Intellectual Works in the Periphery'. *Journal of Sociology*, 38. 167–190.

Connor, U. (1996) *Contrastive Rhetoric: Cross-cultural Aspects of Second-language Writing*, Cambridge: Cambridge University Press.

Connor, U. (2008) 'Mapping multidimensional aspects of research: Reaching to intercultural rhetoric'. In U. Connor, E. Nagelhout and W.V. Rozycki (eds) *Contrastive Rhetoric: Reaching to Intercultural Rhetoric*. Amsterdam: John Benjamins, pp. 219–315.

Cortes, V. (2004) 'Lexical Bundles in Published and Student Disciplinary Writing: Examples from History and Biology'. *English for Specific Purposes*, 23. 397–423.

Coskun, A. (2003) 'Cumhuriyetin ilk yillarinda Turkiye ekonomisi' [The Turkish economy in the first years of the republic]. *Ataturkcu Dusunce Dergisi*, 4. 72–77.

Costa Pinto, A. (2003) 'The Internationalization of Portuguese Historiography'. *E-Journal of Portuguese History*, 1(2).

Cottrell, S. (2003) *The Study Skills Handbook*, Basingstoke: Palgrave Macmillan.

Crane, D. (1967) 'The Gatekeepers of Science: Some Factors Affecting the Selection of Articles for Scientific Journals'. *The American Sociologist*, 2. 195–201.

Cronin, B. (2013) 'Scholarly Publishing: New Models, New Media, New Metrics'. Paper delivered at the *Conferencia sobre calidad de revistas de ciencias sociales y humanidades*, Seville, 9 May. http://www.youtube.com/watch?v=UDVTt_3hYYc. Accessed 22 January 2014.

Cuenca, A. (2013) 'Financial Crisis Cripples Spain Medical Research'. http://phys.org/news/2013-06-financial-crisis-cripples-spain-medical.html. Accessed 16 January 2014.

Curry, M.J. and Lillis, T. (2004) 'Multilingual Scholars and the Imperative to Publish in English: Negotiating Interests, Demands, and Rewards'. *TESOL Quarterly*, 38(4). 663–688.

Curry, M.J. and Lillis, T. (2010) 'Academic Research Networks: Accessing Resources for English-Medium Publishing'. *English for Specific Purposes*, 29. 281–295.

Dahl, T. (2008) 'Contributing to the Academic Conversation: A Study of New Knowledge Claims in Economics and Linguistics'. *Journal of Pragmatics*, 40(7). 1184–1201.

Dall, E. (2007) 'Cooperation and innovation potentials of the WBC'. In J. Nechifor and S. Radošević (eds) *Why Invest in Science in South Eastern Europe?*. Proceedings of the International Conference and High Level Round Table, UNESCO Office Venice: UNESCO, pp. 163–175.

De Angelis, C., Drazen, J.M., Frizelle, F.A., Haug, C., Hoey, J., Horton, R., Kotzin S., Laine C., and Marusic A. International Committee of Medical Journal Editors. (2004) 'Clinical Trial Registration: A Statement from the International Committee of Medical Journal Editors'. *New England Journal of Medicine*, 351. 1250–1251.

De Swaan, A. (2001) 'English in the social sciences'. In U. Ammon (ed.) *The Dominance of English as a Language of Science: Effects on Other Languages and Language Communities*, Berlin and New York: Mouton de Gruyter, pp. 71–83.

De Swaan, A. (2004) 'English in the social sciences'. In P. Drenth and J. Schroots (eds) *ALLEA Biennial Yearbook 2004. Critical Topics in Science and Scholarship.* Amsterdam: ALLEA, pp. 135–146.

Ding, D. (1998) 'Rationality reborn: Historical roots of the passive voice in scientific discourse'. In J.T. Battalio (ed.) *Essays in the Study of Scientific Discourse: Methods, Practice and Pedagogy.* Stanford and London: Ablex, pp. 117–135.

Dittmar, N. (1976) *A Critical Survey of Sociolinguistics: Theory and Application,* New York: St. Martin's Press.

Dontcheva-Navratilova, O. (2012a) 'Cross-cultural differences in the construal of authorial voice in the genre of diploma theses'. In C. Berkenkotter, V. Bhatia and M. Gotti (eds) *Insights into Academic Genres.* Bern: Peter Lang, pp. 301–328.

Dontcheva-Navratilova, O. (2012b) 'Lexical Bundles in Academic Texts by Nonnative Speakers'. *Brno Studies in English*, 38(2). 25–46.

Dontcheva-Navratilova, O. (2013) 'Authorial Presence in Academic Discourse: Functions of Author-Reference Pronouns'. *Linguistica Pragensia*, 23(1). 9–30.

Dontcheva-Navratilova, O. and Povolná, R. (2014) 'Analysing the development of academic writing skills in English as a lingua franca: the case of Czech students'. In C. Haase and N. Orlova (eds) *ELT: Harmony and Diversity.* Newcastle upon Tyne: Cambridge Scholars Publishing, pp. 17–54.

DPT (2006a) Devlet Planlama Teskilati-Tarihce. http://www2.dpt.gov.tr/must/tarihce.asp.

DPT (2006b) 2006 yili programi. http://ekutup.dpt.gov.tr./program/2006/pdf.

Dudley-Evans, T. (1994) 'Genre analysis: An approach to text-analysis for ESP'. In M. Coulthard (ed.) *Advances in Written Text Analysis.* London and New York: Routledge, pp. 219–228.

Duszak, A. (1994) 'Academic Discourse and Intellectual Styles'. *Journal of Pragmatics*, 21. 291–313.

Duszak, A. (ed.) (1997) *Culture and Styles of Academic Discourse,* Berlin: Mouton de Gruyter.

Duszak, A. (1997a) 'Cross-cultural academic communication: A discourse community view'. In A. Duzsak (ed.) *Culture and Styles of Academic Discourse.* Berlin: Mouton de Gruyter, pp. 11–39.

Duszak, A. (1997b) 'Analyzing digressiveness in Polish academic texts'. In A. Duszak (ed.) *Culture and Styles of Academic Discourse.* Berlin: Mouton de Gruyter, pp. 323–342.

Duszak, A. (1998) 'Academic Writing in English and Polish: Comparing and Subverting Genres'. *International Journal of Applied Linguistics.* 8(2). 191–213.

Duszak, A. (2006) 'Looking Globally, Seeing Locally: Exploring Some Myths of Globalization in Academia'. *Revista Canaria de Estudios Ingleses*, 53. 35–45.

Duszak, A. and Lewkowicz, J. (2008) 'Publishing Academic Texts in English: A Polish Perspective'. *Journal of English for Academic Purposes*, 7. 108–120.

Dziubalska-Kołaczyk, K. (2013) 'English or ELFish? A Teaching Dilemma of the 21st century'. In J. Migdał and A. Piotrowska-Wojaczyk (eds). *Cum reverentia, gratia, amicitia… Księga jubileuszowa dedykowana Profesorowi Bogdanowi Walczakowi.* Poznań: Wydawnictwo Rys, pp. 463–469.

Eckert, P. (2008) 'Variation and the Indexical Field'. *Journal of Sociolinguistics*, 12(4). 453–476.

Eco, U. (1997 [1977].) *Como Se Faz uma Tese em Ciência Humanas*, Lisbon: Editorial Presença.

Englander, K. (2011) 'The globalized world of English scientific publishing: An analytical proposal that situates a multilingual scholar'. In G. Pérez Bonilla, and K. Englander (eds) *Discourses and Identities in Context of Educational Changes: Contributions from the USA and Mexico*. New York: Peter Lang, pp. 211–230.

Erichsen, R. (1998) 'Scientific Research and Science Policy in Turkey'. *Cahiers d'Etudes sur la Meditteranee Orientale el le monde Turco-Iranien*, 25. 1–19.

Erickson, E.J. (2006) 'Turkey as Regional Hegemon-2014: Strategic Implications for the United States'. *Turkish Studies*, 5(3). 25–45.

Estrela, E., Soares, M.A. and Leitão, M.J. (2006) *Saber Escrever uma Tese e Outros Textos*, Lisbon: D. Quixote.

Eurydice (2010) 'Organization of the Education System, Turkey 2009–2010'. Available at: http://www.eurodyce.org.

Evan-Zohar, I. (1990/1979), 'Polysystem Theory'. *Poetics Today: International Journal for Theory and Analysis of Literature and Communication*, 11(1). 8–51.

Fairclough, N. and Wodak, R. (1997) 'Critical discourse analysis'. In T. Van Dijk (ed.) *Discourse as Social Interaction*. London: Sage, pp. 258–284.

Fairclough, N. and Wodak, R. (2008) 'The Bologna process and the knowledge-based economy: A critical discourse analysis approach'. In B. Jessop, N. Fairclough and R. Wodak (eds) *Higher Education and the Knowledge Based Economy in Europe*. Rotterdam: Sense Publishers, pp. 109–126.

Ferguson, G. (2007) 'The Global Spread of English, Scientific Communication and ESP: Questions of Equity, Access and Domain Loss'. *Ibérica*, 13. 7–38.

Ferguson, G., Perez-Llantada, C. and Plo, R. (2011) 'English as an International Language of Scientific Publication: A Study of Attitudes'. *World Englishes*, 30(1). 41–59.

Fernández-Quijada, D., Masip, P. and Bergillos, I. (2013) 'El precio de la internacionalidad: la dualidad en los patrones de publicación de los investigadores españoles en comunicación'. *Revista Española de Documentación Científica*, 36 (2), e010.

Fløttum, K., Kinn, T. and Dahl, T. (2006) *Academic Voices: Across Languages and Disciplines*, Amsterdam/Philadelphia: John Benjamins.

Flowerdew, J. (1993) 'An Educational, or Process, Approach to the Teaching of Professional Genres'. *ELT Journal*, 47. 305–316.

Flowerdew, J. (1999a) 'Writing for Scholarly Publication in English: The Case of Hong Kong', *Journal of Second Language Writing*, 8(2). 123–145.

Flowerdew, J. (1999b) 'Problems in Writing for Scholarly Publication in English: The Case of Hong Kong'. *Journal of Second Language Writing*, 8(3). 243–264.

Flowerdew, J. (2000) 'Discourse Community, Legitimate Peripheral Participation, and the Nonnative-English-Speaking Scholar'. *TESOL Quarterly*, 34(1). 127–150.

Flowerdew, J. (2001) 'Attitudes of Journal Editors to Nonnative Speaker Contributions'. *TESOL Quarterly*, 35(1). 121–148.

Flowerdew, J. (ed.) (2002) *Academic Discourse*, London and New York: Longman.

Flowerdew, J. (2007) 'The Non-Anglophone Scholar on the Periphery of Scholarly Publication'. *AILA Review*, 20. 14–27.

Flowerdew, J. (2008) 'Scholarly Writers Who Use English as an Additional Language: What can Goffman's "stigma" Tell Us?'. *Journal of English for Academic Purposes*, 7. 77–86.

Flowerdew, J. (2013) 'Some Thoughts on English for Research Publication Purposes (ERPP) and Related Issues'. *Language Teaching/FirstView*, Article. 1–13. doi: http://dx.doi.org/10.1017/S0261444812000523

Flowerdew, L. (2012) 'Grammar and the research article'. In C. Chapelle (ed.) *Encyclopedia of Applied Linguistics*. Oxford: Wiley-Blackwell, pp. 2394–2399.

Flowerdew, J. and Li, Y. (2009) 'English or Chinese? The trade-off between local and international publication among Chinese academics in the humanities and social sciences'. *Journal of Second Language Writing* 18, 1–16.

Fortanet, I. (2004) 'The Use of *We* in University Lectures: Reference and Function'. *English for Specific Purposes*, 23(1). 45–66.

Fox, H. (1994) *Listening to the World: Cultural Issues in Academic Writing*, Urbana, Illinois: National Council of Teachers of English.

Frattini, R. and Rossi, P. (2012), 'Report sulle Donne nell'Università Italiana', *Meno di Zero, Rivista dell'Università in Movimento*, *III*(8–9). http://www.menodizero. eu/saperepotere-analisi/247-report-sulle-donne-delluniverita-italiana.html. Accessed 6 August 2013.

Friedman, T.L. (2005) *The World is Flat*, London: Penguin Books.

Fry, J. (2004) 'The Cultural Shaping of ICTs Within Academic Fields: Corpus-Based Linguistics as a Case Study'. *Literary and Linguistic Computing*, 19. 303–319.

Gardner, R.C. (1985) *Social Psychology and Second Language Learning: the Role of Attitudes and Motivation*, London: Edward Arnold.

Garrett, P. (2010) *Attitudes to Language*, Cambridge: Cambridge University Press.

Gazzola, M. (2012) 'The Linguistic Implications of Academic Performance Indicators: General Trends and Case Study'. *International Journal of the Sociology of Language*, 216. 131–156.

Giannoni, D.S. (2008) 'Medical Writing at the Periphery: The Case of Italian Journal Editorials'. *Journal of English for Academic Purposes*, 7(2). 97–107.

Gibbs, W.W. (1995) 'Lost Science in the Third World'. *Scientific American*, 1 August. 76–83.

Giltrow, J. and Stein, D. (2009) 'Genres in the internet: Innovation, evolution and genre theory'. In J. Giltrow and D. Stein (eds) *Genres in the Internet: Issues in the Theory of Genre*. Amsterdam/Philadelphia: John Benjamins, pp. 1–25.

Giménez-Toledo, E. (2012) 'Evaluation of Humanities and Social Sciences in Spain: Multi-Indicator Evaluation Models for Scientific Journals and Books'. Lecture. *Research Quality Criteria in the Humanities*. Zurich, 10 May. http://www. psh.ethz.ch/crus/kolloquium/gimenez_EN. Accessed 16 December 2014.

Giménez-Toledo, E., Tejada-Artigas, C. and Mañana-Rodríguez, J (2013) 'Evaluation of Scientific Book Publishers in Social Sciences and Humanities: Results of a Survey'. *Research Evaluation*, 22. 64–77.

Gizycki, R. von (1973) 'Centre and Periphery in the International Scientific Community: Germany, France and Great Britain in the 19th century'. *Minerva*, 11. 479–494.

Glunčić, V., Pulanić, D., Prka, M., Marušić, A. and Marušić, M. (2001) 'Curricular and Extracurricular Activities of Medical Students During War, Zagreb University School of Medicine, 1991–1995'. *Academic Medicine*, 76. 82–87.

Goker, A. (2004) 'Pazar ekonomilerinde bilim ve teknoloji politikalari ve Turkiye' [Science and Technology policies in market economies and Turkey]. Teknoloji, Ankara: TMMOB. 123–220.

Golubić, R., Rudeš, M., Kovačić, N., Marušić, M. and Marušić A. (2008) 'Calculating Impact Factor: How Bibliographical Classification of Journal Items Affects the Impact Factor of Large and Small Journals'. *Science and Engineering Ethics*, 14. 41–49.

Gonerko-Frej, A. (2007) *Culture in the EFL Classroom: A Comparative Analysis of Approaches and Materials in Central and Eastern Europe, 1998–2001*, Szczecin: Zapol.

Gonerko-Frej, A. (2011) 'The importance of being native: The English invasion of the Polish education system – a balance of losses and gains'. In A. Gonerko-Frej, M. Sokół, J. Witkowska and U. Zagratzki (eds) *Us and Them – Them and Us: Constructions of the Other in Cultural Stereotypes*. Aachen: Shaker, pp. 625–639.

Gonerko-Frej, A. (2013) 'Szanse i niebezpieczeństwa języka globalizacji'. In K. Jaworska-Biskup, B. Kijek and A. Szwajczuk (eds) *Interdyscyplinarność w dydaktyce nauczania języków obcych*. Szczecin: Zapol, pp. 33–49.

Gosden, H. (1992) 'Research Writing and NNSs: From the Editors'. *Journal of Second Language Writing*, 1. 123–139.

Gosden, H. (1993) 'Discourse Functions of Subject in Scientific Research Articles'. *Applied Linguistics*, 14. 56–75.

Gotti, M. (2012) 'Cross-Cultural Aspects of Academic Discourse'. *Brno Studies in English*, 38(2). 59–78.

Graddol, D. (1997) *The Future of English?* London: British Council.

Graddol, D. (2006) *English Next*, London: British Council.

Green, L. (1994) 'Missing the post(modern): Cores, peripheries and globalisation'. In L. Green and R. Guinery (eds) *Framing Technology: Society, Choice and Change*. Sydney: Allen and Unwin, pp. 161–175.

Greiner, C. and Sakdapolrak, P. (2013) 'Translocality: Concepts, Applications and Emerging Research Perspectives'. *Geography Compass*, 7. 373–384.

Grieve, J., Biber, D., Friginal, E. and Nekrasova, T. (2010) 'Variation among blogs: A multi-dimensional analysis'. In A. Mehler, S. Sharoff and M. Santini (eds) *Genres on the Web: Computational Models and Empirical Studies*. Berlin: Springer, pp. 303–322.

Gunnarsson, B.L. (2001) 'Swedish, English, French or German – the language situation at Swedish universities'. In U. Ammon (ed.) *The Dominance of English as a Language of Science: Effects on Other Languages and Language Communities*, Berlin: Mouton de Gruyter, pp. 287–316.

Halavais, A. (2006) 'Scholarly blogging: Moving toward the visible college'. In A. Bruns and J. Jacobs (eds) *Uses of Blogs*. New York: Peter Lang, pp. 117–125.

Halliday, M.A.K. and Martin, J.R. (eds) (1993) *Writing Science: Literacy and Discursive Power*. Pittsburgh and London: University of Pittsburgh Press.

Hamel, R.E. (2007) 'The Dominance of English in the International Scientific Periodical Literature and the Future of Language use in Science'. *AILA Review*, 20. 53–71.

Hanauer, D.I. and Englander, K. (2013) *Scientific Writing in a Second Language*, Anderson, SC: Parlor Press.

Hanioglu, M.S. (2008) *A Brief History of the Late Ottoman Empire*, NJ: Princeton University Press.

Harrison, T.M. and Barthel, B. (2009) 'Wielding New Media in Web 2.0: Exploring the History of Engagement with the Collaborative Construction of Media Products'. *New Media and Society*, 11(1–2). 155–178.

Harrison, T.M. and Stephen, T. (1996) 'Computer networking, communication, and scholarship'. In T.M. Harrison and T. Stephen (eds) *Computer Networking and Scholarly Communication in the Twenty-first Century*. New York: State University of New York Press, pp. 3–36.

Harwood, N. (2005a) 'We do not Seem to Have a Theory ... The Theory I Present Here Attempts to Fill This Gap': Inclusive and Exclusive Pronouns in Academic Writing'. *Applied Linguistics*, 26(3). 343–375.

Harwood, N. (2005b) '"I Hoped to Counteract the Memory Problem, but I Made no Impact Whatsoever": Discussing Methods in Computing Science Using *I*'. *English for Specific Purposes*, 24(3). 243–267.

Harwood, N. (2006) '(In)Appropriate Personal Pronoun use in Political Science: A Qualitative Study and a Proposed Heuristic for Future Research'. *Written Communication*, 23. 424–450.

Harwood, N. (2009) 'An Interview-based Study of the Functions of Citations in Academic Writing Across Two Disciplines'. *Journal of Pragmatics*, 41(3). 497–518.

Harzing, A-W (2010) 'Citation Analysis Across Disciplines: The Impact of Different Data Sources and Citation Metrics'. http://www.harzing.com/data_metrics_comparison.htm. Accessed 16 January 2014.

HEC (2004) *Türk yükseköğretiminin bugünkü durumu*. Available at: http://www.yok.gov.tr/egitim/raporlar/kasim2004/turk_yuksekogretim_bugun.doc.

HEC (2010) 'The Higher Education System in Turkey'. Bilkent, Ankara. Available at: http://www.yok.gov.tr.

Herring, S.C., Scheidt, L.A., Bonus, S. and Wright, E. (2004) 'Bridging the gap: A genre analysis of weblogs'. In *Proceedings of the 37th Hawaii International Conference on System Sciences* (CD-ROM), [1/5/2004], Computer Society Press (11 pages) http://ella.slis.indiana.edu/noherring/herring.Scheidt.2004.pdf.

Herring, S.C., Scheidt, L.A., Wright, E. and Bonus, S. (2005) 'Weblogs as a Bridging Genre'. *Information, Technology, and People*, 18(22). 142–171.

Hewings, A. and Coffin, C. (2007) 'Writing in Multi-Party Computer Conferences and Signle Authored Assignments: Exploring the Role of Writer as Thinker'. *Journal of English for Academic Purposes*, 6(2). 126–142.

Hewings, M. and Hewings, A. (2002) ' "It is Interesting to Note That...": A Comparative Study of Anticipatory "it" in Student and Published Writing'. *English for Specific Purposes*, 21. 367–383.

Hewings, A., Lillis, T. and Vladimirou, D. (2010) 'Who's Citing Whose Writings? A Corpus Based Study of Citations as Interpersonal Resource in English Medium National and English Medium International Journals'. *Journal of English for Academic Purposes*, 9. 102–115.

Hicks, B. (2012) 'Poland Scores Late Goals in Education'. *BBC*. 12 June. http://www.bbc.co.uk/news/business-18151512. Accessed 18 March 2014.

Higher Education Law (1981) No: 2547. Available at: http:www.yok.gov.tr/content/view/435/183/lang.tr.

Higher Education Institutions Structure Law (1983) No: 2809. Available at: http:www.yok.gov.tr.

Hoey, J. (2008) 'Crisis at the Croatian Medical Journal: Considering a Proposal for its Destruction'. *Croatian Medical Journal*, 49. 161–163.

Hoffman, E. (1989) *Lost in Translation*, London: Vintage.

Holliday, A.R. (1999) 'Small Cultures'. *Applied Linguistics*, 20(2). 237–264.

Holstein, J.A. and Gubrium, F. (1997) 'Active interviewing'. In D. Silverman (ed.) *Qualitative Research: Theory, Method and Practice*. Thousand Oaks: Sage, pp. 113–129.

Holton, D., Mackridge, P. and Philippaki-Warburton, I. (2002) Γραμματική της Ελληνικής Γλώσσας [transl. of *Greek Grammar: A Comprehensive Grammar of the Modern Language* by V. Spyropoulos]. Athens: Patakis.

House, J. (2003) 'English as a Lingua Franca: A Threat to Multilingualism?'. *Journal of Sociolinguistics*, 7(4). 556–578.

House, J. (2008) 'Global English and the destruction of identity?'. In P. Nikolaou and M.V. Kyritsi (eds). *Translating Selves: Experience and Identity between Languages and Literatures*. London and New York: Continuum, pp. 87–107.

Hovel, R. (2012) 'Professors fume over dominance of English language in Israeli academia'. *Haaretz*, 12 October 2012. www.haaretz.com. Accessed 25 October 2013.

Hrabak, M., Vujaklija, A., Vodopivec, I., Hren, D., Marušić, M. and Marušić, A. (2004) 'Academic Misconduct Among Medical Students in a Post-Communist Country'. *Medical Education*, 38. 276–285.

Hren, D., Lukić, I.K., Marušić, A., Vodopivec, I., Vujaklija, A., Hrabak, M. and Marušić, M. (2004) 'Teaching Research Methodology in Medical Schools: Students' Attitudes Towards and Knowledge About Science'. *Medical Education*, 38. 81–86.

Hren, D., Marušić, M. and Marušić, A. (2011) 'Regression of Moral Reasoning During Medical Education: Combined Design Study to Evaluate the Effect of Clinical Study Years'. PLoS ONE 6, e17406.

Hren, D., Sambunjak, D., Ivaniš, A., Marušić, M. and Marušić, A. (2007) 'Perceptions of Authorship Criteria: Effects of Student Instruction and Scientific Experience'. *Journal of Medical Ethics*, 33. 428–432.

Hren, D., Sambunjak, D., Marušić, M. and Marušić, A. (2013) 'Medical Students' Decisions About Authorship in Disputable Situations: Intervention Study'. *Science and Engineering Ethics*, 19. 641–651.

Hren, D., Vujaklija, A., Ivanišević, R., Knežević, J., Marušić, M. and Marušić, A. (2006) 'Students' Moral Reasoning. Machiavellianism and Socially Desirable Responding: Implications for Teaching Ethics and Research Integrity'. *Medical Education*, 40. 269–277.

Huić, M. (2008) 'Fifteenth Anniversary of the Croatian Medical Journal: Still Moving Ahead'. *Croatian Medical Journal*, 49. 1–7.

Huić, M., Vitezić, D. and Marušić, A. (2011) 'The procedure for the ethical review of protocols for clinical research projects in Croatia'. In EFGCP Ethics Working Party (ed.) *EFGCP Report on the Procedure for the Ethical Review of Protocols for Clinical Research Projects in the European Union*. Brussels: European Forum for Good Clinical Practice. Available at: http://www.efgcp.eu/Downloads/EFGCPReportFiles/Croatia%20definitive%20Updated.pdf. Accessed: 1 June 2014.

Huth, E. (2004) 'A Model of Journal Governance'. *Science Editor*, 27. 102.

Hyland, K. (1998) *Hedging in Scientific Research Articles*, Amsterdam/Philadelphia: John Benjamins.

Hyland, K. (1999) 'Academic Attribution: Citation and the Construction of Disciplinary Knowledge'. *Applied Linguistics*, 20(3). 341–367.

Hyland, K. (2000) *Disciplinary Discourses: Social Interactions in Academic Writing*, Harlow: Longman.

Hyland, K. (2001) 'Humble Servants of the Discipline? Self-Mention in Research Articles'. *English for Specific Purposes*, 18. 207–226.

Hyland, K. (2002a) 'Authority and Invisibility: Authorial Identity in Academic Writing'. *Journal of Pragmatics*, 34. 1091–1112.

Hyland, K. (2002b) 'Options of Identity in Academic Writing'. *English Language Teaching Journal*, 56(4). 351–358.

Hyland, K. (2003) 'Self-Citation and Self-Reference: Credibility and Promotion in Academic Publication'. *Journal of the American Society for Information Science and Technology*, 54(3). 251–259.

Hyland, K. (2005a) 'Stance and Engagement: A Model of Interaction in Academic Discourse'. *Discourse Studies*, 7(2). 173–192.

Hyland, K. (2005b) *Metadiscourse: Exploring Interaction in Writing*, London: Continuum.

Hyland, Ken (2006) 'The "other" English: Thoughts on EAP and Academic Writing'. *The European English Messenger*, 15(2). 34–38.

Hyland, K. (2008) 'As Can be Seen: Lexical Bundles and Disciplinary Variation'. *English for Specific Purposes*, 27. 4–21.

Hyland, K. (2009) *Academic Discourse: English in a Global Context*, London and New York: Continuum.

Hyland, K. (2011) 'Welcome to the Machine: Thoughts on Writing for Scholarly Publication'. *Journal of Second Language Teaching and Research*, 1(1). 58–68.

Hyland, K. (2012) *Disciplinary Identities: Individuality and Community in Academic Discourse*, Cambridge University Press.

Hyland, K. and Tse, P. (2004) 'Metadiscourse in Academic Writing: A Reappraisal'. *Applied Linguistics*, 25. 156–177.

Ilakovac, V., Fišter, K., Marušić, M. and Marušić, A. (2007) 'Reliability of Disclosure Forms of Authors' Contributions'. *Canadian Medical Association Journal*, 176. 41–46.

IMF (2012) 'World Economic Outlook: Growth Resuming, Dangers Remain'. Available at: http://www.imf.org/external/pubs/ft/weo/2012/01/pdf/text.pdf.

IUC-Inter-university Council (2000) 'Doçentlik sınav yönetmeliği'. [Regulation for the associate professorship exam], 01/09/2000. *Resmi Gazette*, No. 24157.

IUC-HEC (2009) 'Doçentlik sınav yönetmeliği' [Regulation for the evaluation for associate professorship], 31/01/2009. *Resmi Gazette*, No. 27127.

Ivaniš, A., Hren, D., Marušić, M. and Marušić, A. (2011) 'Less work, less respect: authors' perceived importance of research contributions and their declared contributions to research articles'. *PLoS ONE* 6, e20206.

Ivaniš, A., Hren, D., Sambunjak, D., Marušić, M. and Marušić, A. (2008) 'Quantification of Authors' Contributions and Eligibility for Authorship: Randomized Study in a General Medical Journal'. *Journal of General and Internal Medicine*, 23. 1303–1310.

Jenkins, H. (2006) *Convergence Culture: Where Old and New Media Collide*, New York and London: New York University Press.

Jenkins, J. (2000) *The Phonology of English as an International Language*. Oxford: Oxford University Press.

Jenkins, J. (2007) *English as a Lingua Franca: Attitude and Identity*, Oxford: Oxford University Press.

Jenkins, J. (2009) 'English as a Lingua Franca: Interpretations and Attitudes'. *World Englishes*, 28(2). 200–207.

Johns, T. (1992) 'It is Presented Initially: Linear Dislocation and Interlanguage Strategies in Brazilian Academic Abstracts in English and Portuguese'. *Revista Ilha do Desterro*, 27. 9–32.

Joseph, J.E. (1987) *Eloquence and Power: The Rise of Language Standards and Standard Languages*, London: Frances Pinter.

Kachru, B. (1985) 'Standards, codification and sociolinguistic realism: The English language in the outer circle'. In R. Quirk and H. Widdowson (eds), *English in the World*. London: Longman, pp. 11–32.

Kachru, B. (2001) 'World Englishes'. In R. Mesthrie (ed.) *Concise Encyclopedia of Sociolinguistics*. New York: Elsevier, pp. 519–524.

Kaplan, R. (1966) 'Cultural Thought Patterns in Intercultural Education'. *Language Learning*, 16(1). 1–20.

Katavić, V. (2006) 'Five-year Report of Croatian Medical Journal's Research Integrity Editor: Policy, Policing, or Policing Policy'. *Croatian Medical Journal*, 47. 220–227.

Kent, M. (1996) *The Great Powers and the End of the Ottoman Empire*, London: Frank Cass.

Kentor, J. (2008) 'The Divergence of Economic and Coercive Power in the world Economy 1960 to 2000: A Measure of Nation-state Position'. IROWS Working Paper #46. http://irows.ucr.edu/papers/irows46/irows46.htm. Accessed 16 January 2014.

Keyder, C. (2009) *The Definition of a Peripheral Economy: Turkey 1923–1929*, Cambridge: Cambridge University Press.

Khosla, I.P. (2001) 'Turkey: The Search for a Role'. *Strategic Analysis*, 25(3). 343–369.

Kim Loi, C. and Evans, M.S. (2010) 'Cultural Differences in the Organization of Research Article Introductions From the Field of Educational Psychology: English and Chinese'. *Journal of Pragmatics*, 42. 2814–2825.

King, D. (2004) 'The Scientific Impact of Nations: What Different Countries Get for Their Research Spending'. *Nature*, 430. 311–316.

Kinzer, S. (2001) *Crescent and Star: Turkey between Two Worlds*, New York: Farrar, Straus and Giroux.

Kiper, M. (2004) 'Teknoloji transfer mekanizmalari ve bu kapsamda universite-sanayi isbirligi'. *Teknoloji*, 59–122.

Kjellberg, S. (2009) 'Scholarly Blogging Practice as Situated Genre: An Analytical Framework Based on Genre Theory'. *Information Research*, 14(3), Paper 410. http://InformationR.net/ir/14-3/paper410.html. Accessed 18 March 2014.

Kjellberg, S. (2010) 'I am a Blogging Researcher: Motivations for Blogging in a Scholarly Context'. *First Monday* 15(8). http://firstmonday.org/article/view/2962/2580#p4. Accessed 18 March 2014.

Kljaković-Gašpić, M., Hren, D., Marušić, A. and Marušić M. (2003) 'Peer Review Time: How Late is Late in a Small Medical Journal?' *Archives of Medical Research*, 34. 439–443.

Kljaković-Gašpić, M., Petrak, J., Rudan, I. and Biloglav, Z. (2007) 'For Free or for Fee? Dilemma of Small Scientific Journals'. *Croatian Medical Journal*, 48. 292–299.

Kohnen, T. (2001) 'Text types as catalysis for language change: The example for the adverbial first participle construction'. In H.-J. Diller and M. Görlach (eds)

*Towards a History of English as a History of Genres*. Heidelberg: Universitätsverlag C. Winter, pp. 111–124.

Koksal, D. and Razi, S. (2011) 'An Investigation into ELT Professional's Research Culture in Turkey'. *Education and Science*, 36. 209–224.

Koku, E., Nazer, N. and Wellman, B. (2001) 'Netting Scholars: Online and Offline'. *American Behavioral Scientist*, 44(10). 1752–1774.

Komorowska, H. (2012) 'The teacher training colleges project in Poland'. In C. Tribble (ed.) *Managing Change in English Language Teaching: Lessons from Experience*. British Council, pp. 147–151.

Kordić, S. (2010) *Jezik i nacionalizam*, Zagreb: Durieux.

Kovačić, N., Huić, M. and Ivaniš, A. (2008) 'Citation analysis of the Croatian Medical Journal: the First 15 years'. *Croatian Medical Journal*, 49. 12–17.

Kramsch, C. (1993) *Context and Culture in Language Teaching*, Oxford: Oxford University Press.

Kramsch, C. (1998) *Language and Culture*, Oxford: Oxford University Press.

Kramsch, C. (2001) 'Intercultural Communication'. In R. Carter and D. Nunan (eds) *The Cambridge Guide to Teaching English to Speakers of Other Languages*. Cambridge: Cambridge University Press, pp. 201–206.

Kreutz, H. and Harres, A. (1997) 'Some observations on the distribution and function of hedging in German and English academic writing'. In A. Duzsak (ed.) *Culture and Styles of Academic Discourse*. Berlin: Mouton de Gruyter, pp. 181–201.

Kubota, R. and Lehner, A. (2004) 'Toward Critical Contrastive Rhetoric'. *Journal of Second Language Writing*, 13. 7–27.

Kulczycki, E. (2012) 'Blogs and scientific services: Scientific communication in culture of convergence'. In I. Sójkowska (ed.) *Materiały konferencyjne EBIB nr 22*. Stowarzyszenie EBIB: Toruń, pp. 1–24.

Kuo, C.-H. (1999) 'The Use of Personal Pronouns: Role Relationships in Scientific Journal Articles'. *English for Specific Purposes*, 18(2). 121–138.

Kutlača, D. (2007) 'The science and technology system in Serbia: Between survival and restructuring'. In J. Nechifor and S. Radošević (eds) *Why Invest in Science in South Eastern Europe?* Proceedings of the International Conference and High Level Round Table. Venice: UNESCO Office, pp. 131–139.

Kuwayama, Takami. (2004) *Native Anthropology: The Japanese Challenge to Western Academic Hegemony*. Melbourne: Trans Pacific Press.

Labov, William (1963) 'The Social Motivation of a Sound Change'. *Word*, 19. 273–309.

Lambert, W.E., Hodgson, R.C., Gardner, R.C. and Fillenbaum, S. (1960) 'Evaluational Reactions to Spoken Language'. *Journal of Abnormal and Social Psychology*, 60. 44–51.

Lang, S. (1998) 'Challenge of Goodness: Twelve Humanitarian Proposals Based on the Experience of 1991–1995 Wars in Croatia and Bosnia and Herzegovina'. *Croatian Medical Journal*, 39. 72–76.

Lang, S. and Marušić, M. (1993) 'Peace and Human Rights: Painful Lessons of the Balkan War'. *International Minds*, 4. 6–13.

Las Heras-Navarro, E. (2013) 'Los libros en humanidades y ciencias sociales: cómo saber que es bueno para los sexenios'. Paper presented at the *Sesión sobre presentación de solicitudes de evaluación de la actividad investigadora a la CNEAI*. Universidad Complutense, Madrid, 16 December.

Lee, L.C., Lin, P.H., Chuang, Y.W. and Lee, Y.Y. (2011) 'Research output and economic productivity: a Granger causality test'. *Scientometrics*, 89. 469–478.

Leki, I. (1991) 'Twenty-five years of contrastive rhetoric: text analysis and writing pedagogues." *TESOL Quarterly*, 25. 123–143.

Lévy, P. (1999) *Collective Intelligence: Mankind's Emerging World in Cyberspace*, Cambridge, MA: Perseus Publishing.

Lévy-Leblond, J.M. and Oustinoff, M. (2007) 'Translation and the Exact Sciences'. *Hermès*, 49. 205–211.

Lillis, T. (1997) 'New Voices in Academia? The Regulative Nature of Academic Writing Conventions'. *Language and Education*, 11(3). 182–199.

Lillis, T. (2012) 'Economies of Signs in Writing for Academic Publication: The Case of English Medium "national" Journals', *Journal of Advanced Composition*, 32. 695–722.

Lillis, T. and Curry, M.J. (2006) 'Professional Academic Writing by Multilingual Scholars: Interactions With Literacy Brokers in the Production of English-Medium texts'. *Written Communication*, 23(1). 3–35.

Lillis, T. and Curry, M.J. (2010) *Academic Writing in a Global Context: The Politics and Practices of Publishing in English*. London and New York: Routledge.

Lillis, T. and Curry, M.J. (2013) 'English, scientific publishing and participation in the global knowledge economy'. In E. Erling, and P. Sargeant (eds) *English and International Development*. Clevedon, UK: Multilingual Matters, pp. 220–242.

Lillis, T.A., Hewings, D. Vladimirou, and M.J. Curry (2010) 'The Geolinguistics of English as an Academic Lingua Franca: Citation Practices Across English-Medium National and English Medium International Journals'. *International Journal of Applied Linguistics*, 20(1). 111–135.

Ljosland, R. (2007) 'English in Norwegian Academia: A Step Towards Diglossia?' *World Englishes*, 26(4). 395–410.

Lorés-Sanz, R., Mur-Dueñas, P., Burgess, S., Rey-Rocha, J. and Moreno, A.I. (2012) 'Publishing in English-medium scientific journals as opportunity: a comparative study of Spanish researchers writing practices in chemistry and business'. Paper presented at the conference *English in Europe: Opportunity or Threat?*. Sheffield, UK, 20–22 April.

MacDonald, S.P. (1994) *Professional Academic Writing in the Humanities and Social Sciences*. Carbondale: Southern Illinois University Press.

Magone, J.M. (2009) *Contemporary Spanish Politics*, London: Routledge.

Manuti, A., Cortini, M. and Mininni, G. (2006), 'Rhetorical argumentation in Italian academic discourse', *Argumentation*, 20. 101–124.

Marcovitch, H. (2008a) 'Croatia is Let Down'. *British Medical Journal* 336. 174.1.

Markovitch, H. (2008b) 'Croatian Minister replies but medical school silent'. Rapid response to Marcovitch, H. (2008a) 'Croatia is Let Down'. *British Medical Journal*, 336. 174.1. http://www.bmj.com/rapid-response/2011/11/01/croatian-minister-replies-medical-school-silent. Accessed 18 March 2014.

Martin, P. and Burgess, S. (2004) 'The Rhetorical Management of Academic Criticism in Research Article Abstracts'. *Text*, 24(2). 171–195.

Marušić, A. (2005a) 'Author Misconduct: Editors as Educators of Research Integrity'. *Medical Education*, 39. 7–11.

Marušić, A. (ed.) (2005b) *Revitalization of Academic Medicine*, Zagreb: Croatian Medical Journal and Medicinska naklada.

Marušić, A. (2008) 'Approaches to the detection of research misconduct: The role of the peer review process'. In F. Wells and M. Farthing (eds) *Fraud and Misconduct in Biomedical Research*. London: The Royal Society of Medicine Press, pp. 135–160.

Marušić A. (2011) 'Good Season Ahead'. *Croatian Medical Journal*, 52. 6–7.

Marušić, A. and Haug, C. (2006) 'The journal editor's perspective'. In M. Foote (ed.) *Clinical Trial Registries. A Practical Guide for Sponsors and Researchers of Medicinal Products*. Basel: Birkhäuser, pp. 13–26.

Marušić, A. and Marušić, M. (1996) 'The Creation of the Croatian Medical Journal and Croatia's Reputation Abroad'. *Journal of Croatian Studies*, 36–37. 149–170.

Marušić, A. and Marušić, M. (1999) 'Small Scientific Journals from Small Countries: Breaking from a Vicious Circle of Inadequacy'. *Croatian Medical Journal*, 40. 508–514.

Marušić, A. and Marušić, M. (2001) 'Good Editorial Practice: Editors as Educators'. *Croatian Medical Journal*, 42. 113–120.

Marušić, A. and Marušić, M. (2002) 'What Can Medical Journal Editors do in War?' *Lancet*, 360 (Suppl), s59–60.

Marušić, A. and Marušić, M. (2003) 'Teaching Students How to Read and Write Science: A Mandatory Course on Scientific Research and Communication in Medicine'. *Academic Medicine*, 78. 1235–1239.

Marušić, A. and Marušić, M. (2012) 'Can Small Journals Provide Leadership?' *Lancet*, 379. 1361–1363.

Marušić, A., Bates, T., Anić, A. and Marušić, M. (2006) 'How the Structure of Contribution Disclosure Statements Affects Validity of Authorship: A Randomized Study in a General Medical Journal'. *Current Medical Research and Opinion*, 22. 1035–1344.

Marušić, A., Katavić, V. and Marušić, M. (2007) 'Role of Editors and Journals in Detecting and Preventing Scientific Misconduct: Strengths, Weaknesses, Opportunities, and Threats'. *Medicine and Law*, 26. 545–566.

Marušić, A., Lukić, I.K., Marušić, M., McNamee, D., Sharp, D. and Horton, R. (2002) 'Peer Review in a Small and a Big Medical Journal: Case Study of the Croatian Medical Journal and the Lancet'. *Croatian Medical Journal*, 43. 286–289.

Marušić, A., Marušić, M. and Lang, S. (1994) 'White Road for Nova Bila and Silver Bosnia: A Chronology of the Humanitarian Convoy'. *Croatian Medical Journal*, 35. 3–7.

Marušić, A., Mišak, A., Kljaković-Gašpić, M. and Marušić, M. (2002) 'Educatione ad Excelentiam: Ten Years of the Croatian Medical Journal'. *Croatian Medical Journal*, 43. 1–7.

Marušić, A., Sambunjak, D., Jerončić, A., Malički, M. and Marušić, M. (2013) 'No Health Research Without Education for Research: Experience from an Integrated Course in Undergraduate Medical Curriculum'. *Medical Teacher*, 35. 609.

Marušić, M. (2008) 'Richard Horton, Editor of the Lancet, Visits Croatia to Support the Croatian Medical Journal'. *Croatian Medical Journal*, 49. 422.

Marušić, M. (2009) 'Conflict of Interest for Editor: Sweet and Sad Choices'. *Croatian Medical Journal*, 50. 342–344.

Marušić, M. (2010a) 'Croatia Moves Away From Fostering Research Integrity'. *Lancet*, 376. 1627–1628.

Marušić, M. (2010b) *Life of an Editor*, Zagreb: Croatian Medical Journal and Medicinska naklada.

Marušić, M. (2011) 'My Life as an Editor'. *European Science Editing*, 37. 19.

Marušić, M. and Marušić A. (2007) 'Threats to the Integrity of the Croatian Medical Journal'. *Croatian Medical Journal*, 48. 779–785.

Marušić, M. and Marušić A. (2008a) 'Threats to the Integrity of the Croatian Medical Journal: An Update'. *Croatian Medical Journal*, 49. 8–11.

Marušić, M. and Marušić A. (2008b) 'Discussing the Future of the Journal'. *Croatian Medical Journal*, 49. 158–160.

Marušić, M., Bošnjak, D., Rulic-Hren, S. and Marušić, A. (2003) 'Legal Regulation of the Croatian Medical Journal: Model for Small Academic Journals'. *Croatian Medical Journal*, 44. 663–673.

Marušić, M., Božikov, J., Katavić, V., Hren, D., Kljaković-Gašpić, M. and Marušić, A. (2004) 'Authorship in a Small Medical Journal: A Study of Contributorship Statements by Corresponding Authors'. *Science and Engineering Ethics*, 10. 493–502.

Marušić, M., Marušić, A., Hren, D., Roso, V. and Donev, D.M. (2010) 'Is Mandatory Training in Research Methodology Associated with Attitudes and Knowledge About Science in Medicine?' *Medical Teacher*, 32. 348.

Marušić, M., Mišak, A., Kljaković-Gašpić, M., Fišter, K., Hren, D. and Marušić, A. (2004) 'Producing a Scientific Journal in a Small Scientific Community: An Author-helpful Policy'. *International Microbiology*, 7. 143–147.

Marušić, M., Sambunjak, D. and Marušić, A. (2006) 'Life of Small Medical Journal: How Bibliographical Indexing and International Visibility Affected Editorial Work in Croatian Medical Journal'. *Croatian Medical Journal*, 47. 372–375.

Matsuda, P.K. and Atkinson, D. (2008) 'A conversation on contrastive rhetoric'. In U. Connor, E. Nagelhout and W.V. Rozycki (eds) *Contrastive Rhetoric: Reaching to Intercultural Rhetoric*. Amsterdam: John Benjamins, pp. 277–298.

Mauranen, A. (1993) 'Contrastive ESP Rhetoric: Metatext in Finnish-English Economic Texts'. *English for Specific Purposes*, 12(3). 3–22.

Mauranen, A. (2012) *Exploring ELF: Academic English Shaped by Non-native Speakers*, Cambridge: Cambridge University Press.

Mauranen, A. (2013) 'ELF for academic publishing: the remaining taboo'. Paper given at the *Sixth International Conference of English as a Lingua Franca*, Rome, 5th September.

Mauranen, A., Hynninen, N. and Ranta, E. (2010) 'English as an Academic Lingua Franca: The ELFA Project'. *English for Specific Purposes*, 29. 183–190.

Mauranen, A. and Ranta, E. (eds) (2009) *English as a Lingua Franca: Studies and Findings*, Newcastle: Cambridge Scholars Publishing.

May, R. (1997) 'The Scientific Wealth of Nations'. *Science*, 275. 793–796.

McGrath, L. and Kuteeva, M. (2012) 'Stance and Engagement in Pure Mathematics Research Articles: Linking Discourse Features to Disciplinary Practices'. *English for Specific Purposes*, 31. 161–173.

McKay, S.L. (2003) 'Reflections on being a gatekeeper'. In C.P. Casanave and S. Vandrick (eds) *Writing for Scholarly Publication: Behind the Scenes in Language Education*. Mahwah, NJ: Lawrence Erlbaum, pp. 91–103.

McNally, J.R. (1969), '"Rector et dux populi": Italian Humanists and the Relationship Between Rhetoric and Logic'. *Modern Philology*, 67(2). 168–176.

Medgyes, P. and Kaplan, R.B. (1992) 'Discourse in a Foreign Language: The Example of Hungarian Scholars'. *International Journal of the Sociology of Language*, 98. 67–100.

Miles, M.B. and Huberman, A.M. (1994) *Qualitative Data Analysis: An Expanded Sourcebook*, 2nd edition. Thousand Oaks: Sage.

Miller, C.R. (1984) 'Genre as Social Action'. *Quarterly Journal of Speech*, 70. 151–167.

Miller, C.R. and Shepherd, D. (2009) 'Questions for genre theory from the blogosphere'. In J. Giltrow and D. Stein (eds) *Genres in the Internet: Issues in the Theory of Genre*. Amsterdam/Philadelphia: John Benjamins, pp. 263–290.

Miller, J. and Glassner, B. (1997) 'The "inside" and the "outside": Finding realities in interviews'. In D. Silverman (ed.) *Qualitative Research: Theory, Method and Practice*. Thousand Oaks: Sage, pp.125–139.

Mišak, A., Marušić, M. and Marušić, A. (2005) 'Manuscript Editing as a Way of Teaching Academic Writing: Experience From a Small Scientific Journal'. *Journal of Second Language Writing*, 14. 122–131.

Mittermayer, R., Huić, M. and Meštrović, J. (2010) 'Quality of Health Care, Accreditation, and Health Technology Assessment in Croatia: Role of Agency for Quality and Accreditation in Health'. [in Croatian]. *Acta Medica Croatica*, 64. 425–434.

MIUR (2003) 'Guidelines for the Evaluation of Research', http://vtr2006.cineca.it/documenti/linee_guida_EN.pdf. Accessed 29 July 2013.

MIUR (2009) 'Il Personale Docente di Ruolo nelle Università', *Notiziario Statistico, 2009*(5). http://statistica.miur.it/data/notiziario_5_2009.pdf. Accessed August 3 2013.

Mocikat, R., Hasse, W. and Dieter, H.H. (2005) 'Sieben Thesen zur deutschen Sprache'. http://www.7thesenwissenschaftssprache.de. Accessed 25 October 2013.

Molino, A. (2010) 'Personal and Impersonal Authorial References: A Contrastive Study of English and Italian Linguistics Research Articles'. *Journal of English for Academic Purposes*, 9(2). 86–101.

Mollin, S. (2006) *Euro-English: Assessing Variety Status*. Tübingen: Gunter Narr.

Monteleone, S. and Torrisi, B. (2012) 'Italian Researchers Abroad: A Multivariate Analysis of Migration Trends', *Rivista Italiana degli Economisti XVII*. 101–127.

Morano Foadi, S. (2006) 'Key Issues and Causes of the Italian Brain Drain'. *Innovation*, 19(2). 209–223.

Moreno, A.I. (2013) 'Compiling Comparable Corpora of Research Articles for Writing Teaching Purposes Through Interdisciplinary Collaboration'. Paper Presented at the *7th Conference of the European Association for the Teaching of Academic Writing* (EATAW), Budapest, Hungary, 27–29 June.

Moreno, A.I. and Suárez, L. (2008) 'A Study of Critical Attitude Across English and Spanish Academic Book Reviews'. *Journal of English for Academic Purposes*, 7. 15–26.

Moreno, A.I., Burgess, S., Sachdev, I., López-Navarro, I. and Rey-Rocha, J. (2013) 'The ENEIDA Questionnaire: Publication Experiences in Scientific Journals in English and Spanish'. http://eneida.unileon.es/eneidaquestionnaire.php. Accessed 6 February 2014.

Mortensen, T. and Walker, J. (2002) 'Blogging thoughts: Personal publication as an online research tool'. In A. Morrison (ed.) *Researching ICTs in Context*. Oslo: InterMedia, University of Oslo, pp. 249–279.

Mühlhäusler, P. (1996) *Linguistic Ecology. Language Change and Linguistic Imperialism in the Pacific Rim*, London: Routledge.

Mur-Dueñas, P. (2007) 'I/we Focus on...: A Cross-Cultural Analysis of Self-Mentions in Business Management Research Articles'. *Journal of English for Academic Purposes*, 6. 143–162.

Mur-Dueñas, P., Lorés-Sanz, R., Burgess, S., Rey-Rocha, J. and Moreno, A.I (2012) 'Publishing in English-Medium Scientific Journals as Challenge: A Comparative Study of Spanish Researchers Writing Practices in Chemistry and Business'. Paper presented at the conference *English in Europe: Opportunity or Threat?* Sheffield, 20–22 April.

Muresan, L. (2009) 'Dimensions of Teacher Development in a Romanian Higher Education Context'. *Cambridge ESOL Research Notes*, 38. 18–23.

Muresan, L. (2013) 'How to promote high quality multilingualism in an English-dominated research world? Challenges and opportunities'. In I. Roceanu, B. Logofatu, M. Stanescu, M. Blaga, & A. Colibaba (eds), *Quality and Efficiency in eLearning: Proceedings of the 9th International Scientific Conference e-Learning and Software for Education, Bucharest*, Bucharest: Editura Universitatii Nationale de Aparare "Carol I" 3. 278–283.

Muresan, L.M. and Pérez-Llantada, C. (2014) 'English for Research Publication and Dissemination in Bi-/Multiliterate Environments: The Case of Romanian Academics'. *Journal of English for Academic Purposes*, 13. 53–64.

Murray, H. and Dingwall, S (2001) 'The dominance of English at European universities: Switzerland and Sweden compared'. In U. Ammon (ed.) *The Dominance of English as a Language of Science: Effects on Other Languages and Language Communities*. Berlin: Mouton de Gruyter, pp. 85–112.

Myers, G. (1989) 'The Pragmatics of Politeness in Scientific Articles'. *Applied Linguistics*, 10. 1–35.

Myers, G. (1990) *Writing Biology: Texts in the Social Construction of Scientific Knowledge*, Madison, WI: University of Wisconsin Press.

Myers, G. (2010) *The Discourse of Blogs and Wikis*, London and New York: Continuum.

Nava, S. (2009) *La Fuga dei Talenti*, Alba, Italy: San Paolo Edizioni. http://fugade-italenti.wordpress.com/il-libro/. Accessed 1 August 2013.

Negretti, R. (2012) 'Metacognition in Student Academic Writing: a Longitudinal Study of Metacognitive Awareness and its Relation to Task Perception and Evaluation of Performance'. *Written Communication*, 29(2). 142–179.

Negretti, R. and Kuteeva, M. (2011) 'Fostering Metacognitive Genre Awareness in L2 Academic Reading and Writing: A Case Study of Pre-service English Teachers', *Journal of Second Language Writing*, 20. 95–110.

Newmeyer, F. (2001) 'The Prague School and North American Functionalist Approach to Syntax'. *Journal of Linguistics*, 37. 101–126.

Nikam, K. and Rajendra, B.H. (2009) 'Moving from Script to Science 2.0 for Scholarly Communication'. *Webology*, 6(1), Article 68. http://www.webology.org/2009/v6n1/a68.html. Accessed 18 March 2014.

Nunes, J.A. and Gonçalves, M.E. (eds) (2001) *Enteados de Galileu? A Semiperiferia no Sistema Mundial da Ciência*, Porto: Edições Afrontamento.

Nylenna, M., Hagve, T.-A. and Marušić, A. (2003) 'Small journals and non-English journals'. In F. Godlee and T. Jefferson (eds) *Peer Review in Health Sciences*. London: BMJ Books, pp. 140–150.

O'Reilly, T. (2005) 'What is Web 2.0: Design Patterns and Business Models for the Next Generation of Software'. http://oreilly.com/web2/archive/what-is-web-20.html. Accessed 18 March 2014.

Ortaş, I. (2009) 'Bilimsel yayinlar sounu' [The problem of scientific publications]. http://www.makaleler.com/bilim-makaleleri/bilimsel-yayinlar-sorunu.htm.

Otero, J. (1995) 'Una nueva mirada al índice de importancia internacional de las lenguas'. In *El peso de la lengua española en el mundo*. Instituto Virtual Cervantes. http://cvc.cervantes.es/lengua/peso_lengua/otero.htm#np75. Accessed 15 October 2014.

Pais Ribeiro, J.L., Martins da Silva, A., Kochen, S., Mota Gomes, M., Valia-Bueno, A. and Silvério Marques, M. (2011) *Manifesto: pela universalidade da divulgação da produção científica*, Lisbon: Placebo, Editora LDA.

Paltridge, B. and Starfield, S. (2007) *Thesis and Dissertation Writing in a Second Language. A Handbook for Supervisors*, London and New York: Routledge.

Patton, M.Q. (2002) *Qualitative Research and Evaluation Methods*, 2nd edition. Thousand Oaks: Sage.

Pavlidou, T. -S. (2008) 'Εμείς και η συνομιλιακή συγκρότηση (έμφυλων)συλλογικοτήτων'. ['We' and the discursive construction of (gendered) collectivities]. In Maria Theodoropoulou (ed.) *Light and Warmth: In Memory of A.-Ph. Christidis*. Thessaloniki: Center for the Greek Language, pp. 437–453.

Pavlidou, T.-S. (2012) 'Collective aspects of subjectivity: The subject pronoun *εμείς* ("we") in Modern Greek'. In N. Baumgarten, I. Du Bois and J. House (eds) *Subjectivity in Language and in Discourse*, Leiden: Brill, pp. 33–65.

Pazarlıoğlu, M.V. and Özkoç, H. (2009) 'The Econometric Analysis of International Publications of Turkey Between 1983–2004'. *Sosyal Bilimler*, 7(2). 45–58.

Pérez-Llantada, C. (2012) *Scientific Discourse and the Rhetoric of Globalization: The Impact of Culture and Language*, London: Continuum.

Pérez-Llantada, C., Plo, R. and Ferguson, G.R. (2011) ' "You Don't Say What you Know, Only What You Can": The Perceptions and Practices of Senior Spanish Academics Regarding Research Dissemination in English'. *English for Specific Purposes*, 30(1). 18–30.

Petrić, B. (2005) 'Contrastive Rhetoric in the Writing Classroom: A Case Study'. *English for Specific Purposes*, 24. 213–228.

Petrovečki, M. and Scheetz, M.D. (2001) 'Croatian Medical Journal Introduces Culture, Control, and the Study of Research Integrity'. *Croatian Medical Journal*, 42. 7–13.

Phillipson, R. (1992) *Linguistic Imperialism*, Oxford: Oxford University Press.

Phillipson, R. and Skutnabb-Kangas, T. (1997) 'Linguistic Human Rights and English in Europe'. *World Englishes*, 16(1). 27–43.

Pirandello, L. (1908) *L'umorismo. Saggio*, Lanciano: Carabba.

Piras, R. (2013) 'Can the Augmented Solow Model with Migration Explain the Italian Internal Brain Drain?'. *Labour*, 27(2). 140–163.

Polo, F.J.F. and Varela, M.C. (2009) 'English for Research Purposes at the University of Santiago de Compostela: A Survey'. *Journal of English for Academic Purposes*, 8(3). 152–164.

Povolná, R. (2012a) 'Causal and Contrastive Discourse Markers in Novice Academic Writing'. *Brno Studies in English*, 38(2). 105–122.

Povolná, R. (2012b) 'Cross-cultural differences in the use of discourse markers by Czech and German students of English in the genre of Master's Theses'. In C. Berkenkotter, V. Bhatia and M. Gotti (eds) *Insights into Academic Genres*. Bern: Peter Lang, pp.329–351.

Prodromou, L. (2008) English as a Lingua Franca. A Corpus-based Analysis. London, New York: Continuum.

Przygoński, K. (2012) *Sociolinguistic aspects of the functioning of English in post-1989 Poland*. Frankfurt: Peter Lang.

Puljak, L. (2007) 'Croatia Founded a National Body for Ethics in Science'. *Science and Engineering Ethics*, 13. 191–193.

Puljak, L. and Rako, D. (2009) 'Enhancing Medical Practice in Croatia Through the Cochrane Collaboration'. *Biochemia Medica*, 19. 260–265.

Quirk, R., Greenbaum, S., Leech, G. and Svartvik, J. (1985) *A Comprehensive Grammar of the English Language*. London and New York: Longman.

Radošević, S. (2010) 'Southeast Europe'. In *UNESCO Science Report 2010: The Current Status of Science Around the World*. Paris: UNESCO, pp. 183–218.

Ramos-Torre, R. and Callejo-Gallego, J. (2013) 'El español en las ciencias sociales'. In J.L. García Delgado, J.A. Alonso and J.C. Jiménez (eds) *El español, lengua de comunicación científica*. Madrid: Ariel and Fundación Telefónica, pp. 29–74.

Reichelt, M. (2005a) 'English in Poland'. *World Englishes*, 24 (2). 217–225.

Reichelt, M. (2005b) 'English Language Writing Instruction in Poland'. *Journal of Second Language Writing*, 14. 215–232.

Reichelt, M., Lefkowitz, N., Rinnert, C. and Schultz, J.M. (2012) 'Key Issues in Foreign Language Writing'. *Foreign Language Annals*, 45(1). 22–41.

Rey-Rocha, J. and Martín-Sempere, M.J. (1999) 'The Role of Domestic Journals in Geographically-Oriented Disciplines: The Case of Spanish Journals on Earth Sciences'. *Scientometrics*, 45. 203–216.

Ribeiro, G.L. and Escobar, A. (eds) (2008) *Antropologías del mundo: transformaciones disciplinarias dentro de sistemas de poder*, London: Berg.

Ripley, A. (2013) *The Brightest Kids in the World and How they Got That Way*, New York: Simon and Schuster.

Römer, U. (2009) 'English in Academia: Does Nativeness Matter?'. *Anglistik: International Journal of English Studies*, 20(2). 89–100.

Rounds, P.L. (1987) 'Multifunctional Personal Pronoun Use in an Educational Setting'. *English for Specific Purposes*, 6. 13–29.

Rowley-Jolivet, E. (2012) 'An analysis of web-mediated protocols'. In S. Campagna, G. Garzone, C. Ilie and E. Rowley-Jolivet (eds) *Evolving Genres in Web-mediated Communication*. Bern: Peter Lang, pp. 127–149.

Salager-Meyer, F. (2008) 'Scientific Publishing in Developing Countries: Challenges for the Future'. *Journal of English for Academic Purposes*, 7. 121–132.

Salager-Meyer, F. (2014) 'Writing and Publishing in Peripheral Scholarly Journals: How to Enhance the Global Influence of Multilingual Scholars?'. *Journal of English for Academic Purposes*, 13. 78–82.

Sambunjak, D. and Ivaniš, A. (2005) 'Is There a Demand for Science Communication Courses? The Experience of Croatian Medical Journal'. *European Science Editing*, 31. 117–119.

Sambunjak, D. and Ivaniš, A. (2006) 'Survive, Help, Learn: Experience of a Medical Journal in War and Post-war Times'. *Journal of Public Health Policy*, 27. 124–135.

Sambunjak, D. and Marušić, M. (2011) 'Between Forwarding and Mentoring: A Qualitative Study of Recommending Medical Doctors for International Postdoctoral Research Positions'. *BMC Medical Education*, 11. 31.

Sambunjak, D., Huić, M., Hren, D., Katić, M., Marušić, A. and Marušić, M. (2009) 'What do Medical Professionals Know and Think About National and International Journals: A Cross-Sectional Study'. *Learned Publishers*, 22. 57–70.

Sambunjak, D., Ivaniš, A., Marušić, A. and Marušić, M. (2008) 'Representation of Journals from Five Neighboring European Countries in the Journal Citation Reports'. *Scientometrics*, 76. 261–271.

Sambunjak, D. and Šimunović, V. (2007) 'Peace Through Medical Education in Bosnia and Herzegovina'. *Lancet*, 369. 905.

Samraj, B. (2008) 'A Discourse Analysis of Master's Theses Across Disciplines With a Focus on Introductions'. *English for Academic Purposes*, 7. 55–67.

Scheuer, S. (2010) 'Can (an) ELF Have a Life of its Own?'. *Poznań Studies in Contemporary Linguistics*, 46(3). 331–349.

Schiltz, M., Truyen, F. and Coppens, H. (2007) 'Cutting the Trees of Knowledge: Social Software, Information Architecture and Their Epistemic Consequences'. *Thesis Eleven*, 89(1). 94–114.

Schwab, K. (ed.) (2012) *Global Competitiveness Report 2012–2013*, Geneva: World Economic Forum.

Scollon, R. (1993) 'Maxims of Stance: Channel, Relationship, and Main Topic in Discourse'. *Research Report*, 26. City Polytechnic of Hong Kong, Department of English.

Scollon, S. (2000) 'Not to waste words or students: Confucian and Socratic discourse in the tertiary classroom'. In E. Hinkel (ed.) *Culture in Second Language Teaching and Learning*. Cambridge: Cambridge University Press, pp. 13–28.

Seidlhofer, B. (2011) *Understanding English as a Lingua Franca*, Oxford: Oxford University Press.

Seidlhofer, B., Jenkins, J. and Mauranen, A. (2012) 'Editorial', *Journal of English as a Lingua Franca* 1. p. 1–3.

Shanghai Ranking (2013) *Academic Ranking of World Universities*. http://www.shanghairanking.com/ARWU2013.html. Accessed 18 March 2014.

Shaw, P. and Vassileva, I. (2009) 'Co-Evolving Academic Rhetoric Across Culture: Britain, Bulgaria, Denmark, Germany in the 20th Century'. *Journal of Pragmatics*, 4(2). 290–305.

Shaw, S. and Shaw, K.E. (1977) *History of the Ottoman Empire and Modern Turkey. Reform, Revolution and Republic: The Rise of Modern Turkey 1808–1975*, Cambridge: Cambridge University Press.

Sibbald, B. and Flegel, K. (2008) 'Integrity at the Croatian Medical Journal'. *Canadian Medical Association Journal*, 178. 1637–1640.

Siewierska, A. (2004) *Person*, Cambridge: Cambridge University Press.

Šimunović, V.J., Sonntag, H.G., Hren, D., Dorup, J., Krivokuća, Z., Bokonjić, D., Verhaaren, H., Horsch, A., Mimica, M., Vojniković, B., Selesković, H., Marz, R., Marušić, A. and Marušić, M. (2006) 'A Comprehensive Assessment of Medical Schools in Bosnia and Herzegovina'. *Medical Education*, 40. 1162–1172.

Škaričić N. (2009) 'Human Rights Organization Condemns University's Attempt to Discredit One of its Staff'. *British Medical Journal*, 338. b2455.

Skutnabb-Kangas, T. and Phillipson, R. (eds) (1995) *Linguistic Human Rights: Overcoming Linguistic Discrimination*, Berlin: Mouton de Gruyter.

Skutnabb-Kangas, T. and Phillipson, R. (2008) 'A human rights perspective on language ecology'. In A. Creese, P. Martin and N.H. Hornberger (eds) *Encyclopedia of Language and Education*, 2nd Edition. New York: Springer, pp. 3–14.

Snell-Hornby, M. (1999) 'Communicating in the Global Village: On Language, Translation and Cultural Identity'. *Current Issues in Language and Society*, 6(2). 103–120.

Sobkowiak, W. (2008) 'Why not LFC?' In Dziubalska-Kolaczyk, K. and Przedlacka, J. (Ed.) *English Pronunciation Models: A Changing Scene*. Peter Lang International Academic Publishers. Bern.

Sokół, M. (2012) 'Metadiscourse and the construction of the author's voices in the blogosphere: Academic weblogs as a form of self-promotion'. In S. Campagna, G. Garzone, C. Ilie and E. Rowley-Jolivet (eds) *Evolving Genres in Web-mediated Communication*. Bern: Peter Lang, pp. 265–287.

Sousa Santos, B. (1985) 'Estado e sociedade na semiperiferia do sistema mundial: o caso português'. *Análise Social*, XXI (87–88–89), 3.4.5: 869–901.

Sousa Santos, Boaventura de (1996) 'The fall of the Angelus Novus: Beyond the modern game of roots and options'. *Working Paper Series on Political Economy of Legal Change* 3, University of Wisconsin-Madison.

Sousa Santos, Boaventura de (2001) 'Towards an Epistemology of Blindness: Why the New Forms of "ceremonial adequacy" Neither Regulate nor Emancipate'. *European Journal of Social Theory*, 4(3). 251–279.

Stašková, J. (2005) 'Options of identity: Authorial presence in research articles abstracts'. In M. Huttová (ed.) *Slovak Studies in English 1*. Bratislava: Univerzita Komenského, pp. 201–207.

Swales, J. (1986) 'Citation Analysis and Discourse Analysis'. *Applied Linguistics*, 7(1). 39–56.

Swales, J. (1987) 'Utilizing the Literatures in Teaching a Research Paper'. *TESOL Quarterly*, 31(1). 41–68.

Swales, J. (1990) *Genre Analysis*, Cambridge: Cambridge University Press.

Swales, J. (1997) 'English as Tyrannosaurus Rex'. *World Englishes*, 16(3). 373–382.

Swales, J. (2004) *Research Genres*, Cambridge: Cambridge University Press.

Swales, J.M. and Feak, C.B. (2008) *Academic Writing for Graduate Students*. 2nd edition. Ann Arbor. The University of Michigan Press.

Tang, R. and John, S. (1999) 'The "I" in Identity: Exploring Writer Identity in Student Academic Writing Through the First-Person Pronoun'. *English for Specific Purposes*, 18. 23–39.

Tardy, C. (2004) 'The role of English in Scientific Communication: Lingua Franca or Tyrannosaurus Rex?'. *Journal of English for Academic Purposes*, 3. 247–269.

Tatalović, M. (2011) 'Editors of Croatian Medical Journal Resign amid Long-Running Feud'. *Science Insider* http://news.sciencemag.org/sciencein-sider/2011/07/cmj-resign.html#more. Accessed 18 March 2014.

Taylor, G. and Chen, T. (1991) 'Linguistic, Cultural, and Subcultural Issues in Contrastive Discourse Analysis: Anglo-American and Chinese Scientific Texts'. *Applied Linguistics*, 12(3). 319–336.

Terra-Figari, L. (2009) *Information and Communication Technology for the Dissemination of Scholarly Knowledge in a Public University on the Periphery: the case of social sciences and humanities in the Universidad de la Republica, Uruguay*. Unpublished Doctoral Dissertation, University of British Columbia.

Thompson, G. (2001) 'Interaction in Academic Writing: Learning to Argue with the Reader'. *Applied Linguistics*, 22(1). 58–78.

Thompson, P. (2005) 'Points of Focus and Position: Intertextual Reference in Ph D Theses'. *Journal of English for Academic Purposes*, 4. 307–323.

Truchot, C. (1990) *L'Anglais dans le Monde contemporain*, Paris: Robert.

TUBITAK (1993) Türk Bilim ve Teknoloji Politikası, (1993–2003) Ankara, 1993 http://www.tubitak.gov.tr/tubitak_content_files/BTYPD/btyk/2/2btyk_karar.pdf.

TUBITAK (2005) Bilim ve Teknoloji Yüksek Kurulu Onbirinci Toplantısı 10 Mart 2005: Gelişmelere ilişkin değerlendirmeler ve kararlar. Available at: http://www. tubitak.gov.tr/tubitak_content_files/BTYPD/btyk/11/11btyk_karar.pdf.

TUBITAK (2012) Tubitak tarihcesi. http://www.tubitak.gov.tr/home.do?sid=334. http://www.tubitak.gov.tr/home.do?sid=334.

TUBITAK-ULAKBIM (2011) *Turkish Publication Statistics*. Available at: http://www. ulakbim.gov.tr/cabim/yayin/tr-veri.uhtml.

Tugwell, P. (2004) 'The Campaign to Revitalize Academic Medicine Kicks Off: We Need a Deep and Broad International Debate to Begin'. *Croatian Medical Journal*, 45. 241–242.

Ucuzsatar, N.U. (2002) 'The Dissolution of the Ottoman Empire and the Foundation of Modern Turkey Under the Leadership of Mustafa Kemal Ataturk'. *Journal of Istanbul Kultur University*, 2. 55–68.

ULAKBIM (2010) UBYT uygulama esaslarinda degisiklik [Change in the principles of application of Ulakbim publication incentives], *191 sayili Bilim Kurulu Karari*. Available at: http//www.ulakbim.gov.tr/cabim/ubyt/haberler.uhtml.

Uzuner, S. (2008) 'Multilingual Scholars' Participation in Core/ Global Academic Communities: A Literature Review'. *Journal of English for Academic Purposes*, 7. 250–263.

van Weijen, D. (2012) 'The Language of (future) Scientific Communication'. *Research Trends*, 31. http://www.researchtrends.com/issue-31-november-2012/the-language-of-future-scientific-communication. Accessed 15 May 2013.

Vassileva, I. (1998) 'Who am I/who are we in Academic Writing?'. *International Journal of Applied Linguistics*, 8(2). 163–192.

Vassileva, I. (2000) *Who is the Author? A Contrastive Analysis of Authorial Presence in English, German, French, Russian and Bulgarian Academic Discourse*, Sankt Augustin: Asgard.

Vázquez, I. and Giner, D. (2008) 'Beyond Mood and Modality: Epistemic Modality Markers as Hedges in Research Articles: A Cross-Disciplinary Study'. *Revista Alicantina de Estudios Ingleses*, 21. 171–190.

Vázquez, I. and Giner, D. (2009) 'Writing with Conviction: The Use of Boosters in Modelling Persuasion in Academic Discourses'. *Revista Alicantina de Estudios Ingleses*, 22. 219–237.

Vergaro, C. (2011) 'Shades of Impersonality: Rhetorical Positioning in the Academic Writing of Italian Students of English'. *Linguistics and Education*, 22(2). 118–132.

Vladimirou, D. (2008) *Personal Reference in Linguistics Journal Articles: Exploring the English-speaking vs. the Greek-speaking Academic Communities*. Unpublished Ph.D. Thesis, Lancaster University.

Vladimirou, D. (2014) 'Author positioning and audience addressivity by means of "we" in Greek academic discourse'. In T.S. Pavlidou (ed.) *Constructing Collectivity: 'We' across Languages and Contexts*. Amsterdam and Philadelphia: John Benjamins.

Vogel, R. (2008) 'Sentence Linkers in Essays and Papers by Native vs. Non-native Writers'. *Discourse and Interaction*, 1(2). 119–126.

Vujaklija, A., Hren, D., Sambunjak, D., Vodopivec, I., Ivaniš, A., Marušić, A. and Marušić M. (2010) 'Can Teaching Research Methodology Influence Students' Attitude Toward Science? Cohort Study and Nonrandomized Trial in a Single Medical School'. *Journal of Investigative Medicine*, 58. 282–286.

Waldrop, M.M. (2008) 'Science 2.0: Great New Tool, or Great Risk?' *Scientific American.* 9 January. http://www.scientificamerican.com/article/science-2-point-0-great-new-tool-or-great-risk. Accessed 18 March 2014.

Wales, K. (1996) *Personal Pronouns in Present-Day English,* Cambridge: Cambridge University Press.

Walker, J. (2006) 'Blogging from inside the ivory tower'. In A. Bruns and J. Jacobs (eds) *Uses of Blogs.* New York: Peter Lang, pp. 127–137.

Wallerstein, I. (1984) *The Politics of the World-Economy: The States, the Movements and the Civilizations,* Cambridge: Cambridge University Press.

Wallerstein, I. (1997) 'The Time of Space and the Space of Time: The Future of Social Science'. Publications of the Fernand Braudel Centre, Binghamton University. http://www2.binghamton.edu/fbc/archive/iwtynesi.htm. Accessed 18 March 2013.

Wallerstein, I. (2001) *Unthinking Social Science,* 2nd edition. Philadelphia: Temple University Press.

Wallerstein, I. (2004) *World-Systems Analysis: An Introduction,* Durham and London: Duke University Press.

Webometrics (2013) 'Ranking Web of Universities'. http://www.webometrics.info. Accessed 7 October 2013.

White, H.D. (2004) 'Citation Analysis and Discourse Analysis Revisited'. *Applied Linguistics,* 25(1). 89–116.

Whitehand, J.W.R. (2005) 'The Problem of Anglophone Squint'. *Area,* 37. 228–230.

Widdowson, H. (1987) 'The Ownership of English'. *TESOL Quarterly,* 28(2). 377–88.

Wierzbicka, A. (1991) *Cross-cultural Pragmatics: The Semantics of Human Interaction,* Berlin: Mouton de Gruyter.

Wierzbicka, A. (2010) *Experience, Evidence and Sense,* New York: Oxford University Press.

Willey, I. and Tanimoto, K. (2013) ' "Convenience editors" as Legitimate Participants in the Practice of Scientific Editing: An Interview Study'. *Journal of English for Academic Purposes,* 12. 23–32.

Yakhontova, T. (2006) 'Cultural and Disciplinary Variation in Academic Discourse: The Issue of Influencing Factors'. *Journal of English for Academic Purposes,* 5. 153–167.

Yucel, I.H. (2006) Turkiye'de Bilim Teknoloji politikalari ve iktisadi gelismenin yonu. DPT: 2690. Available at: http://ekutup.dpt.gov.tr/bilim/yucelih/bilim/pdf

Yus, F. (2007a) 'Weblogs: web pages in search of a genre?' In S. Posteguillo, M.J. Esteve, and M.L. Gea-Valor (eds) *The Texture of Internet: Netlinguistics in Progress.* Newcastle: Cambridge Scholars Publishing, pp. 118–142.

Yus, F. (2007b) 'Towards a Pragmatics of Weblogs'. *Quaderns de Filologia. Estudis Lingüístics,* XII. 15–33.

# Index

Printed by Printforce, United Kingdom